**The Quran With
Tafsir Ibn Kathir
Part 8 of 30:
Al An'am 111 To
Al A'raf 087**

The Quran With Tafsir Ibn Kathir Part 8 of 30: Al An'am 111 To Al A'raf 087

With
Arabic Script, Transliteration of Arabic, Meaning in English and Ibn Kathir's Abridged Tafsir (Explanation)

Muhammad Saed Abdul-Rahman

BSc, DipHE

© Muhammad Saed Abdul-Rahman,2012
ISBN 978-1-86179-849-7

All Rights reserved

British Library Cataloguing in Publication Data. A Catalogue record for this book is available from the British Library

Designed, Typeset and produced by:
MSA Publication Limited, 4 Bello Close, Herne Hill,
London SE24 9BW
United Kingdom

Cover design: Houriyah Abdul-Rahman

TABLE OF CONTENTS

TABLE OF CONTENTS V

PRELUDE XIII

    OPENING SERMAN XIII
    OUR MISSION XIV
    BIOGRAPHY OF HAFIZ IBN KATHIR (701 H - 774 H) XIV
        Ibn Kathir's Teachers xiv
        Ibn Kathir's Students xv
        Ibn Kathir's Books xv
        Ibn Kathir's Death xvi

PREFACE XVII

    ABOUT THIS BOOK XVII
    PERFORMING PROSTRATION WHILE READING THE QUR'AN XVII

PART 8 FULL ARABIC TEXT 1

INTRODUCTION TO CHAPTER (SURAH) 6: AL-AN'AM (CATTLE, LIVESTOCK) 12

    IBN KATHIR'S INTRODUCTION 12
        The Virtue of Surat Al-An`am and When it Was Revealed 12

CHAPTER (SURAH) 6: AL-AN'AM (CATTLE, LIVESTOCK), VERSES 111-165 12

    Surah: 6 Ayah: 111 13
        Tafsir Ibn Kathir: 13
    Surah: 6 Ayah: 112 & Ayah: 113 14
        Tafsir Ibn Kathir: 14
        Every Prophet Has Enemies 14
    Surah: 6 Ayah: 114 & Ayah: 115 16
        Tafsir Ibn Kathir: 16
    Surah: 6 Ayah: 116 & Ayah: 117 17
        Tafsir Ibn Kathir: 17
        Most People are Misguided 17
    Surah: 6 Ayah: 118 & Ayah: 119 18
        Tafsir Ibn Kathir: 18
        Allowing What was Slaughtered in the Name of Allah 18
    Surah: 6 Ayah: 120 19
        Tafsir Ibn Kathir: 19
    Surah: 6 Ayah: 121 20
        Tafsir Ibn Kathir: 20
        The Prohibition of what was Slaughtered in other than Allah's Name 20
        The Devil's Inspiration 21
        Giving Preference to Anyone's Saying Over the Legislation of Allah is Shirk 22

- Surah: 6 Ayah: 122 22
  - Tafsir Ibn Kathir: 23
    - The Parable of the Disbeliever and the Believer 23
- Surah: 6 Ayah: 123 & Ayah: 124 24
  - Tafsir Ibn Kathir: 24
    - Evil Plots of the Leaders of the Criminals and their Subsequent Demise 24
    - The Disbelievers Admit to the Prophet's Nobility of Lineage 26
- Surah: 6 Ayah: 125 28
  - Tafsir Ibn Kathir: 28
- Surah: 6 Ayah: 126 & Ayah: 127 29
  - Tafsir Ibn Kathir: 29
- Surah: 6 Ayah: 128 30
  - Tafsir Ibn Kathir: 30
- Surah: 6 Ayah: 129 31
  - Tafsir Ibn Kathir: 31
    - The Wrongdoers Are the Supporters of Each other 31
- Surah: 6 Ayah: 130 32
  - Tafsir Ibn Kathir: 32
    - Chastising the Jinns and Humans after their Admission that Allah Sent Messengers to Them 32
- Surah: 6 Ayah: 131 & Ayah: 132 33
  - Tafsir Ibn Kathir: 34
- Surah: 6 Ayah: 133, Ayah: 134 & Ayah: 135 35
  - Tafsir Ibn Kathir: 35
    - If They Disobey, They Will Perish 35
- Surah: 6 Ayah: 136 37
  - Tafsir Ibn Kathir: 37
    - Some Acts of Shirk 37
- Surah: 6 Ayah: 137 39
  - Tafsir Ibn Kathir: 39
    - Shaytan Lured the Idolators to Kill Their Children 39
- Surah: 6 Ayah: 138 40
  - Tafsir Ibn Kathir: 40
    - The Idolators Forbade Certain Types of Cattle 40
- Surah: 6 Ayah: 139 41
  - Tafsir Ibn Kathir: 41
- Surah: 6 Ayah: 140 42
  - Tafsir Ibn Kathir: 42
    - Allah says that those who committed these evil acts have earned the loss of this life and the Hereafter. 42
- Surah: 6 Ayah: 141 & Ayah: 142 43
  - Tafsir Ibn Kathir: 43
    - Allah Created the Produce, Seed Grains and Cattle 43
    - Prohibiting Extravagance 44

Table of Contents

- Benefits of Cattle 45
  - Eat the Meat of These Cattle, But Do Not Follow Shaytan's Law Concerning Them 45
- *Surah: 6 Ayah: 143 & Ayah: 144* 46
  - Tafsir Ibn Kathir: 47
  - These Ayat demonstrate the ignorance of the Arabs before Islam. 47
- *Surah: 6 Ayah: 145* 48
  - Tafsir Ibn Kathir: 48
  - Forbidden Things 48
- *Surah: 6 Ayah: 146* 50
  - Tafsir Ibn Kathir: 50
  - Foods that were Prohibited for the Jews Because of their Transgression 50
  - The Tricks of the Jews, and Allah's Curse 51
- *Surah: 6 Ayah: 147* 52
  - Tafsir Ibn Kathir: 52
- *Surah: 6 Ayah: 148, Surah: 6 Ayah: 149 & Ayah: 150* 53
  - Tafsir Ibn Kathir: 54
  - A False Notion and its Rebuttal 54
- *Surah: 6 Ayah: 151* 55
  - Tafsir Ibn Kathir: 56
  - Ten Commandments 56
  - Shirk is Forbidden 57
  - The Order for Kindness to Parents 58
  - Killing Children is Forbidden 59
  - The Prohibition of Unjustified Killing 60
- *Surah: 6 Ayah: 152* 61
  - Tafsir Ibn Kathir: 62
  - The Prohibition of Consuming the Orphan's Property 62
  - The Command to Give Full Measure and Full Weight with Justice 62
  - The Order for Just Testimony 63
  - Fulfilling the Covenant of Allah is an Obligation 63
- *Surah: 6 Ayah: 153* 63
  - Tafsir Ibn Kathir: 64
  - The Command to Follow Allah's Straight Path and to Avoid All Other Paths 64
- *Surah: 6 Ayah: 154 & Ayah: 155* 66
  - Tafsir Ibn Kathir: 66
  - Praising the Tawrah and the Qur'an 66
- *Surah: 6 Ayah: 156 & Ayah: 157* 68
  - Tafsir Ibn Kathir: 68
  - The Qur'an is Allah's Proof Against His Creation 68
- *Surah: 6 Ayah: 158* 69
  - Tafsir Ibn Kathir: 70
  - The Disbelievers Await the Commencement of the Hereafter, or Some of its Portents ... 70
- *Surah: 6 Ayah: 159* 72
  - Tafsir Ibn Kathir: 72
  - Criticizing Division in the Religion 72

Surah: 6 Ayah: 160 73
    Tafsir Ibn Kathir: 73
        The Good Deed is Multiplied Tenfold, While the Sin is Recompensed with the Same 73
Surah: 6 Ayah: 161, Ayah: 162 & Ayah: 163 76
    Tafsir Ibn Kathir: 76
        Islam is the Straight Path 76
        The Command for Sincerity in Worship 77
        Islam is the Religion of all Prophets 77
Surah: 6 Ayah: 164 79
    Tafsir Ibn Kathir: 79
        The Command to Sincerely Trust in Allah 79
        Every Person Carries His Own Burden 80
Surah: 6 Ayah: 165 81
    Tafsir Ibn Kathir: 81
        Allah Made Mankind Dwellers on the earth, Generation After Generation, of Various Grades, in order to Test Them 81

CHAPTER (SURAH) 7: AL-ARAF (THE HEIGHTS), VERSES 001 - 087 83

Surah: 7 Ayah: 1, Ayah: 2 & Ayah: 3 84
    Tafsir Ibn Kathir: 84
        Which was revealed in Makkah 84
Surah: 7 Ayah: 4, Ayah: 5, Ayah: 6 & Ayah: 7 85
    Tafsir Ibn Kathir: 86
        Nations that were destroyed 86
Surah: 7 Ayah: 8 & Ayah: 9 87
    Tafsir Ibn Kathir: 88
        The Meaning of weighing the Deeds 88
Surah: 7 Ayah: 10 89
    Tafsir Ibn Kathir: 89
        All Bounties in the Heavens and Earth are for the Benefit of Mankind 89
Surah: 7 Ayah: 11 90
    Tafsir Ibn Kathir: 90
        Prostration of the Angels to Adam and Shaytan's Arrogance 90
Surah: 7 Ayah: 12 91
    Tafsir Ibn Kathir: 91
        Iblis was the First to use Qiyas (Analogical Comparison) 92
Surah: 7 Ayah: 13, Ayah: 14 & Ayah: 15 92
    Tafsir Ibn Kathir: 92
Surah: 7 Ayah: 16 & Ayah: 17 93
    Tafsir Ibn Kathir: 93
Surah: 7 Ayah: 18 95
    Tafsir Ibn Kathir: 96
Surah: 7 Ayah: 19, Ayah: 20 & Ayah: 21 96
    Tafsir Ibn Kathir: 97

Table of Contents

Shaytan's Deceit with Adam and Hawwa' and Their eating from the Forbidden Tree 97
Surah: 7 Ayah: 22 & Ayah: 23 98
    Tafsir Ibn Kathir: 98
Surah: 7 Ayah: 24 & Ayah: 25 99
    Tafsir Ibn Kathir: 99
        Sending Them All Down to Earth 99
Surah: 7 Ayah: 26 100
    Tafsir Ibn Kathir: 100
        Bestowing Raiment and Adornment on Mankind 100
Surah: 7 Ayah: 27 101
    Tafsir Ibn Kathir: 101
        Warning against the Lures of Shaytan 101
Surah: 7 Ayah: 28, Ayah: 29 & Ayah: 30 101
    Tafsir Ibn Kathir: 102
        Disbelievers commit Sins and claim that Allah commanded Them to do so! 102
        Allah does not order Fahsha', but orders Justice and Sincerity 103
        The Meaning of being brought into Being in the Beginning and brought back again 103
Surah: 7 Ayah: 31 106
    Tafsir Ibn Kathir: 106
        Allah commands taking Adornment when going to the Masjid 106
        Prohibiting Extravagance 107
Surah: 7 Ayah: 32 108
    Tafsir Ibn Kathir: 108
        Allah refutes those who prohibit any type of food, drink or clothes according to their own understanding, without relying on what Allah has legislated, ... 108
Surah: 7 Ayah: 33 109
    Tafsir Ibn Kathir: 109
        Fahishah, Sin, Transgression, Shirk and Lying about Allah are prohibited 109
Surah: 7 Ayah: 34, Ayah: 35 & Ayah: 36 110
    Tafsir Ibn Kathir: 110
Surah: 7 Ayah: 37 111
    Tafsir Ibn Kathir: 111
        Idolators enjoy Their destined Share in This Life, but will lose Their Supporters upon Death 111
Surah: 7 Ayah: 38 & Ayah: 39 112
    Tafsir Ibn Kathir: 113
        People of the Fire will dispute and curse Each Other Allah mentioned what He will say to those who associate others with Him, invent lies about Him, and reject His Ayat, ... 113
Surah: 7 Ayah: 40 & Ayah: 41 114
    Tafsir Ibn Kathir: 115
        Doors of Heaven shall not open for Those Who deny Allah's Ayat, and They shall never enter Paradise 115
Surah: 7 Ayah: 42 & Ayah: 43 116
    Tafsir Ibn Kathir: 116

Destination of Righteous Believers 116
Surah: 7 Ayah: 44 & Ayah: 45 118
   Tafsir Ibn Kathir: 118
      People of Hellfire will feel Anguish upon Anguish 118
Surah: 7 Ayah: 46 & Ayah: 47 120
   Tafsir Ibn Kathir: 120
      The People of Al-A`raf 120
Surah: 7 Ayah: 48 & Ayah: 49 121
   Tafsir Ibn Kathir: 121
Surah: 7 Ayah: 50 & Ayah: 51 122
   Tafsir Ibn Kathir: 122
      The Favors of paradise are Prohibited for the People of the Fire 122
Surah: 7 Ayah: 52 & Ayah: 53 124
   Tafsir Ibn Kathir: 124
      The Idolators have no Excuse 124
Surah: 7 Ayah: 54 125
   Tafsir Ibn Kathir: 126
      The Universe was created in Six Days 126
      Meaning of Istawa 126
      The Day and the Night are among the Signs of Allah 127
Surah: 7 Ayah: 55 & Ayah: 56 128
   Tafsir Ibn Kathir: 128
      Encouraging supplicating to Allah 128
      Forbidding Aggression in Supplications 129
      The Prohibition of causing Mischief in the Land 129
Surah: 7 Ayah: 57 & Ayah: 58 130
   Tafsir Ibn Kathir: 130
      Among Allah's Signs, He sends down the Rain and brings forth the Produce 130
Surah: 7 Ayah: 59, Ayah: 60, Ayah: 61 & Ayah: 62 132
   Tafsir Ibn Kathir: 133
      The Story of Nuh and His People 133
Surah: 7 Ayah: 63 & Ayah: 64 134
   Tafsir Ibn Kathir: 134
Surah: 7 Ayah: 65, Ayah: 66, Ayah: 67, Ayah: 68 & Ayah: 69 135
   Tafsir Ibn Kathir: 136
      The Story of Hud, Peace be upon Him, and the Lineage of the People of `Ad 136
      The Land of `Ad 136
      Debate between Hud and his People 137
Surah: 7 Ayah: 70, Ayah: 71 & Ayah: 72 138
   Tafsir Ibn Kathir: 139
      Allah mentions the rebellion, defiance and stubbornness of Hud's people, and their opposition to him, peace be upon him, ... 139
      The End of `Ad 139
      Story of the Emissary of `Ad 140

Table of Contents

Surah: 7 Ayah: 73, Ayah: 74, Ayah: 75, Ayah: 76, Ayah: 77 & Ayah: 78 141
    Tafsir Ibn Kathir: 142
        Thamud: Their Land and Their Lineage 142
        The Story of Prophet Salih and Thamud 143
        Thamud asked that a Camel appear from a Stone, and it did 143
        Thamud kills the She-Camel 144
        The Wicked Ones Plot to Kill Prophet Salih, But the Torment descended on Them........ 145
Surah: 7 Ayah: 79 146
    Tafsir Ibn Kathir: 147
Surah: 7 Ayah: 80 & Ayah: 81 147
    Tafsir Ibn Kathir: 148
        The Story of Prophet Lut, upon Him be Peace, and His People 148
Surah: 7 Ayah: 82 149
    Tafsir Ibn Kathir: 149
Surah: 7 Ayah: 83 & Ayah: 84 149
    Tafsir Ibn Kathir: 149
        Allah says, We saved Lut and his family, for only his household believed in him............ 149
Surah: 7 Ayah: 85 150
    Tafsir Ibn Kathir: 151
        Story of Shu`ayb, upon him be Peace, and the Land of Madyan 151
Surah: 7 Ayah: 86 & Ayah: 87 151
    Tafsir Ibn Kathir: 152
        Prophet Shu`ayb forbade his people from setting up blockades on the roads, saying, ..152

PRELUDE

Opening Serman

Indeed, all praise is due to Allah. We praise Him and seek His help and forgiveness. We seek refuge with Allah from our soul's evil and our wrong doings. He whom Allah guides, no one can misguide; and he whom He misguides, no one can guide

I bear witness that there is no (true) god except Allah – alone without a partner, and I bear witness that Muhammad (peace and blessings of Allah be upon him) is His 'abd (servant) and messenger.

يَٰٓأَيُّهَا ٱلَّذِينَ ءَامَنُواْ ٱتَّقُواْ ٱللَّهَ حَقَّ تُقَاتِهِۦ وَلَا تَمُوتُنَّ إِلَّا وَأَنتُم مُّسْلِمُونَ ۝

O you who believe! Fear Allâh (by doing all that He has ordered and by abstaining from all that He has forbidden) as He should be feared. (Obey Him, be thankful to Him, and remember Him always), and die not except in a state of Islâm (as Muslims (with complete submission to Allâh)).

يَٰٓأَيُّهَا ٱلنَّاسُ ٱتَّقُواْ رَبَّكُمُ ٱلَّذِى خَلَقَكُم مِّن نَّفْسٍ وَٰحِدَةٍ وَخَلَقَ مِنْهَا زَوْجَهَا وَبَثَّ مِنْهُمَا رِجَالًا كَثِيرًا وَنِسَآءً ۚ وَٱتَّقُواْ ٱللَّهَ ٱلَّذِى تَسَآءَلُونَ بِهِۦ وَٱلْأَرْحَامَ ۚ إِنَّ ٱللَّهَ كَانَ عَلَيْكُمْ رَقِيبًا ۝

O mankind! Be dutiful to your Lord, Who created you from a single person (Adam), and from him (Adam) He created his wife (Hawwâ (Eve)) and from them both He created many men and women; and fear Allâh through Whom you demand (your mutual rights), and (do not cut the relations of) the wombs (kinship). Surely, Allâh is Ever an All-Watcher over you.

يُصْلِحْ لَكُمْ أَعْمَٰلَكُمْ وَيَغْفِرْ لَكُمْ ذُنُوبَكُمْ ۗ وَمَن يُطِعِ ٱللَّهَ وَرَسُولَهُۥ فَقَدْ فَازَ فَوْزًا عَظِيمًا ۝

He will direct you to do righteous good deeds and will forgive you your sins. And whosoever obeys Allâh and His Messenger (peace be upon him), he has indeed achieved a great achievement (i.e. he will be saved from the Hell-fire and will be admitted to Paradise).

Indeed, the best speech is Allah's Book and the best guidance is Muhammad's () guidance. The worst affairs (of religion) are those innovated (by people), for every such innovation is an act of misguidance leading to the Fire

Our Mission

Our mission is to gather in one place, for the English-speaking public, all relevant information needed to make the Qur'an more understandable and easier to study. This book tries to do this by providing the following:

1. The Arabic Text for those who are able to read Arabic
2. Transliteration of the Arabic text for those who are unable to read the Arabic script. This will give them a sample of the sound of the Qur'an, which they could not otherwise comprehend from reading the English meaning.
3. The meaning of the qur'an (translated by Dr. Muhammad Taqi-ud-Din Al-Hilali, Ph.D. and Dr. Muhammad Muhsin Khan)
4. Explanation (abridged Tafsir) by Ibn Kathir (translated by Safi-ur-Rahman al-Mubarakpuri)

We hope that by doing this an ordinary English-speaker will be able to pick up a copy of this book and study and comprehend The Glorious Qur'an in a way that is acceptable to the understanding of the Rightly-guided Muslim Ummah (Community).

Biography of Hafiz Ibn Kathir
(701 H - 774 H)

By the Honored Shaykh `Abdul-Qadir Al-Arna'ut, may Allah protect him.

He is the respected Imam, Abu Al-Fida', `Imad Ad-Din Isma il bin 'Umar bin Kathir Al-Qurashi Al-Busrawi - Busraian in origin; Dimashqi in training, learning and residence.

Ibn Kathir was born in the city of Busra in 701 H. His father was the Friday speaker of the village, but he died while Ibn Kathir was only four years old. Ibn Kathir's brother, Shaykh Abdul-Wahhab, reared him and taught him until he moved to Damascus in 706 H., when he was five years old.

Ibn Kathir's Teachers

Ibn Kathir studied Fiqh - Islamic jurisprudence - with Burhan Ad-Din, Ibrahim bin `Abdur-Rahman Al-Fizari, known as Ibn Al-Firkah (who died in 729 H). Ibn Kathir heard Hadiths from `Isa bin Al-Mutim, Ahmad bin Abi Talib, (Ibn Ash-Shahnah) (who died in 730 H), Ibn Al-Hajjar, (who died in 730 H), and the Hadith narrator of Ash-Sham (modern day Syria and surrounding areas); Baha Ad-Din Al-Qasim bin Muzaffar bin `Asakir (who died in 723 H), and Ibn Ash-Shirdzi, Ishaq bin Yahya Al-Ammuddi, also known as `Afif Ad-Din, the Zahiriyyah Shaykh who died in 725 H, and Muhammad bin Zarrad. He remained with Jamal Ad-Din, Yusuf bin Az-Zaki AlMizzi who died in 724 H, he benefited from his knowledge and also married his daughter. He also read with Shaykh Al-Islam, Taqi Ad-Din Ahmad bin `Abdul-Halim bin `Abdus-Salam bin Taymiyyah who died in 728 H. He also read with the Imam Hafiz and historian Shams Ad-Din, Muhammad bin Ahmad bin Uthman bin Qaymaz Adh-Dhahabi, who died in 748 H. Also, Abu Musa Al-Qarafai, Abu Al-Fath Ad-Dabbusi and

'Ali bin `Umar As-Suwani and others who gave him permission to transmit the knowledge he learned with them in Egypt.

In his book, Al-Mu jam Al-Mukhtas, Al-Hafiz Adh-Dhaliabi wrote that Ibn Kathir was, "The Imam, scholar of jurisprudence, skillful scholar of Hadith, renowned Faqih and scholar of Tafsir who wrote several beneficial books."

Further, in Ad-Durar Al-Kdminah, Al-Hafiz Ibn Hajar AlAsqalani said, "Ibn Kathir worked on the subject of the Hadith in the areas of texts and chains of narrators. He had a good memory, his books became popular during his lifetime, and people benefited from them after his death."

Also, the renowned historian Abu Al-Mahasin, Jamal Ad-Din Yusuf bin Sayf Ad-Din (Ibn Taghri Bardi), said in his book, AlManhal As-Safi, "He is the Shaykh, the Imam, the great scholar `Imad Ad-Din Abu Al-Fida'. He learned extensively and was very active in collecting knowledge and writing. He was excellent in the areas of Fiqh, Tafsfr and Hadith. He collected knowledge, authored (books), taught, narrated Hadith and wrote. He had immense knowledge in the fields of Hadith, Tafsir, Fiqh, the Arabic language, and so forth. He gave Fatawa (religious verdicts) and taught until he died, may Allah grant him mercy. He was known for his precision and vast knowledge, and as a scholar of history, Hadith and Tafsir."

Ibn Kathir's Students

Ibn Hajji was one of Ibn Kathir's students, and he described Ibn Kathir: "He had the best memory of the Hadith texts. He also had the most knowledge concerning the narrators and authenticity, his contemporaries and teachers admitted to these qualities. Every time I met him I gained some benefit from him."

Also, Ibn Al-`Imad Al-Hanbali said in his book, Shadhardt Adh-Dhahab, "He is the renowned Hafiz `Imad Ad-Din, whose memory was excellent, whose forgetfulness was miniscule, whose understanding was adequate, and who had good knowledge in the Arabic language." Also, Ibn Habib said about Ibn Kathir, "He heard knowledge and collected it and wrote various books. He brought comfort to the ears with his Fatwas and narrated Hadith and brought benefit to other people. The papers that contained his Fatwas were transmitted to the various (Islamic) provinces. Further, he was known for his precision and encompassing knowledge."

Ibn Kathir's Books

1 - One of the greatest books that Ibn Kathir wrote was his Tafsir of the Noble Qur'an, which is one of the best Tafsir that rely on narrations [of Ahadith, the Tafsir of the Companions, etc.]. The Tafsir by Ibn Kathir was printed many times and several scholars have summarized it.

2- The History Collection known as Al-Biddyah, which was printed in 14 volumes under the name Al-Bidayah wanNihdyah, and contained the stories of the Prophets and previous nations, the Prophet's Seerah (life story) and Islamic history until his time. He also added a book Al-Fitan, about the Signs of the Last Hour.

3- At-Takmil ft Ma`rifat Ath-Thiqat wa Ad-Du'afa wal Majdhil which Ibn Kathir collected from the books of his two Shaykhs Al-Mizzi and Adh-Dhahabi; Al-Kdmal and Mizan Al-Ftiddl. He added several benefits regarding the subject of Al-Jarh and AtT'adil.

4- Al-Hadi was-Sunan ft Ahadith Al-Masdnfd was-Sunan which is also known by, Jami` Al-Masdnfd. In this book, Ibn Kathir collected the narrations of Imams Ahmad bin Hanbal, Al-Bazzar, Abu Ya`la Al-Mawsili, Ibn Abi Shaybah and from the six collections of Hadith: the Two Sahihs [Al-Bukhari and Muslim] and the Four Sunan [Abu Dawud, At-Tirmidhi, AnNasa and Ibn Majah]. Ibn Kathir divided this book according to areas of Fiqh.

5-Tabaqat Ash-Shaf iyah which also contains the virtues of Imam Ash-Shafi.

6- Ibn Kathir wrote references for the Ahadith of Adillat AtTanbfh, from the Shafi school of Fiqh.

7- Ibn Kathir began an explanation of Sahih Al-Bukhari, but he did not finish it.

8- He started writing a large volume on the Ahkam (Laws), but finished only up to the Hajj rituals.

9- He summarized Al-Bayhaqi's 'Al-Madkhal. Many of these books were not printed.

10- He summarized `Ulum Al-Hadith, by Abu `Amr bin AsSalah and called it Mukhtasar `Ulum Al-Hadith. Shaykh Ahmad Shakir, the Egyptian Muhaddith, printed this book along with his commentary on it and called it Al-Ba'th Al-Hathfth fi Sharh Mukhtasar `Ulum Al-Hadith.

11- As-Sfrah An-Nabawiyyah, which is contained in his book Al-Biddyah, and both of these books are in print.

12- A research on Jihad called Al-Ijtihad ft Talabi Al-Jihad, which was printed several times.

Ibn Kathir's Death

Al-Hafiz Ibn Hajar Al-Asgalani said, "Ibn Kathir lost his sight just before his life ended. He died in Damascus in 774 H." May Allah grant mercy upon Ibn Kathir and make him among the residents of His Paradise.

PREFACE

In the name of Allah, Most Gracious, Most Merciful.

About this book

The previous publication of this book included some background information to the chapters of the Qur'an by an Islamic scholar known as Abul Ala Maududi. This information was used to shed more light on the chapters by giving a summery of why each chapter was given its name, It's period of revelation and the circumstances surrounding its revelatiom. However, some Muslims objected to the inclusion of the contributions of Maududi.

In this new publication of Tafsir Ibn Kathir, we have removed all traces of the contribution of Abul Ala Maududi. Personally, I do not know the reasons for the objections to Maududi, but this work concerns only the tafsir of Ibn Kathir, so we have not included anything from Maududi in it. We have also corrected all the typing and formatting errors found in the previous publication. We have not alter the structure of the book. The reader is still able to read the full Arabic Text of the thirty Parts of the Qur'an and follow its meanings in the English language. The transliteration of the Arabic text should also give the reader a taste of the sound of the original Arabic.

May Almighty Allah accept this effort from us, and make it a source of blessings for us in this world and in the next. I bear witness that there is none worthy of worship but Allah and I bear witness that Muhammad (may the peace and blessings of Allah be upon him) is the slave and messenger of Allah.

Performing Prostration While Reading the Qur'an

Question:

Could you please give a list of the Qur'anic verses when a prostration is recommended? What happens if we read these verses and not perform a prostration?

A. Jalil

Answer:

There are 15 verses in the Qur'an that mention prostration before God Almighty as a good action by God-fearing believers. Therefore, it is strongly recommended to perform such a prostration when we read or listen to any of these verses, whether during prayer or in any situation.

Some scholars are of the view that even if one has not performed ablution, one should prostrate oneself. These verses are given here, starting with the Arabic title of the surah which is followed by two numbers, the first indicating the surah, and the second indicating the verse,: Al-Araf 7: 206; Al-Raad 13: 15; Al-Nahl 16: 50; Al-Isra 17: 109; Maryam 19: 58; Al-Hajj 22: 18 & 22: 77; Al-Furqan 25: 60; Al-Naml 27: 26;

Al-Sajdah 32: 15; Saad 38: 25; Fussilat 41: 38; Al-Najm 53: 62; Al-Inshiqaq 84: 21 and Al-Alaq 96: 19.

If you do not perform a prostration when you read or listen to any of these verses, you have done badly because you miss out on the reward of performing a prostration for God. You incur no sin and violate no divine order.

Reference:
http://archive.arabnews.com/?page=5&section=0&article=97811&d=1&m=7&y=2007

The Glorious Qur'an Juz' 8 (Part 8): Chapter (Surah) 6: Al-An'am (Cattle, Livestock) 111 To Chapter (Surah) 7: Al-A'raf (The Heights) 087

PART 8 FULL ARABIC TEXT

Chapter (Surah) 6: An-An'am 111-165

۞ وَلَوْ أَنَّنَا نَزَّلْنَا إِلَيْهِمُ ٱلْمَلَٰٓئِكَةَ وَكَلَّمَهُمُ ٱلْمَوْتَىٰ وَحَشَرْنَا عَلَيْهِمْ كُلَّ شَىْءٍ قُبُلًا مَّا كَانُوا۟ لِيُؤْمِنُوٓا۟ إِلَّآ أَن يَشَآءَ ٱللَّهُ وَلَٰكِنَّ أَكْثَرَهُمْ يَجْهَلُونَ ۝ وَكَذَٰلِكَ جَعَلْنَا لِكُلِّ نَبِىٍّ عَدُوًّا شَيَٰطِينَ ٱلْإِنسِ وَٱلْجِنِّ يُوحِى بَعْضُهُمْ إِلَىٰ بَعْضٍ زُخْرُفَ ٱلْقَوْلِ غُرُورًا ۚ وَلَوْ شَآءَ رَبُّكَ مَا فَعَلُوهُ ۖ فَذَرْهُمْ وَمَا يَفْتَرُونَ ۝ وَلِتَصْغَىٰٓ إِلَيْهِ أَفْـِٔدَةُ ٱلَّذِينَ لَا يُؤْمِنُونَ بِٱلْـَٔاخِرَةِ وَلِيَرْضَوْهُ وَلِيَقْتَرِفُوا۟ مَا هُم مُّقْتَرِفُونَ ۝ أَفَغَيْرَ ٱللَّهِ أَبْتَغِى حَكَمًا وَهُوَ ٱلَّذِىٓ أَنزَلَ إِلَيْكُمُ ٱلْكِتَٰبَ مُفَصَّلًا ۚ وَٱلَّذِينَ ءَاتَيْنَٰهُمُ ٱلْكِتَٰبَ يَعْلَمُونَ أَنَّهُۥ مُنَزَّلٌ مِّن رَّبِّكَ بِٱلْحَقِّ ۖ فَلَا تَكُونَنَّ مِنَ ٱلْمُمْتَرِينَ ۝ وَتَمَّتْ كَلِمَتُ رَبِّكَ صِدْقًا وَعَدْلًا ۚ لَّا مُبَدِّلَ لِكَلِمَٰتِهِۦ ۚ وَهُوَ ٱلسَّمِيعُ ٱلْعَلِيمُ ۝ وَإِن تُطِعْ أَكْثَرَ مَن فِى ٱلْأَرْضِ يُضِلُّوكَ عَن سَبِيلِ ٱللَّهِ ۚ إِن يَتَّبِعُونَ إِلَّا ٱلظَّنَّ وَإِنْ هُمْ إِلَّا يَخْرُصُونَ ۝ إِنَّ رَبَّكَ هُوَ أَعْلَمُ مَن يَضِلُّ عَن سَبِيلِهِۦ ۖ وَهُوَ أَعْلَمُ بِٱلْمُهْتَدِينَ ۝ فَكُلُوا۟ مِمَّا ذُكِرَ ٱسْمُ ٱللَّهِ عَلَيْهِ إِن كُنتُم بِـَٔايَٰتِهِۦ مُؤْمِنِينَ ۝ وَمَا لَكُمْ أَلَّا تَأْكُلُوا۟ مِمَّا ذُكِرَ ٱسْمُ ٱللَّهِ عَلَيْهِ وَقَدْ فَصَّلَ لَكُم مَّا حَرَّمَ عَلَيْكُمْ إِلَّا مَا ٱضْطُرِرْتُمْ إِلَيْهِ ۗ وَإِنَّ كَثِيرًا لَّيُضِلُّونَ بِأَهْوَآئِهِم بِغَيْرِ عِلْمٍ ۗ إِنَّ رَبَّكَ هُوَ أَعْلَمُ بِٱلْمُعْتَدِينَ ۝ وَذَرُوا۟ ظَٰهِرَ ٱلْإِثْمِ وَبَاطِنَهُۥٓ ۚ إِنَّ ٱلَّذِينَ يَكْسِبُونَ ٱلْإِثْمَ

سَيُجْزَوْنَ بِمَا كَانُواْ يَقْتَرِفُونَ ۝ وَلاَ تَأْكُلُواْ مِمَّا لَمْ يُذْكَرِ اسْمُ اللَّهِ عَلَيْهِ وَإِنَّهُ لَفِسْقٌ وَإِنَّ الشَّيَاطِينَ لَيُوحُونَ إِلَى أَوْلِيَآئِهِمْ لِيُجَـدِلُوكُمْ وَإِنْ أَطَعْتُمُوهُمْ إِنَّكُمْ لَمُشْرِكُونَ ۝ أَوَ مَن كَانَ مَيْتًا فَأَحْيَيْنَـهُ وَجَعَلْنَا لَهُ نُورًا يَمْشِى بِهِ فِى النَّاسِ كَمَن مَّثَلُهُ فِى الظُّلُمَـتِ لَيْسَ بِخَارِجٍ مِّنْهَا كَذَلِكَ زُيِّنَ لِلْكَـفِرِينَ مَا كَانُواْ يَعْمَلُونَ ۝ وَكَذَلِكَ جَعَلْنَا فِى كُلِّ قَرْيَةٍ أَكَـبِرَ مُجْرِمِيهَا لِيَمْكُرُواْ فِيهَا وَمَا يَمْكُرُونَ إِلاَّ بِأَنفُسِهِمْ وَمَا يَشْعُرُونَ ۝ وَإِذَا جَآءَتْهُمْ ءَايَةٌ قَالُواْ لَن نُّؤْمِنَ حَتَّى نُؤْتَى مِثْلَ مَا أُوتِىَ رُسُلُ اللَّهِ اللَّهُ أَعْلَمُ حَيْثُ يَجْعَلُ رِسَالَتَهُ سَيُصِيبُ الَّذِينَ أَجْرَمُواْ صَغَارٌ عِندَ اللَّهِ وَعَذَابٌ شَدِيدٌ بِمَا كَانُواْ يَمْكُرُونَ ۝ فَمَن يُرِدِ اللَّهُ أَن يَهْدِيَهُ يَشْرَحْ صَدْرَهُ لِلإِسْلَـمِ وَمَن يُرِدْ أَن يُضِلَّهُ يَجْعَلْ صَدْرَهُ ضَيِّقًا حَرَجًا كَأَنَّمَا يَصَّعَّدُ فِى السَّمَآءِ كَذَلِكَ يَجْعَلُ اللَّهُ الرِّجْسَ عَلَى الَّذِينَ لاَ يُؤْمِنُونَ ۝ وَهَـذَا صِرَاطُ رَبِّكَ مُسْتَقِيمًا قَدْ فَصَّلْنَا الاٌّيَـتِ لِقَوْمٍ يَذَّكَّرُونَ ۝ لَهُمْ دَارُ السَّلَـمِ عِندَ رَبِّهِمْ وَهُوَ وَلِيُّهُمْ بِمَا كَانُواْ يَعْمَلُونَ ۝ وَيَوْمَ يَحْشُرُهُمْ جَمِيعًا يَـمَعْشَرَ الْجِنِّ قَدِ اسْتَكْثَرْتُم مِّنَ الإِنسِ وَقَالَ أَوْلِيَآؤُهُم مِّنَ الإِنسِ رَبَّنَا اسْتَمْتَعَ بَعْضُنَا بِبَعْضٍ وَبَلَغْنَا أَجَلَنَا الَّذِى أَجَّلْتَ لَنَا قَالَ النَّارُ مَثْوَاكُمْ خَـلِدِينَ فِيهَآ إِلاَّ مَا شَآءَ اللَّهُ إِنَّ رَبَّكَ حَكِيمٌ عَلِيمٌ ۝ وَكَذَلِكَ نُوَلِّى بَعْضَ الظَّـلِمِينَ بَعْضًا بِمَا كَانُواْ يَكْسِبُونَ ۝ يَـمَعْشَرَ الْجِنِّ وَالإِنسِ أَلَمْ يَأْتِكُمْ رُسُلٌ مِّنكُمْ يَقُصُّونَ عَلَيْكُمْ ءَايَـتِى وَيُنذِرُونَكُمْ لِقَآءَ يَوْمِكُمْ هَـذَا قَالُواْ شَهِدْنَا عَلَى أَنفُسِنَا وَغَرَّتْهُمُ الْحَيَوةُ الدُّنْيَا وَشَهِدُواْ عَلَى أَنفُسِهِمْ أَنَّهُمْ كَانُواْ كَـفِرِينَ ۝ ذَلِكَ أَن لَّمْ يَكُن رَّبُّكَ مُهْلِكَ الْقُرَى بِظُلْمٍ وَأَهْلُهَا غَـفِلُونَ ۝ وَلِكُلٍّ دَرَجَـتٌ مِّمَّا عَمِلُواْ وَمَا رَبُّكَ بِغَـفِلٍ

عَمَّا يَعْمَلُونَ ۝ وَرَبُّكَ ٱلْغَنِىُّ ذُو ٱلرَّحْمَةِ ۚ إِن يَشَأْ يُذْهِبْكُمْ وَيَسْتَخْلِفْ مِنۢ بَعْدِكُم مَّا يَشَآءُ كَمَآ أَنشَأَكُم مِّن ذُرِّيَّةِ قَوْمٍ ءَاخَرِينَ ۝ إِنَّ مَا تُوعَدُونَ لَءَاتٍ ۖ وَمَآ أَنتُم بِمُعْجِزِينَ ۝ قُلْ يَٰقَوْمِ ٱعْمَلُوا۟ عَلَىٰ مَكَانَتِكُمْ إِنِّى عَامِلٌ ۖ فَسَوْفَ تَعْلَمُونَ مَن تَكُونُ لَهُۥ عَٰقِبَةُ ٱلدَّارِ ۗ إِنَّهُۥ لَا يُفْلِحُ ٱلظَّٰلِمُونَ ۝ وَجَعَلُوا۟ لِلَّهِ مِمَّا ذَرَأَ مِنَ ٱلْحَرْثِ وَٱلْأَنْعَٰمِ نَصِيبًا فَقَالُوا۟ هَٰذَا لِلَّهِ بِزَعْمِهِمْ وَهَٰذَا لِشُرَكَآئِنَا ۖ فَمَا كَانَ لِشُرَكَآئِهِمْ فَلَا يَصِلُ إِلَى ٱللَّهِ ۖ وَمَا كَانَ لِلَّهِ فَهُوَ يَصِلُ إِلَىٰ شُرَكَآئِهِمْ ۗ سَآءَ مَا يَحْكُمُونَ ۝ وَكَذَٰلِكَ زَيَّنَ لِكَثِيرٍ مِّنَ ٱلْمُشْرِكِينَ قَتْلَ أَوْلَٰدِهِمْ شُرَكَآؤُهُمْ لِيُرْدُوهُمْ وَلِيَلْبِسُوا۟ عَلَيْهِمْ دِينَهُمْ ۖ وَلَوْ شَآءَ ٱللَّهُ مَا فَعَلُوهُ ۖ فَذَرْهُمْ وَمَا يَفْتَرُونَ ۝ وَقَالُوا۟ هَٰذِهِۦٓ أَنْعَٰمٌ وَحَرْثٌ حِجْرٌ لَّا يَطْعَمُهَآ إِلَّا مَن نَّشَآءُ بِزَعْمِهِمْ وَأَنْعَٰمٌ حُرِّمَتْ ظُهُورُهَا وَأَنْعَٰمٌ لَّا يَذْكُرُونَ ٱسْمَ ٱللَّهِ عَلَيْهَا ٱفْتِرَآءً عَلَيْهِ ۚ سَيَجْزِيهِم بِمَا كَانُوا۟ يَفْتَرُونَ ۝ وَقَالُوا۟ مَا فِى بُطُونِ هَٰذِهِ ٱلْأَنْعَٰمِ خَالِصَةٌ لِّذُكُورِنَا وَمُحَرَّمٌ عَلَىٰٓ أَزْوَٰجِنَا ۖ وَإِن يَكُن مَّيْتَةً فَهُمْ فِيهِ شُرَكَآءُ ۚ سَيَجْزِيهِمْ وَصْفَهُمْ ۚ إِنَّهُۥ حَكِيمٌ عَلِيمٌ ۝ قَدْ خَسِرَ ٱلَّذِينَ قَتَلُوٓا۟ أَوْلَٰدَهُمْ سَفَهًۢا بِغَيْرِ عِلْمٍ وَحَرَّمُوا۟ مَا رَزَقَهُمُ ٱللَّهُ ٱفْتِرَآءً عَلَى ٱللَّهِ ۚ قَدْ ضَلُّوا۟ وَمَا كَانُوا۟ مُهْتَدِينَ ۝ ۞ وَهُوَ ٱلَّذِىٓ أَنشَأَ جَنَّٰتٍ مَّعْرُوشَٰتٍ وَغَيْرَ مَعْرُوشَٰتٍ وَٱلنَّخْلَ وَٱلزَّرْعَ مُخْتَلِفًا أُكُلُهُۥ وَٱلزَّيْتُونَ وَٱلرُّمَّانَ مُتَشَٰبِهًا وَغَيْرَ مُتَشَٰبِهٍ ۚ كُلُوا۟ مِن ثَمَرِهِۦٓ إِذَآ أَثْمَرَ وَءَاتُوا۟ حَقَّهُۥ يَوْمَ حَصَادِهِۦ ۖ وَلَا تُسْرِفُوٓا۟ ۚ إِنَّهُۥ لَا يُحِبُّ ٱلْمُسْرِفِينَ ۝ وَمِنَ ٱلْأَنْعَٰمِ حَمُولَةً وَفَرْشًا ۚ كُلُوا۟ مِمَّا رَزَقَكُمُ ٱللَّهُ وَلَا تَتَّبِعُوا۟ خُطُوَٰتِ ٱلشَّيْطَٰنِ ۚ إِنَّهُۥ لَكُمْ عَدُوٌّ مُّبِينٌ

ثَمَٰنِيَةَ أَزْوَٰجٍ ۖ مِّنَ ٱلضَّأْنِ ٱثْنَيْنِ وَمِنَ ٱلْمَعْزِ ٱثْنَيْنِ ۗ قُلْ ءَآلذَّكَرَيْنِ حَرَّمَ أَمِ ٱلْأُنثَيَيْنِ أَمَّا ٱشْتَمَلَتْ عَلَيْهِ أَرْحَامُ ٱلْأُنثَيَيْنِ ۖ نَبِّـُٔونِى بِعِلْمٍ إِن كُنتُمْ صَٰدِقِينَ ۝ وَمِنَ ٱلْإِبِلِ ٱثْنَيْنِ وَمِنَ ٱلْبَقَرِ ٱثْنَيْنِ ۗ قُلْ ءَآلذَّكَرَيْنِ حَرَّمَ أَمِ ٱلْأُنثَيَيْنِ أَمَّا ٱشْتَمَلَتْ عَلَيْهِ أَرْحَامُ ٱلْأُنثَيَيْنِ ۖ أَمْ كُنتُمْ شُهَدَآءَ إِذْ وَصَّىٰكُمُ ٱللَّهُ بِهَٰذَا ۚ فَمَنْ أَظْلَمُ مِمَّنِ ٱفْتَرَىٰ عَلَى ٱللَّهِ كَذِبًا لِّيُضِلَّ ٱلنَّاسَ بِغَيْرِ عِلْمٍ ۗ إِنَّ ٱللَّهَ لَا يَهْدِى ٱلْقَوْمَ ٱلظَّٰلِمِينَ ۝ قُل لَّآ أَجِدُ فِى مَآ أُوحِىَ إِلَىَّ مُحَرَّمًا عَلَىٰ طَاعِمٍ يَطْعَمُهُۥٓ إِلَّآ أَن يَكُونَ مَيْتَةً أَوْ دَمًا مَّسْفُوحًا أَوْ لَحْمَ خِنزِيرٍ فَإِنَّهُۥ رِجْسٌ أَوْ فِسْقًا أُهِلَّ لِغَيْرِ ٱللَّهِ بِهِۦ ۚ فَمَنِ ٱضْطُرَّ غَيْرَ بَاغٍ وَلَا عَادٍ فَإِنَّ رَبَّكَ غَفُورٌ رَّحِيمٌ ۝ وَعَلَى ٱلَّذِينَ هَادُوا۟ حَرَّمْنَا كُلَّ ذِى ظُفُرٍ ۖ وَمِنَ ٱلْبَقَرِ وَٱلْغَنَمِ حَرَّمْنَا عَلَيْهِمْ شُحُومَهُمَآ إِلَّا مَا حَمَلَتْ ظُهُورُهُمَآ أَوِ ٱلْحَوَايَآ أَوْ مَا ٱخْتَلَطَ بِعَظْمٍ ۚ ذَٰلِكَ جَزَيْنَٰهُم بِبَغْيِهِمْ ۖ وَإِنَّا لَصَٰدِقُونَ ۝ فَإِن كَذَّبُوكَ فَقُل رَّبُّكُمْ ذُو رَحْمَةٍ وَٰسِعَةٍ وَلَا يُرَدُّ بَأْسُهُۥ عَنِ ٱلْقَوْمِ ٱلْمُجْرِمِينَ ۝ سَيَقُولُ ٱلَّذِينَ أَشْرَكُوا۟ لَوْ شَآءَ ٱللَّهُ مَآ أَشْرَكْنَا وَلَآ ءَابَآؤُنَا وَلَا حَرَّمْنَا مِن شَىْءٍ ۚ كَذَٰلِكَ كَذَّبَ ٱلَّذِينَ مِن قَبْلِهِمْ حَتَّىٰ ذَاقُوا۟ بَأْسَنَا ۗ قُلْ هَلْ عِندَكُم مِّنْ عِلْمٍ فَتُخْرِجُوهُ لَنَآ ۖ إِن تَتَّبِعُونَ إِلَّا ٱلظَّنَّ وَإِنْ أَنتُمْ إِلَّا تَخْرُصُونَ ۝ قُلْ فَلِلَّهِ ٱلْحُجَّةُ ٱلْبَٰلِغَةُ ۖ فَلَوْ شَآءَ لَهَدَىٰكُمْ أَجْمَعِينَ ۝ قُلْ هَلُمَّ شُهَدَآءَكُمُ ٱلَّذِينَ يَشْهَدُونَ أَنَّ ٱللَّهَ حَرَّمَ هَٰذَا ۖ فَإِن شَهِدُوا۟ فَلَا تَشْهَدْ مَعَهُمْ ۚ وَلَا تَتَّبِعْ أَهْوَآءَ ٱلَّذِينَ كَذَّبُوا۟ بِـَٔايَٰتِنَا وَٱلَّذِينَ لَا يُؤْمِنُونَ بِٱلْءَاخِرَةِ وَهُم بِرَبِّهِمْ يَعْدِلُونَ ۝ ۞ قُلْ تَعَالَوْا۟ أَتْلُ مَا حَرَّمَ رَبُّكُمْ عَلَيْكُمْ ۖ أَلَّا تُشْرِكُوا۟ بِهِۦ شَيْـًٔا ۖ وَبِٱلْوَٰلِدَيْنِ إِحْسَٰنًا ۖ وَلَا تَقْتُلُوٓا۟ أَوْلَٰدَكُم مِّنْ إِمْلَٰقٍ ۖ نَّحْنُ

نَرْزُقُكُمْ وَإِيَّاهُمْ ۖ وَلَا تَقْرَبُوا۟ ٱلْفَوَٰحِشَ مَا ظَهَرَ مِنْهَا وَمَا بَطَنَ ۖ وَلَا تَقْتُلُوا۟ ٱلنَّفْسَ ٱلَّتِى حَرَّمَ ٱللَّهُ إِلَّا بِٱلْحَقِّ ۚ ذَٰلِكُمْ وَصَّىٰكُم بِهِۦ لَعَلَّكُمْ تَعْقِلُونَ ۝١٥١ وَلَا تَقْرَبُوا۟ مَالَ ٱلْيَتِيمِ إِلَّا بِٱلَّتِى هِىَ أَحْسَنُ حَتَّىٰ يَبْلُغَ أَشُدَّهُۥ ۖ وَأَوْفُوا۟ ٱلْكَيْلَ وَٱلْمِيزَانَ بِٱلْقِسْطِ ۖ لَا نُكَلِّفُ نَفْسًا إِلَّا وُسْعَهَا ۖ وَإِذَا قُلْتُمْ فَٱعْدِلُوا۟ وَلَوْ كَانَ ذَا قُرْبَىٰ ۖ وَبِعَهْدِ ٱللَّهِ أَوْفُوا۟ ۚ ذَٰلِكُمْ وَصَّىٰكُم بِهِۦ لَعَلَّكُمْ تَذَكَّرُونَ ۝١٥٢ وَأَنَّ هَٰذَا صِرَٰطِى مُسْتَقِيمًا فَٱتَّبِعُوهُ ۖ وَلَا تَتَّبِعُوا۟ ٱلسُّبُلَ فَتَفَرَّقَ بِكُمْ عَن سَبِيلِهِۦ ۚ ذَٰلِكُمْ وَصَّىٰكُم بِهِۦ لَعَلَّكُمْ تَتَّقُونَ ۝١٥٣ ثُمَّ ءَاتَيْنَا مُوسَى ٱلْكِتَٰبَ تَمَامًا عَلَى ٱلَّذِىٓ أَحْسَنَ وَتَفْصِيلًا لِّكُلِّ شَىْءٍ وَهُدًى وَرَحْمَةً لَّعَلَّهُم بِلِقَآءِ رَبِّهِمْ يُؤْمِنُونَ ۝١٥٤ وَهَٰذَا كِتَٰبٌ أَنزَلْنَٰهُ مُبَارَكٌ فَٱتَّبِعُوهُ وَٱتَّقُوا۟ لَعَلَّكُمْ تُرْحَمُونَ ۝١٥٥ أَن تَقُولُوٓا۟ إِنَّمَآ أُنزِلَ ٱلْكِتَٰبُ عَلَىٰ طَآئِفَتَيْنِ مِن قَبْلِنَا وَإِن كُنَّا عَن دِرَاسَتِهِمْ لَغَٰفِلِينَ ۝١٥٦ أَوْ تَقُولُوا۟ لَوْ أَنَّآ أُنزِلَ عَلَيْنَا ٱلْكِتَٰبُ لَكُنَّآ أَهْدَىٰ مِنْهُمْ ۚ فَقَدْ جَآءَكُم بَيِّنَةٌ مِّن رَّبِّكُمْ وَهُدًى وَرَحْمَةٌ ۚ فَمَنْ أَظْلَمُ مِمَّن كَذَّبَ بِـَٔايَٰتِ ٱللَّهِ وَصَدَفَ عَنْهَا ۗ سَنَجْزِى ٱلَّذِينَ يَصْدِفُونَ عَنْ ءَايَٰتِنَا سُوٓءَ ٱلْعَذَابِ بِمَا كَانُوا۟ يَصْدِفُونَ ۝١٥٧ هَلْ يَنظُرُونَ إِلَّآ أَن تَأْتِيَهُمُ ٱلْمَلَٰٓئِكَةُ أَوْ يَأْتِىَ رَبُّكَ أَوْ يَأْتِىَ بَعْضُ ءَايَٰتِ رَبِّكَ ۗ يَوْمَ يَأْتِى بَعْضُ ءَايَٰتِ رَبِّكَ لَا يَنفَعُ نَفْسًا إِيمَٰنُهَا لَمْ تَكُنْ ءَامَنَتْ مِن قَبْلُ أَوْ كَسَبَتْ فِىٓ إِيمَٰنِهَا خَيْرًا ۗ قُلِ ٱنتَظِرُوٓا۟ إِنَّا مُنتَظِرُونَ ۝١٥٨ إِنَّ ٱلَّذِينَ فَرَّقُوا۟ دِينَهُمْ وَكَانُوا۟ شِيَعًا لَّسْتَ مِنْهُمْ فِى شَىْءٍ ۚ إِنَّمَآ أَمْرُهُمْ إِلَى ٱللَّهِ ثُمَّ يُنَبِّئُهُم بِمَا كَانُوا۟ يَفْعَلُونَ ۝١٥٩ مَن جَآءَ بِٱلْحَسَنَةِ فَلَهُۥ عَشْرُ أَمْثَالِهَا ۖ وَمَن جَآءَ بِٱلسَّيِّئَةِ فَلَا يُجْزَىٰٓ إِلَّا مِثْلَهَا وَهُمْ لَا يُظْلَمُونَ ۝١٦٠ قُلْ إِنَّنِى هَدَىٰنِى رَبِّىٓ إِلَىٰ صِرَٰطٍ مُّسْتَقِيمٍ دِينًا قِيَمًا مِّلَّةَ إِبْرَٰهِيمَ حَنِيفًا ۚ وَمَا كَانَ مِنَ ٱلْمُشْرِكِينَ ۝١٦١ قُلْ إِنَّ صَلَاتِى وَنُسُكِى

وَمَحْيَايَ وَمَمَاتِي لِلَّهِ رَبِّ الْعَالَمِينَ ۝ لَا شَرِيكَ لَهُ ۖ وَبِذَٰلِكَ أُمِرْتُ وَأَنَا۠ أَوَّلُ الْمُسْلِمِينَ ۝ قُلْ أَغَيْرَ اللَّهِ أَبْغِي رَبًّا وَهُوَ رَبُّ كُلِّ شَيْءٍ ۚ وَلَا تَكْسِبُ كُلُّ نَفْسٍ إِلَّا عَلَيْهَا ۚ وَلَا تَزِرُ وَازِرَةٌ وِزْرَ أُخْرَىٰ ۚ ثُمَّ إِلَىٰ رَبِّكُم مَّرْجِعُكُمْ فَيُنَبِّئُكُم بِمَا كُنتُمْ فِيهِ تَخْتَلِفُونَ ۝ وَهُوَ الَّذِي جَعَلَكُمْ خَلَائِفَ الْأَرْضِ وَرَفَعَ بَعْضَكُمْ فَوْقَ بَعْضٍ دَرَجَاتٍ لِّيَبْلُوَكُمْ فِي مَا آتَاكُمْ ۗ إِنَّ رَبَّكَ سَرِيعُ الْعِقَابِ وَإِنَّهُ لَغَفُورٌ رَّحِيمٌ ۝

(Al-An'am 111-165)

Chapter (Surah) 7: Al A'raf 001-087

بِسْمِ اللَّهِ الرَّحْمَٰنِ الرَّحِيمِ

المص ۝ كِتَابٌ أُنزِلَ إِلَيْكَ فَلَا يَكُن فِي صَدْرِكَ حَرَجٌ مِّنْهُ لِتُنذِرَ بِهِ وَذِكْرَىٰ لِلْمُؤْمِنِينَ ۝ اتَّبِعُوا مَا أُنزِلَ إِلَيْكُم مِّن رَّبِّكُمْ وَلَا تَتَّبِعُوا مِن دُونِهِ أَوْلِيَاءَ ۗ قَلِيلًا مَّا تَذَكَّرُونَ ۝ وَكَم مِّن قَرْيَةٍ أَهْلَكْنَاهَا فَجَاءَهَا بَأْسُنَا بَيَاتًا أَوْ هُمْ قَائِلُونَ ۝ فَمَا كَانَ دَعْوَاهُمْ إِذْ جَاءَهُم بَأْسُنَا إِلَّا أَن قَالُوا إِنَّا كُنَّا ظَالِمِينَ ۝ فَلَنَسْأَلَنَّ الَّذِينَ أُرْسِلَ إِلَيْهِمْ وَلَنَسْأَلَنَّ الْمُرْسَلِينَ ۝ فَلَنَقُصَّنَّ عَلَيْهِم بِعِلْمٍ ۖ وَمَا كُنَّا غَائِبِينَ ۝ وَالْوَزْنُ يَوْمَئِذٍ الْحَقُّ ۚ فَمَن ثَقُلَتْ مَوَازِينُهُ فَأُولَٰئِكَ هُمُ الْمُفْلِحُونَ ۝ وَمَنْ خَفَّتْ مَوَازِينُهُ فَأُولَٰئِكَ الَّذِينَ خَسِرُوا أَنفُسَهُم بِمَا كَانُوا بِآيَاتِنَا يَظْلِمُونَ ۝ وَلَقَدْ مَكَّنَّاكُمْ فِي الْأَرْضِ وَجَعَلْنَا لَكُمْ فِيهَا مَعَايِشَ ۗ قَلِيلًا مَّا تَشْكُرُونَ ۝ وَلَقَدْ خَلَقْنَاكُمْ ثُمَّ صَوَّرْنَاكُمْ ثُمَّ قُلْنَا لِلْمَلَائِكَةِ اسْجُدُوا لِآدَمَ فَسَجَدُوا إِلَّا إِبْلِيسَ لَمْ يَكُن مِّنَ السَّاجِدِينَ ۝ قَالَ مَا مَنَعَكَ أَلَّا تَسْجُدَ إِذْ أَمَرْتُكَ ۖ قَالَ أَنَا۠ خَيْرٌ مِّنْهُ خَلَقْتَنِي مِن نَّارٍ وَخَلَقْتَهُ مِن طِينٍ ۝ قَالَ فَاهْبِطْ مِنْهَا فَمَا يَكُونُ لَكَ أَن تَتَكَبَّرَ فِيهَا فَاخْرُجْ إِنَّكَ مِنَ الصَّاغِرِينَ ۝ قَالَ أَنظِرْنِي إِلَىٰ يَوْمِ يُبْعَثُونَ ۝

قَالَ إِنَّكَ مِنَ ٱلْمُنظَرِينَ ۝ قَالَ فَبِمَآ أَغْوَيْتَنِى لَأَقْعُدَنَّ لَهُمْ صِرَٰطَكَ ٱلْمُسْتَقِيمَ ۝ ثُمَّ لَءَاتِيَنَّهُم مِّنۢ بَيْنِ أَيْدِيهِمْ وَمِنْ خَلْفِهِمْ وَعَنْ أَيْمَٰنِهِمْ وَعَن شَمَآئِلِهِمْ ۖ وَلَا تَجِدُ أَكْثَرَهُمْ شَٰكِرِينَ ۝ قَالَ ٱخْرُجْ مِنْهَا مَذْءُومًا مَّدْحُورًا ۖ لَّمَن تَبِعَكَ مِنْهُمْ لَأَمْلَأَنَّ جَهَنَّمَ مِنكُمْ أَجْمَعِينَ ۝ وَيَٰٓـَٔادَمُ ٱسْكُنْ أَنتَ وَزَوْجُكَ ٱلْجَنَّةَ فَكُلَا مِنْ حَيْثُ شِئْتُمَا وَلَا تَقْرَبَا هَٰذِهِ ٱلشَّجَرَةَ فَتَكُونَا مِنَ ٱلظَّٰلِمِينَ ۝ فَوَسْوَسَ لَهُمَا ٱلشَّيْطَٰنُ لِيُبْدِىَ لَهُمَا مَا وُۥرِىَ عَنْهُمَا مِن سَوْءَٰتِهِمَا وَقَالَ مَا نَهَىٰكُمَا رَبُّكُمَا عَنْ هَٰذِهِ ٱلشَّجَرَةِ إِلَّآ أَن تَكُونَا مَلَكَيْنِ أَوْ تَكُونَا مِنَ ٱلْخَٰلِدِينَ ۝ وَقَاسَمَهُمَآ إِنِّى لَكُمَا لَمِنَ ٱلنَّٰصِحِينَ ۝ فَدَلَّىٰهُمَا بِغُرُورٍ ۚ فَلَمَّا ذَاقَا ٱلشَّجَرَةَ بَدَتْ لَهُمَا سَوْءَٰتُهُمَا وَطَفِقَا يَخْصِفَانِ عَلَيْهِمَا مِن وَرَقِ ٱلْجَنَّةِ ۖ وَنَادَىٰهُمَا رَبُّهُمَآ أَلَمْ أَنْهَكُمَا عَن تِلْكُمَا ٱلشَّجَرَةِ وَأَقُل لَّكُمَآ إِنَّ ٱلشَّيْطَٰنَ لَكُمَا عَدُوٌّ مُّبِينٌ ۝ قَالَا رَبَّنَا ظَلَمْنَآ أَنفُسَنَا وَإِن لَّمْ تَغْفِرْ لَنَا وَتَرْحَمْنَا لَنَكُونَنَّ مِنَ ٱلْخَٰسِرِينَ ۝ قَالَ ٱهْبِطُوا۟ بَعْضُكُمْ لِبَعْضٍ عَدُوٌّ ۖ وَلَكُمْ فِى ٱلْأَرْضِ مُسْتَقَرٌّ وَمَتَٰعٌ إِلَىٰ حِينٍ ۝ قَالَ فِيهَا تَحْيَوْنَ وَفِيهَا تَمُوتُونَ وَمِنْهَا تُخْرَجُونَ ۝ يَٰبَنِىٓ ءَادَمَ قَدْ أَنزَلْنَا عَلَيْكُمْ لِبَاسًا يُوَٰرِى سَوْءَٰتِكُمْ وَرِيشًا ۖ وَلِبَاسُ ٱلتَّقْوَىٰ ذَٰلِكَ خَيْرٌ ۚ ذَٰلِكَ مِنْ ءَايَٰتِ ٱللَّهِ لَعَلَّهُمْ يَذَّكَّرُونَ ۝ يَٰبَنِىٓ ءَادَمَ لَا يَفْتِنَنَّكُمُ ٱلشَّيْطَٰنُ كَمَآ أَخْرَجَ أَبَوَيْكُم مِّنَ ٱلْجَنَّةِ يَنزِعُ عَنْهُمَا لِبَاسَهُمَا لِيُرِيَهُمَا سَوْءَٰتِهِمَآ ۗ إِنَّهُۥ يَرَىٰكُمْ هُوَ وَقَبِيلُهُۥ مِنْ حَيْثُ لَا تَرَوْنَهُمْ ۗ إِنَّا جَعَلْنَا ٱلشَّيَٰطِينَ أَوْلِيَآءَ لِلَّذِينَ لَا يُؤْمِنُونَ ۝ وَإِذَا فَعَلُوا۟ فَٰحِشَةً قَالُوا۟ وَجَدْنَا عَلَيْهَآ ءَابَآءَنَا وَٱللَّهُ أَمَرَنَا بِهَا ۗ قُلْ إِنَّ ٱللَّهَ لَا يَأْمُرُ بِٱلْفَحْشَآءِ ۖ أَتَقُولُونَ عَلَى ٱللَّهِ مَا لَا تَعْلَمُونَ ۝ قُلْ أَمَرَ رَبِّى بِٱلْقِسْطِ ۖ وَأَقِيمُوا۟ وُجُوهَكُمْ عِندَ كُلِّ مَسْجِدٍ وَٱدْعُوهُ مُخْلِصِينَ لَهُ ٱلدِّينَ ۚ كَمَا بَدَأَكُمْ تَعُودُونَ ۝ فَرِيقًا هَدَىٰ

وَفَرِيقًا حَقَّ عَلَيْهِمُ ٱلضَّلَـٰلَةُ ۗ إِنَّهُمُ ٱتَّخَذُوا۟ ٱلشَّيَـٰطِينَ أَوْلِيَآءَ مِن دُونِ ٱللَّهِ وَيَحْسَبُونَ أَنَّهُم مُّهْتَدُونَ ۝ يَـٰبَنِىٓ ءَادَمَ خُذُوا۟ زِينَتَكُمْ عِندَ كُلِّ مَسْجِدٍ وَكُلُوا۟ وَٱشْرَبُوا۟ وَلَا تُسْرِفُوٓا۟ ۚ إِنَّهُۥ لَا يُحِبُّ ٱلْمُسْرِفِينَ ۝ قُلْ مَنْ حَرَّمَ زِينَةَ ٱللَّهِ ٱلَّتِىٓ أَخْرَجَ لِعِبَادِهِۦ وَٱلطَّيِّبَـٰتِ مِنَ ٱلرِّزْقِ ۚ قُلْ هِىَ لِلَّذِينَ ءَامَنُوا۟ فِى ٱلْحَيَوٰةِ ٱلدُّنْيَا خَالِصَةً يَوْمَ ٱلْقِيَـٰمَةِ ۗ كَذَٰلِكَ نُفَصِّلُ ٱلْـَٔايَـٰتِ لِقَوْمٍ يَعْلَمُونَ ۝ قُلْ إِنَّمَا حَرَّمَ رَبِّىَ ٱلْفَوَٰحِشَ مَا ظَهَرَ مِنْهَا وَمَا بَطَنَ وَٱلْإِثْمَ وَٱلْبَغْىَ بِغَيْرِ ٱلْحَقِّ وَأَن تُشْرِكُوا۟ بِٱللَّهِ مَا لَمْ يُنَزِّلْ بِهِۦ سُلْطَـٰنًا وَأَن تَقُولُوا۟ عَلَى ٱللَّهِ مَا لَا تَعْلَمُونَ ۝ وَلِكُلِّ أُمَّةٍ أَجَلٌ ۖ فَإِذَا جَآءَ أَجَلُهُمْ لَا يَسْتَأْخِرُونَ سَاعَةً ۖ وَلَا يَسْتَقْدِمُونَ ۝ يَـٰبَنِىٓ ءَادَمَ إِمَّا يَأْتِيَنَّكُمْ رُسُلٌ مِّنكُمْ يَقُصُّونَ عَلَيْكُمْ ءَايَـٰتِى ۙ فَمَنِ ٱتَّقَىٰ وَأَصْلَحَ فَلَا خَوْفٌ عَلَيْهِمْ وَلَا هُمْ يَحْزَنُونَ ۝ وَٱلَّذِينَ كَذَّبُوا۟ بِـَٔايَـٰتِنَا وَٱسْتَكْبَرُوا۟ عَنْهَآ أُو۟لَـٰٓئِكَ أَصْحَـٰبُ ٱلنَّارِ ۖ هُمْ فِيهَا خَـٰلِدُونَ ۝ فَمَنْ أَظْلَمُ مِمَّنِ ٱفْتَرَىٰ عَلَى ٱللَّهِ كَذِبًا أَوْ كَذَّبَ بِـَٔايَـٰتِهِۦٓ ۚ أُو۟لَـٰٓئِكَ يَنَالُهُمْ نَصِيبُهُم مِّنَ ٱلْكِتَـٰبِ ۖ حَتَّىٰٓ إِذَا جَآءَتْهُمْ رُسُلُنَا يَتَوَفَّوْنَهُمْ قَالُوٓا۟ أَيْنَ مَا كُنتُمْ تَدْعُونَ مِن دُونِ ٱللَّهِ ۖ قَالُوا۟ ضَلُّوا۟ عَنَّا وَشَهِدُوا۟ عَلَىٰٓ أَنفُسِهِمْ أَنَّهُمْ كَانُوا۟ كَـٰفِرِينَ ۝ قَالَ ٱدْخُلُوا۟ فِىٓ أُمَمٍ قَدْ خَلَتْ مِن قَبْلِكُم مِّنَ ٱلْجِنِّ وَٱلْإِنسِ فِى ٱلنَّارِ ۖ كُلَّمَا دَخَلَتْ أُمَّةٌ لَّعَنَتْ أُخْتَهَا ۖ حَتَّىٰٓ إِذَا ٱدَّارَكُوا۟ فِيهَا جَمِيعًا قَالَتْ أُخْرَىٰهُمْ لِأُولَىٰهُمْ رَبَّنَا هَـٰٓؤُلَآءِ أَضَلُّونَا فَـَٔاتِهِمْ عَذَابًا ضِعْفًا مِّنَ ٱلنَّارِ ۖ قَالَ لِكُلٍّ ضِعْفٌ وَلَـٰكِن لَّا تَعْلَمُونَ ۝ وَقَالَتْ أُولَىٰهُمْ لِأُخْرَىٰهُمْ فَمَا كَانَ لَكُمْ عَلَيْنَا مِن فَضْلٍ فَذُوقُوا۟ ٱلْعَذَابَ بِمَا كُنتُمْ تَكْسِبُونَ ۝ إِنَّ ٱلَّذِينَ كَذَّبُوا۟ بِـَٔايَـٰتِنَا وَٱسْتَكْبَرُوا۟ عَنْهَا لَا تُفَتَّحُ لَهُمْ أَبْوَٰبُ ٱلسَّمَآءِ وَلَا يَدْخُلُونَ ٱلْجَنَّةَ حَتَّىٰ يَلِجَ ٱلْجَمَلُ فِى سَمِّ ٱلْخِيَاطِ ۚ وَكَذَٰلِكَ نَجْزِى ٱلْمُجْرِمِينَ ۝ لَهُم مِّن جَهَنَّمَ مِهَادٌ

وَمِن فَوْقِهِمْ غَوَاشٍ ۚ وَكَذَٰلِكَ نَجْزِى ٱلظَّٰلِمِينَ ۝ وَٱلَّذِينَ ءَامَنُوا۟ وَعَمِلُوا۟ ٱلصَّٰلِحَٰتِ لَا نُكَلِّفُ نَفْسًا إِلَّا وُسْعَهَآ أُو۟لَٰٓئِكَ أَصْحَٰبُ ٱلْجَنَّةِ ۖ هُمْ فِيهَا خَٰلِدُونَ ۝ وَنَزَعْنَا مَا فِى صُدُورِهِم مِّنْ غِلٍّ تَجْرِى مِن تَحْتِهِمُ ٱلْأَنْهَٰرُ ۖ وَقَالُوا۟ ٱلْحَمْدُ لِلَّهِ ٱلَّذِى هَدَىٰنَا لِهَٰذَا وَمَا كُنَّا لِنَهْتَدِىَ لَوْلَآ أَنْ هَدَىٰنَا ٱللَّهُ ۖ لَقَدْ جَآءَتْ رُسُلُ رَبِّنَا بِٱلْحَقِّ ۖ وَنُودُوٓا۟ أَن تِلْكُمُ ٱلْجَنَّةُ أُورِثْتُمُوهَا بِمَا كُنتُمْ تَعْمَلُونَ ۝ وَنَادَىٰٓ أَصْحَٰبُ ٱلْجَنَّةِ أَصْحَٰبَ ٱلنَّارِ أَن قَدْ وَجَدْنَا مَا وَعَدَنَا رَبُّنَا حَقًّا فَهَلْ وَجَدتُّم مَّا وَعَدَ رَبُّكُمْ حَقًّا ۖ قَالُوا۟ نَعَمْ ۚ فَأَذَّنَ مُؤَذِّنٌۢ بَيْنَهُمْ أَن لَّعْنَةُ ٱللَّهِ عَلَى ٱلظَّٰلِمِينَ ۝ ٱلَّذِينَ يَصُدُّونَ عَن سَبِيلِ ٱللَّهِ وَيَبْغُونَهَا عِوَجًا وَهُم بِٱلْءَاخِرَةِ كَٰفِرُونَ ۝ وَبَيْنَهُمَا حِجَابٌ ۚ وَعَلَى ٱلْأَعْرَافِ رِجَالٌ يَعْرِفُونَ كُلًّۢا بِسِيمَىٰهُمْ ۚ وَنَادَوْا۟ أَصْحَٰبَ ٱلْجَنَّةِ أَن سَلَٰمٌ عَلَيْكُمْ ۚ لَمْ يَدْخُلُوهَا وَهُمْ يَطْمَعُونَ ۝ ۞ وَإِذَا صُرِفَتْ أَبْصَٰرُهُمْ تِلْقَآءَ أَصْحَٰبِ ٱلنَّارِ قَالُوا۟ رَبَّنَا لَا تَجْعَلْنَا مَعَ ٱلْقَوْمِ ٱلظَّٰلِمِينَ ۝ وَنَادَىٰٓ أَصْحَٰبُ ٱلْأَعْرَافِ رِجَالًا يَعْرِفُونَهُم بِسِيمَىٰهُمْ قَالُوا۟ مَآ أَغْنَىٰ عَنكُمْ جَمْعُكُمْ وَمَا كُنتُمْ تَسْتَكْبِرُونَ ۝ أَهَٰٓؤُلَآءِ ٱلَّذِينَ أَقْسَمْتُمْ لَا يَنَالُهُمُ ٱللَّهُ بِرَحْمَةٍ ۚ ٱدْخُلُوا۟ ٱلْجَنَّةَ لَا خَوْفٌ عَلَيْكُمْ وَلَآ أَنتُمْ تَحْزَنُونَ ۝ وَنَادَىٰٓ أَصْحَٰبُ ٱلنَّارِ أَصْحَٰبَ ٱلْجَنَّةِ أَنْ أَفِيضُوا۟ عَلَيْنَا مِنَ ٱلْمَآءِ أَوْ مِمَّا رَزَقَكُمُ ٱللَّهُ ۚ قَالُوٓا۟ إِنَّ ٱللَّهَ حَرَّمَهُمَا عَلَى ٱلْكَٰفِرِينَ ۝ ٱلَّذِينَ ٱتَّخَذُوا۟ دِينَهُمْ لَهْوًا وَلَعِبًا وَغَرَّتْهُمُ ٱلْحَيَوٰةُ ٱلدُّنْيَا ۚ فَٱلْيَوْمَ نَنسَىٰهُمْ كَمَا نَسُوا۟ لِقَآءَ يَوْمِهِمْ هَٰذَا وَمَا كَانُوا۟ بِـَٔايَٰتِنَا يَجْحَدُونَ ۝ وَلَقَدْ جِئْنَٰهُم بِكِتَٰبٍ فَصَّلْنَٰهُ عَلَىٰ عِلْمٍ هُدًى وَرَحْمَةً لِّقَوْمٍ يُؤْمِنُونَ ۝ هَلْ يَنظُرُونَ إِلَّا تَأْوِيلَهُۥ ۚ يَوْمَ يَأْتِى تَأْوِيلُهُۥ يَقُولُ ٱلَّذِينَ نَسُوهُ مِن قَبْلُ قَدْ جَآءَتْ رُسُلُ رَبِّنَا بِٱلْحَقِّ فَهَل لَّنَا مِن شُفَعَآءَ فَيَشْفَعُوا۟ لَنَآ أَوْ نُرَدُّ فَنَعْمَلَ غَيْرَ ٱلَّذِى كُنَّا نَعْمَلُ ۚ قَدْ

خَسِرُوٓاْ أَنفُسَهُمْ وَضَلَّ عَنْهُم مَّا كَانُواْ يَفْتَرُونَ ۝ إِنَّ رَبَّكُمُ ٱللَّهُ ٱلَّذِى خَلَقَ ٱلسَّمَـٰوَٰتِ وَٱلْأَرْضَ فِى سِتَّةِ أَيَّامٍ ثُمَّ ٱسْتَوَىٰ عَلَى ٱلْعَرْشِ يُغْشِى ٱلَّيْلَ ٱلنَّهَارَ يَطْلُبُهُۥ حَثِيثًا وَٱلشَّمْسَ وَٱلْقَمَرَ وَٱلنُّجُومَ مُسَخَّرَٰتٍۭ بِأَمْرِهِۦٓ أَلَا لَهُ ٱلْخَلْقُ وَٱلْأَمْرُ تَبَارَكَ ٱللَّهُ رَبُّ ٱلْعَـٰلَمِينَ ۝ ٱدْعُواْ رَبَّكُمْ تَضَرُّعًا وَخُفْيَةً إِنَّهُۥ لَا يُحِبُّ ٱلْمُعْتَدِينَ ۝ وَلَا تُفْسِدُواْ فِى ٱلْأَرْضِ بَعْدَ إِصْلَـٰحِهَا وَٱدْعُوهُ خَوْفًا وَطَمَعًا إِنَّ رَحْمَتَ ٱللَّهِ قَرِيبٌ مِّنَ ٱلْمُحْسِنِينَ ۝ وَهُوَ ٱلَّذِى يُرْسِلُ ٱلرِّيَـٰحَ بُشْرًۢا بَيْنَ يَدَىْ رَحْمَتِهِۦ حَتَّىٰٓ إِذَآ أَقَلَّتْ سَحَابًا ثِقَالًا سُقْنَـٰهُ لِبَلَدٍ مَّيِّتٍ فَأَنزَلْنَا بِهِ ٱلْمَآءَ فَأَخْرَجْنَا بِهِۦ مِن كُلِّ ٱلثَّمَرَٰتِ كَذَٰلِكَ نُخْرِجُ ٱلْمَوْتَىٰ لَعَلَّكُمْ تَذَكَّرُونَ ۝ وَٱلْبَلَدُ ٱلطَّيِّبُ يَخْرُجُ نَبَاتُهُۥ بِإِذْنِ رَبِّهِۦ وَٱلَّذِى خَبُثَ لَا يَخْرُجُ إِلَّا نَكِدًا كَذَٰلِكَ نُصَرِّفُ ٱلْـَٔايَـٰتِ لِقَوْمٍ يَشْكُرُونَ ۝ لَقَدْ أَرْسَلْنَا نُوحًا إِلَىٰ قَوْمِهِۦ فَقَالَ يَـٰقَوْمِ ٱعْبُدُواْ ٱللَّهَ مَا لَكُم مِّنْ إِلَـٰهٍ غَيْرُهُۥٓ إِنِّىٓ أَخَافُ عَلَيْكُمْ عَذَابَ يَوْمٍ عَظِيمٍ ۝ قَالَ ٱلْمَلَأُ مِن قَوْمِهِۦٓ إِنَّا لَنَرَىٰكَ فِى ضَلَـٰلٍ مُّبِينٍ ۝ قَالَ يَـٰقَوْمِ لَيْسَ بِى ضَلَـٰلَةٌ وَلَـٰكِنِّى رَسُولٌ مِّن رَّبِّ ٱلْعَـٰلَمِينَ ۝ أُبَلِّغُكُمْ رِسَـٰلَـٰتِ رَبِّى وَأَنصَحُ لَكُمْ وَأَعْلَمُ مِنَ ٱللَّهِ مَا لَا تَعْلَمُونَ ۝ أَوَعَجِبْتُمْ أَن جَآءَكُمْ ذِكْرٌ مِّن رَّبِّكُمْ عَلَىٰ رَجُلٍ مِّنكُمْ لِيُنذِرَكُمْ وَلِتَتَّقُواْ وَلَعَلَّكُمْ تُرْحَمُونَ ۝ فَكَذَّبُوهُ فَأَنجَيْنَـٰهُ وَٱلَّذِينَ مَعَهُۥ فِى ٱلْفُلْكِ وَأَغْرَقْنَا ٱلَّذِينَ كَذَّبُواْ بِـَٔايَـٰتِنَآ إِنَّهُمْ كَانُواْ قَوْمًا عَمِينَ ۝ ۞ وَإِلَىٰ عَادٍ أَخَاهُمْ هُودًا قَالَ يَـٰقَوْمِ ٱعْبُدُواْ ٱللَّهَ مَا لَكُم مِّنْ إِلَـٰهٍ غَيْرُهُۥٓ أَفَلَا تَتَّقُونَ ۝ قَالَ ٱلْمَلَأُ ٱلَّذِينَ كَفَرُواْ مِن قَوْمِهِۦٓ إِنَّا لَنَرَىٰكَ فِى سَفَاهَةٍ وَإِنَّا لَنَظُنُّكَ مِنَ ٱلْكَـٰذِبِينَ ۝ قَالَ يَـٰقَوْمِ لَيْسَ بِى سَفَاهَةٌ وَلَـٰكِنِّى رَسُولٌ مِّن رَّبِّ ٱلْعَـٰلَمِينَ ۝ أُبَلِّغُكُمْ رِسَـٰلَـٰتِ رَبِّى وَأَنَا۠ لَكُمْ نَاصِحٌ أَمِينٌ ۝ أَوَعَجِبْتُمْ أَن جَآءَكُمْ ذِكْرٌ مِّن رَّبِّكُمْ عَلَىٰ رَجُلٍ مِّنكُمْ

لِيُنذِرَكُمْ ۚ وَٱذْكُرُوٓاْ إِذْ جَعَلَكُمْ خُلَفَآءَ مِنۢ بَعْدِ قَوْمِ نُوحٍ وَزَادَكُمْ فِى ٱلْخَلْقِ بَصۜطَةً ۖ فَٱذْكُرُوٓاْ ءَالَآءَ ٱللَّهِ لَعَلَّكُمْ تُفْلِحُونَ ۝ قَالُوٓاْ أَجِئْتَنَا لِنَعْبُدَ ٱللَّهَ وَحْدَهُۥ وَنَذَرَ مَا كَانَ يَعْبُدُ ءَابَآؤُنَا ۖ فَأْتِنَا بِمَا تَعِدُنَآ إِن كُنتَ مِنَ ٱلصَّـٰدِقِينَ ۝ قَالَ قَدْ وَقَعَ عَلَيْكُم مِّن رَّبِّكُمْ رِجْسٌ وَغَضَبٌ ۖ أَتُجَـٰدِلُونَنِى فِىٓ أَسْمَآءٍ سَمَّيْتُمُوهَآ أَنتُمْ وَءَابَآؤُكُم مَّا نَزَّلَ ٱللَّهُ بِهَا مِن سُلْطَـٰنٍ ۚ فَٱنتَظِرُوٓاْ إِنِّى مَعَكُم مِّنَ ٱلْمُنتَظِرِينَ ۝ فَأَنجَيْنَـٰهُ وَٱلَّذِينَ مَعَهُۥ بِرَحْمَةٍ مِّنَّا وَقَطَعْنَا دَابِرَ ٱلَّذِينَ كَذَّبُواْ بِـَٔايَـٰتِنَا ۖ وَمَا كَانُواْ مُؤْمِنِينَ ۝ وَإِلَىٰ ثَمُودَ أَخَاهُمْ صَـٰلِحًا ۗ قَالَ يَـٰقَوْمِ ٱعْبُدُواْ ٱللَّهَ مَا لَكُم مِّنْ إِلَـٰهٍ غَيْرُهُۥ ۖ قَدْ جَآءَتْكُم بَيِّنَةٌ مِّن رَّبِّكُمْ ۖ هَـٰذِهِۦ نَاقَةُ ٱللَّهِ لَكُمْ ءَايَةً ۖ فَذَرُوهَا تَأْكُلْ فِىٓ أَرْضِ ٱللَّهِ ۖ وَلَا تَمَسُّوهَا بِسُوٓءٍ فَيَأْخُذَكُمْ عَذَابٌ أَلِيمٌ ۝ وَٱذْكُرُوٓاْ إِذْ جَعَلَكُمْ خُلَفَآءَ مِنۢ بَعْدِ عَادٍ وَبَوَّأَكُمْ فِى ٱلْأَرْضِ تَتَّخِذُونَ مِن سُهُولِهَا قُصُورًا وَتَنْحِتُونَ ٱلْجِبَالَ بُيُوتًا ۖ فَٱذْكُرُوٓاْ ءَالَآءَ ٱللَّهِ وَلَا تَعْثَوْاْ فِى ٱلْأَرْضِ مُفْسِدِينَ ۝ قَالَ ٱلْمَلَأُ ٱلَّذِينَ ٱسْتَكْبَرُواْ مِن قَوْمِهِۦ لِلَّذِينَ ٱسْتُضْعِفُواْ لِمَنْ ءَامَنَ مِنْهُمْ أَتَعْلَمُونَ أَنَّ صَـٰلِحًا مُّرْسَلٌ مِّن رَّبِّهِۦ ۚ قَالُوٓاْ إِنَّا بِمَآ أُرْسِلَ بِهِۦ مُؤْمِنُونَ ۝ قَالَ ٱلَّذِينَ ٱسْتَكْبَرُوٓاْ إِنَّا بِٱلَّذِىٓ ءَامَنتُم بِهِۦ كَـٰفِرُونَ ۝ فَعَقَرُواْ ٱلنَّاقَةَ وَعَتَوْاْ عَنْ أَمْرِ رَبِّهِمْ وَقَالُواْ يَـٰصَـٰلِحُ ٱئْتِنَا بِمَا تَعِدُنَآ إِن كُنتَ مِنَ ٱلْمُرْسَلِينَ ۝ فَأَخَذَتْهُمُ ٱلرَّجْفَةُ فَأَصْبَحُواْ فِى دَارِهِمْ جَـٰثِمِينَ ۝ فَتَوَلَّىٰ عَنْهُمْ وَقَالَ يَـٰقَوْمِ لَقَدْ أَبْلَغْتُكُمْ رِسَالَةَ رَبِّى وَنَصَحْتُ لَكُمْ وَلَـٰكِن لَّا تُحِبُّونَ ٱلنَّـٰصِحِينَ ۝ وَلُوطًا إِذْ قَالَ لِقَوْمِهِۦٓ أَتَأْتُونَ ٱلْفَـٰحِشَةَ مَا سَبَقَكُم بِهَا مِنْ أَحَدٍ مِّنَ ٱلْعَـٰلَمِينَ ۝ إِنَّكُمْ لَتَأْتُونَ ٱلرِّجَالَ شَهْوَةً مِّن دُونِ ٱلنِّسَآءِ ۚ بَلْ أَنتُمْ قَوْمٌ مُّسْرِفُونَ ۝ وَمَا كَانَ جَوَابَ قَوْمِهِۦٓ إِلَّآ أَن

$$\text{قَالُوٓاْ أَخْرِجُوهُم مِّن قَرْيَتِكُمْ ۖ إِنَّهُمْ أُنَاسٌ يَتَطَهَّرُونَ ۝ فَأَنجَيْنَاهُ وَأَهْلَهُۥٓ إِلَّا ٱمْرَأَتَهُۥ كَانَتْ مِنَ ٱلْغَابِرِينَ ۝ وَأَمْطَرْنَا عَلَيْهِم مَّطَرًا ۖ فَٱنظُرْ كَيْفَ كَانَ عَٰقِبَةُ ٱلْمُجْرِمِينَ ۝ وَإِلَىٰ مَدْيَنَ أَخَاهُمْ شُعَيْبًا ۗ قَالَ يَٰقَوْمِ ٱعْبُدُوا۟ ٱللَّهَ مَا لَكُم مِّنْ إِلَٰهٍ غَيْرُهُۥ ۖ قَدْ جَآءَتْكُم بَيِّنَةٌ مِّن رَّبِّكُمْ ۖ فَأَوْفُوا۟ ٱلْكَيْلَ وَٱلْمِيزَانَ وَلَا تَبْخَسُوا۟ ٱلنَّاسَ أَشْيَآءَهُمْ وَلَا تُفْسِدُوا۟ فِى ٱلْأَرْضِ بَعْدَ إِصْلَٰحِهَا ۚ ذَٰلِكُمْ خَيْرٌ لَّكُمْ إِن كُنتُم مُّؤْمِنِينَ ۝ وَلَا تَقْعُدُوا۟ بِكُلِّ صِرَٰطٍ تُوعِدُونَ وَتَصُدُّونَ عَن سَبِيلِ ٱللَّهِ مَنْ ءَامَنَ بِهِۦ وَتَبْغُونَهَا عِوَجًا ۚ وَٱذْكُرُوٓا۟ إِذْ كُنتُمْ قَلِيلًا فَكَثَّرَكُمْ ۖ وَٱنظُرُوا۟ كَيْفَ كَانَ عَٰقِبَةُ ٱلْمُفْسِدِينَ ۝ وَإِن كَانَ طَآئِفَةٌ مِّنكُمْ ءَامَنُوا۟ بِٱلَّذِىٓ أُرْسِلْتُ بِهِۦ وَطَآئِفَةٌ لَّمْ يُؤْمِنُوا۟ فَٱصْبِرُوا۟ حَتَّىٰ يَحْكُمَ ٱللَّهُ بَيْنَنَا ۚ وَهُوَ خَيْرُ ٱلْحَٰكِمِينَ ۝}$$

(Al-A'raf 001-087)

INTRODUCTION TO CHAPTER (SURAH) 6: AL-AN'AM (CATTLE, LIVESTOCK)

Ibn kathir's Introduction

The Virtue of Surat Al-An`am and When it Was Revealed

Al-`Awfi, `Ikrimah and `Ata' said that Ibn `Abbas said, "Surat Al-An`am was revealed in Makkah" At-Tabarani recorded that Ibn `Abbas said, "All of Surat Al-An`am was revealed in Makkah at night, accompanied by seventy thousand angels, raising their voices in glorification of Allah" As-Suddi said that Murrah said that `Abdullah said, "Surat Al-An`am was revealed in the company of seventy thousand angels."

CHAPTER (SURAH) 6: AL-AN'AM (CATTLE, LIVESTOCK), VERSES 111-165

$$\text{﴿ بِسْمِ ٱللَّهِ ٱلرَّحْمَٰنِ ٱلرَّحِيمِ ۝ ﴾}$$

In the Name of Allâh, the Most Gracious, the Most Merciful.

Surah: 6 Ayah: 111

﴿ ۞ وَلَوْ أَنَّنَا نَزَّلْنَا إِلَيْهِمُ ٱلْمَلَٰٓئِكَةَ وَكَلَّمَهُمُ ٱلْمَوْتَىٰ وَحَشَرْنَا عَلَيْهِمْ كُلَّ شَىْءٍ قُبُلًا مَّا كَانُوا۟ لِيُؤْمِنُوٓا۟ إِلَّآ أَن يَشَآءَ ٱللَّهُ وَلَٰكِنَّ أَكْثَرَهُمْ يَجْهَلُونَ ﴿١١١﴾ ﴾

111. And even if We had sent down unto them angels, and the dead had spoken unto them, and We had gathered together all things before their very eyes, they would not have believed, unless Allâh willed, but most of them behave ignorantly.

Transliteration

111. Walaw annana nazzalna ilayhimu almala-ikata wakallamahumu almawta wahasharna AAalayhim kulla shay-in qubulan ma kanoo liyu/minoo illa an yashaa Allahu walakinna aktharahum yajhaloona

Tafsir Ibn Kathir:

Allah says: `Had We accepted what the disbelievers asked for,' that is -- those who swore their strongest oaths by Allah that if a miracle came to them they would believe in it -- `had We sent down angels, ' to convey to them Allah's Message, in order to support the truth of the Messengers, as they asked, when they said,

(or you bring Allah and the angels before (us) face to face.) (17:92)

(They said: "We shall not believe until we receive the like of that which the Messengers of Allah had received.") (6:124) and,

(And those who expect not a meeting with Us said: "Why are not the angels sent down to us, or why do we not see our Lord" Indeed they think too highly of themselves, and are scornful with great pride.) (25:21) Allah said,

(and the dead had spoken unto them,) This is, to inform them of the truth of what the Messengers brought them;

(and We had gathered together all things before them,) before their eyes, as `Ali bin Abi Talhah and Al-`Awfi reported from Ibn `Abbas. This is the view of Qatadah and `Abdur-Rahman bin Zayd bin Aslam. This Ayah means, if all nations were gathered before them, one after the other, and each one testifies to the truth of what the Messengers came with,

(they would not have believed, unless Allah willed,) for guidance is with Allah not with them. Certainly, Allah guides whom He wills and misguides whom He wills, and He does what He wills,

(He cannot be questioned about what He does, while they will be questioned.) (21:23), This is due to His knowledge, wisdom, power, supreme authority and irresistibility. Similarly, Allah said,

(Truly, those, against whom the Word (wrath) of your Lord has been justified, will not believe. Even if every sign should come to them, until they see the painful torment.) (10:96-97)

Surah: 6 Ayah: 112 & Ayah: 113

﴿ وَكَذَٰلِكَ جَعَلْنَا لِكُلِّ نَبِيٍّ عَدُوًّا شَيَاطِينَ ٱلْإِنسِ وَٱلْجِنِّ يُوحِى بَعْضُهُمْ إِلَىٰ بَعْضٍ زُخْرُفَ ٱلْقَوْلِ غُرُورًا ۚ وَلَوْ شَآءَ رَبُّكَ مَا فَعَلُوهُ ۖ فَذَرْهُمْ وَمَا يَفْتَرُونَ ۝

112. And so We have appointed for every Prophet enemies - Shayâtin (devils) among mankind and jinn, inspiring one another with adorned speech as a delusion (or by way of deception). If your Lord had so willed, they would not have done it; so leave them alone with their fabrications. (Tafseer Qurtubi)

﴿ وَلِتَصْغَىٰٓ إِلَيْهِ أَفْـِٔدَةُ ٱلَّذِينَ لَا يُؤْمِنُونَ بِٱلْءَاخِرَةِ وَلِيَرْضَوْهُ وَلِيَقْتَرِفُوا۟ مَا هُم مُّقْتَرِفُونَ ۝

113. (And this is in order) that the hearts of those who disbelieve in the Hereafter may incline to such (deceit), and that they may remain pleased with it, and that they may commit what they are committing (all kinds of sins and evil deeds).

Transliteration

112. Wakathalika jaAAalna likulli nabiyyin AAaduwwan shayateena al-insi waaljinni yoohee baAAduhum ila baAAdin zukhrufa alqawli ghurooran walaw shaa rabbuka ma faAAaloohu fatharhum wama yaftaroona 113. Walitasgha ilayhi af-idatu allatheena la yu/minoona bial-akhirati waliyardawhu waliyaqtarifoo ma hum muqtarifoona

Tafsir Ibn Kathir:

Every Prophet Has Enemies

Allah says, just as We made enemies for you, O Muhammad, who will oppose and rebel against you and become your adversaries, We also made enemies for every Prophet who came before you. Therefore, do not be saddened by this fact. Allah said in other Ayat:

(Verily, Messengers were denied before you, but with patience they bore the denial, and they were hurt...) (6:34), and,

(Nothing is said to you except what was said to the Messengers before you. Verily, your Lord is the Possessor of forgiveness, and (also) the Possessor of painful punishment.) (41:43) and,

(Thus have We made for every Prophet an enemy among the criminals.) (25:31). Waraqah bin Nawfal said to Allah's Messenger , "None came with what you came with but he was the subject of enmity." Allah's statement,

(Shayatin among mankind...) refers to,

(enemies. ..) meaning, the Prophets have enemies among the devils of mankind and the devils of the Jinns. The word, Shaytan, describes one who is dissimilar to his kind due to his or her wickedness. Indeed, only the Shayatin, may Allah humiliate and curse them, from among mankind and the Jinns oppose the Messengers. `Abdur-Razzaq said that Ma`mar narrated that Qatadah commented on Allah's statement,

(Shayatin (devils) among mankind and Jinn...) "There are devils among the Jinns and devils among mankind who inspire each other." Allah's statement,

(inspiring one another with adorned speech as a delusion.) means, they inspire each other with beautified, adorned speech that deceives the ignorant who hear it,

(If your Lord had so willed, they would not have done it;) for all this occurs by Allah's decree, will and decision, that every Prophet had enemies from these devils,

(so leave them alone with their fabrications.) and lies. This Ayah orders patience in the face of the harm of the wicked and to trust in Allah against their enmity, for, "Allah shall suffice for you (O Muhammad) and aid you against them." Allah's statement,

(And Tasgha to it.) means, according to Ibn `Abbas, "incline to it."

(the hearts of those who do not believe in the Hereafter...) their hearts, mind and hearing. As-Suddi said that this Ayah refers to the hearts of the disbelievers.

(And that they may remain pleased with it.) they like and adore it. Only those who disbelieve in the Hereafter accept this evil speech, being enemies of the Prophets, etc., just as Allah said in other Ayat,

(So, verily, you (pagans) and those whom you worship (idols). Cannot lead astray. Except those who are predestined to burn in Hell!) (37:161-163) and,

(Certainly, you have different ideas. Turned aside therefrom is he who is turned aside.) (51:8-9) Allah said;

(And that they may commit what they are committing.) meaning, "let them earn whatever they will earn", according to `Ali bin Abi Talhah who reported this from Ibn `Abbas. As-Suddi and Ibn Zayd also commented, "Let them do whatever they will do."

Surah: 6 Ayah: 114 & Ayah: 115

﴿ أَفَغَيْرَ ٱللَّهِ أَبْتَغِى حَكَمًا وَهُوَ ٱلَّذِى أَنزَلَ إِلَيْكُمُ ٱلْكِتَـٰبَ مُفَصَّلًا ۚ وَٱلَّذِينَ ءَاتَيْنَـٰهُمُ ٱلْكِتَـٰبَ يَعْلَمُونَ أَنَّهُۥ مُنَزَّلٌ مِّن رَّبِّكَ بِٱلْحَقِّ ۖ فَلَا تَكُونَنَّ مِنَ ٱلْمُمْتَرِينَ ﴾

114. (Say (O Muhammad (peace be upon him))) "Shall I seek a judge other than Allâh while it is He Who has sent down unto you the Book (The Qur'ân), explained in detail." Those unto whom We gave the Scripture (the Taurât (Torah) and the Injeel (Gospel)) know that it is revealed from your Lord in truth. So be not you of those who doubt.

﴿ وَتَمَّتْ كَلِمَتُ رَبِّكَ صِدْقًا وَعَدْلًا ۚ لَّا مُبَدِّلَ لِكَلِمَـٰتِهِۦ ۚ وَهُوَ ٱلسَّمِيعُ ٱلْعَلِيمُ ﴾

115. And the Word of your Lord has been fulfilled in truth and in justice. None can change His Words. And He is the All-Hearer, the All-Knower.

Transliteration

114. Afaghayra Allahi abtaghee hakaman wahuwa allathee anzala ilaykumu alkitaba mufassalan waallatheena ataynahumu alkitaba yaAAlamoona annahu munazzalun min rabbika bialhaqqi fala takoonanna mina almumtareena   115. Watammat kalimatu rabbika sidqan waAAadlan la mubaddila likalimatihi wahuwa alssameeAAu alAAaleemu

Tafsir Ibn Kathir:

Allah tells His Prophet to say to these polytheists who worship others besides Allah,

(Shall I seek a judge other than Allah...) between you and I,

(while it is He Who has sent down unto you the Book, explained...) in detail,

(and those unto whom We gave the Scripture) the Jews and the Christians,

(know that it is revealed from your Lord in truth.) because the previous Prophets have conveyed the good news of you coming to them. Allah's statement,

(So be not you of those who doubt.) is similar to His other statement,

(So if you are in doubt concerning that which We have revealed unto you, then ask those who are reading the Book before you. Verily, the truth has come to you from your Lord. So be not of those who doubt (it).) (10:94) The conditional `if' in this Ayah does not mean that `doubt' will ever occur to the Prophet . Allah said,

(And the Word of your Lord has been fulfilled in truth and in justice.) Qatadah commented, "In truth concerning what He stated and in justice concerning what He decided." Surely, whatever Allah says is the truth and He is Most Just in what He commands. All of Allah's statements are true, there is no doubt or cause for speculation about this fact, and all His commandments are pure justice, besides which there is no justice. All that He forbade is evil, for He only forbids what brings about evil consequences. Allah said in another Ayah,

(He commands them with good; and forbids them from evil...) (7:157) until the end of the Ayah.

(None can change His Words.) meaning, none can avert Allah's judgment whether in this life or the Hereafter,

(And He is the All-Hearer,) Hearing, His servants' statements,

(The All-Knower.) of their activities and lack of activity, Who awards each according to their deeds.

Surah: 6 Ayah: 116 & Ayah: 117

﴿ وَإِن تُطِعْ أَكْثَرَ مَن فِي ٱلْأَرْضِ يُضِلُّوكَ عَن سَبِيلِ ٱللَّهِ ۚ إِن يَتَّبِعُونَ إِلَّا ٱلظَّنَّ وَإِنْ هُمْ إِلَّا يَخْرُصُونَ ﴾

116. And if you obey most of those on the earth, they will mislead you far away from Allâh's Path. They follow nothing but conjectures, and they do nothing but lie.

﴿ إِنَّ رَبَّكَ هُوَ أَعْلَمُ مَن يَضِلُّ عَن سَبِيلِهِ ۖ وَهُوَ أَعْلَمُ بِٱلْمُهْتَدِينَ ﴾

117. Verily, your Lord! It is He Who knows best who strays from His Way, and He knows best the rightly guided ones.

Transliteration

116. Wa-in tutiAA akthara man fee al-ardi yudillooka AAan sabeeli Allahi in yattabiAAoona illa alththanna wa-in hum illa yakhrusoona 117. Inna rabbaka huwa aAAlamu man yadillu AAan sabeelihi wahuwa aAAlamu bialmuhtadeena

Tafsir Ibn Kathir:

Most People are Misguided

Allah states that most of the people of the earth, are misguided. Allah said in other Ayat,

(And indeed most of the men of old went astray before them.) (37:71) and,

(And most of mankind will not believe even if you eagerly desire it.)(12:103) They are misguided, yet they have doubts about their way, and they rely on wishful thinking and delusions.

(They follow nothing but conjecture, and they do nothing but lie.) Thus, they fulfill Allah's decree and decision concerning them,

(It is He Who knows best who strays from His way.) and facilitates that for him,

(And He knows best the rightly guided.) He facilitates that for them, all of them are facilitated for what He created them.

Surah: 6 Ayah: 118 & Ayah: 119

﴿ فَكُلُواْ مِمَّا ذُكِرَ ٱسْمُ ٱللَّهِ عَلَيْهِ إِن كُنتُم بِـَٔايَـٰتِهِۦ مُؤْمِنِينَ ۝ ﴾

118. So eat of that (meat) on which Allâh's Name has been pronounced (while slaughtering the animal), if you are believers in His Ayât (proofs, evidences, verses, lessons, signs, revelations, etc.).

﴿ وَمَا لَكُمْ أَلَّا تَأْكُلُواْ مِمَّا ذُكِرَ ٱسْمُ ٱللَّهِ عَلَيْهِ وَقَدْ فَصَّلَ لَكُم مَّا حَرَّمَ عَلَيْكُمْ إِلَّا مَا ٱضْطُرِرْتُمْ إِلَيْهِ ۗ وَإِنَّ كَثِيرًا لَّيُضِلُّونَ بِأَهْوَآئِهِم بِغَيْرِ عِلْمٍ ۗ إِنَّ رَبَّكَ هُوَ أَعْلَمُ بِٱلْمُعْتَدِينَ ۝ ﴾

119. And why should you not eat of that (meat) on which Allâh's Name has been pronounced (at the time of slaughtering the animal), while He has explained to you in detail what is forbidden to you, except under compulsion of necessity? And surely many do lead (mankind) astray by their own desires through lack of knowledge. Certainly your Lord knows best the transgressors.

Transliteration

118. Fakuloo mimma thukira ismu Allahi AAalayhi in kuntum bi-ayatihi mu/mineena
119. Wama lakum alla ta/kuloo mimma thukira ismu Allahi AAalayhi waqad fassala lakum ma harrama AAalaykum illa ma idturirtum ilayhi wa-inna katheeran layudilloona bi-ahwa-ihim bighayri AAilmin inna rabbaka huwa aAAlamu bialmuAAtadeena

Tafsir Ibn Kathir:

Allowing What was Slaughtered in the Name of Allah

This is a statement of permission from Allah, for His servants, allowing them to eat the slaughtered animals werein His Name was mentioned when slaughtering them. It is understood from it that He has not allowed that over which Allah's Name was not mentioned when slaughtering. This was the practice of the pagans of Quraysh who used to eat dead animals and eat what was slaughtered for the idols. Allah next encourages eating from the meat of sacrificed animals on which His Name was mentioned upon slaughtering,

(And why should you not eat of that on which Allah's Name has been mentioned, while He has explained to you what is forbidden to you...) meaning, He has explained and made clear to you what He has prohibited for you in detail,

(except under compulsion of necessity.) In which case, you are allowed to eat whatever you can find. Allah next mentions the ignorance of the idolators in their misguided ideas, such as eating dead animals and what was sacrificed while other than Allah's Name was mentioned when slaughtering them. Allah said,

(And surely, many do lead astray by their own desires through lack of knowledge. Certainly your Lord knows best the transgressors.) He has complete knowledge of their transgression, lies and inventions.

Surah: 6 Ayah: 120

﴿ وَذَرُواْ ظَٰهِرَ ٱلْإِثْمِ وَبَاطِنَهُۥٓ ۚ إِنَّ ٱلَّذِينَ يَكْسِبُونَ ٱلْإِثْمَ سَيُجْزَوْنَ بِمَا كَانُواْ يَقْتَرِفُونَ ﴾

120. Leave (O mankind, all kinds of) sin, open and secret. Verily, those who commit sin will get due recompense for that which they used to commit.

Transliteration

120. Watharoo thahira al-ithmi wabatinahu inna allatheena yaksiboona al-ithma sayujzawna bima kanoo yaqtarifoona

Tafsir Ibn Kathir:

Mujahid said that, (Leave evil, open and secret...) refers to all kinds of sins committed in public and secret. Qatadah said that,

(Leave sin, open and secret...) encompasses sins committed in public and secret, whether few or many. In another statement, Allah said,

(Say: "(But) the things that my Lord has indeed forbidden are Al-Fawahish (evil sins) whether committed openly or secretly.) (7:33) This is why Allah said,

(Verily, those who commit sin will get due recompense for that which they used to commit.) Whether the sins they committed were public or secret, Allah will compensate them for these sins. Ibn Abi Hatim recorded that An-Nawwas bin Sam`an said, "I asked Allah's Messenger about Al-Ithm. He said,

«الْإِثْمُ مَا حَاكَ فِي صَدْرِكَ وَكَرِهْتَ أَنْ يَطَّلِعَ النَّاسُ عَلَيْهِ»

(The sin is that which you find in your heart and you dislike that people become aware of it.)

Surah: 6 Ayah: 121

$$﴿ وَلَا تَأْكُلُوا۟ مِمَّا لَمْ يُذْكَرِ ٱسْمُ ٱللَّهِ عَلَيْهِ وَإِنَّهُۥ لَفِسْقٌ ۗ وَإِنَّ ٱلشَّيَٰطِينَ لَيُوحُونَ إِلَىٰٓ أَوْلِيَآئِهِمْ لِيُجَٰدِلُوكُمْ ۖ وَإِنْ أَطَعْتُمُوهُمْ إِنَّكُمْ لَمُشْرِكُونَ ﴿١٢١﴾ ﴾$$

121. Eat not (O believers) of that (meat) on which Allâh's Name has not been pronounced (at the time of the slaughtering of the animal), for sure it is Fisq (a sin and disobedience of Allâh). And certainly, the Shayâtin (devils) do inspire their friends (from mankind) to dispute with you, and if you obey them (by making Al-Maitah (a dead animal) legal by eating it), then you would indeed be Mushrikûn (polytheists); (because they (devils and their friends) made lawful to you to eat that which Allâh has made unlawful to eat and you obeyed them by considering it lawful to eat, and by doing so you worshipped them; and to worship others besides Allâh is polytheism).

Transliteration

121. Wala ta/kuloo mimma lam yuthkari ismu Allahi AAalayhi wa-innahu lafisqun wa-inna alshshayateena layoohoona ila awliya-ihim liyujadilookum wa-in ataAAtumoohum innakum lamushrikoona

Tafsir Ibn Kathir:

The Prohibition of what was Slaughtered in other than Allah's Name

This Ayah is used to prove that slaughtered animals are not lawful when Allah's Name is not mentioned over them -- even if slaughtered by a Muslim. The Ayah about hunting game,

(So eat of what they (trained hunting dogs or birds of prey) catch for you, but pronounce the Name of Allah over it.) (5:4) supports this. The Ayah here emphasized this ruling, when Allah said,

(for surely it is disobedience.) They say that "it" refers to eating it, and others say that it refers to the sacrifice for other than Allah. There are various Hadiths that order mentioning Allah's Name when slaughtering and hunting. The Hadith narrated by `Adi bin Hatim and Abu Tha`labah (that the Prophet said);

«إِذَا أَرْسَلْتَ كَلْبَكَ الْمُعَلَّمَ وَذَكَرْتَ اسْمَ اللهِ عَلَيْهِ فَكُلْ مَا أَمْسَكَ عَلَيْكَ»

(When you send your trained hunting dog and mention Allah's Name on releasing it, then eat from whatever it catches for you.) This Hadith was collected in the Two Sahihs. The Rafi` bin Khadij narrated that the Prophet said;

«مَا أَنْهَرَ الدَّمَ وَذُكِرَ اسْمُ اللهِ عَلَيْهِ فَكُلُوه»

Chapter 6: Al-An'am (Cattle, Livestock), Verses 111-165

(You can use what would make blood flow (i. e., slaughter) and you can eat what is slaughtered and the Name of Allah is mentioned at the time of slaughtering.) This Hadith was also collected in the Two Sahihs. Ibn Mas`ud narrated that Allah's Messenger said to the Jinns.

«لَكُمْ كُلُّ عَظْمٍ ذُكِرَ اسْمُ اللهِ عَلَيْهِ»

((For food) you have every bone on which Allah's Name was mentioned on slaughtering.) Muslim collected this Hadith. Jundub bin Sufyan Al-Bajali said that the Messenger of Allah said,

«مَنْ ذَبَحَ قَبْلَ أَنْ يُصَلِّيَ فَلْيَذْبَحْ مَكَانَهَا أُخْرَى، وَمَنْ لَمْ يَكُنْ ذَبَحَ، حَتَّى صَلَّيْنَا فَلْيَذْبَحْ بِاسْمِ اللهِ»

(Whoever slaughtered before he prayed (the `Id prayer), let him slaughter another sacrifice in its place. Whoever did not offer the sacrifice before we finished the prayer, let him slaughter and mention Allah's Name.) The Two Sahihs recorded this Hadith.

The Devil's Inspiration

Allah said,

(And certainly, the Shayatin do inspire their friends to dispute with you,) Ibn Abi Hatim recorded that Abu Ishaq said that a man said to Ibn `Umar that Al-Mukhtar claimed that he received revelation. So Ibn `Umar said, "He has said the truth," and recited this Ayah,

(And certainly, the Shayatin do inspire their friends...) Abu Zamil said, "I was sitting next to Ibn `Abbas at a time when Al-Mukhtar bin Abi `Ubayd was performing Hajj. So a man came to Ibn `Abbas and said, `O Ibn `Abbas! Abu Ishaq (Al-Mukhtar) claimed that he received revelation this night.' Ibn `Abbas said, He has said the truth.' I was upset and said, `Ibn `Abbas says that Al-Mukhtar has said the truth' Ibn `Abbas replied, `There are two types of revelation, one from Allah and one from the devil. Allah's revelation came to Muhammad , while the Shaytan's revelation comes to his friends.' He then recited,

(And certainly, the Shayatin do inspire their friends...) We also mentioned `Ikrimah's commentary on the Ayah,

(Inspiring one another with adorned speech as a delusion.) Allah said next,

(to dispute with you,) Ibn Jarir recorded that Ibn `Abbas commented;

(Eat not of that on which Allah's Name has not been mentioned...) until,

(...to dispute with you,) "The devils inspire their loyal supporters, `Do you eat from what you kill but not from what Allah causes to die'" As-Suddi said; "Some idolators said to the Muslims, `You claim that you seek Allah's pleasure. Yet, you do not eat what Allah causes to die, but you eat what you slaughter' Allah said,

(and if you obey them...), and eat dead animals,

(then you would indeed be polytheists.) Similar was said by Mujahid, Ad-Dahhak and several others among scholars of the Salaf.

Giving Preference to Anyone's Saying Over the Legislation of Allah is Shirk

Allah's statement,

(and if you obey them, then you would indeed be polytheists.) means, when you turn away from Allah's command and Legislation to the saying of anyone else, preferring other than what Allah has said, then this constitutes Shirk. Allah said in another Ayah,

(They (Jews and Christians) took their rabbis and their monks to be their lords besides Allah.)(9:31) In explanation of this Ayah, At-Tirmidhi recorded that `Adi bin Hatim said, "O Allah's Messenger! They did not worship them." The Prophet said,

«بَلَى إِنَّهُمْ أَحَلُّوا لَهُمُ الْحَرَامَ وَحَرَّمُوا عَلَيْهِمُ الْحَلَالَ فَاتَّبَعُوهُمْ فَذَلِكَ عِبَادَتُهُمْ إِيَّاهُم»

(Yes they did. They (monks and rabbis) allowed the impermissible for them and they prohibited the lawful for them, and they followed them in that. That was their worship of them.)

Surah: 6 Ayah: 122

﴿أَوَمَن كَانَ مَيْتًا فَأَحْيَيْنَـهُ وَجَعَلْنَا لَهُ نُورًا يَمْشِى بِهِ فِى ٱلنَّاسِ كَمَن مَّثَلُهُ فِى ٱلظُّلُمَـٰتِ لَيْسَ بِخَارِجٍ مِّنْهَا كَذَٰلِكَ زُيِّنَ لِلْكَـٰفِرِينَ مَا كَانُوا۟ يَعْمَلُونَ﴾

122. Is he who was dead (without Faith by ignorance and disbelief) and We gave him life (by knowledge and Faith) and set for him a light (of Belief) whereby he can walk amongst men - like him who is in the darkness (of disbelief, polytheism and hypocrisy) from which he can never come out? Thus it is made fair-seeming to the disbelievers that which they used to do.

Transliteration

122. Awa man kana maytan faahyaynahu wajaAAalna lahu nooran yamshee bihi fee alnnasi kaman mathaluhu fee alththulumati laysa bikharijin minha kathalika zuyyina lilkafireena ma kanoo yaAAmaloona

Tafsir Ibn Kathir:

The Parable of the Disbeliever and the Believer

This is an example that Allah has given of the believer who was dead, meaning, wandering in confusion and misguidance. Then, Allah brought life to him, by bringing life to his heart with faith, guiding him to it and guiding him to obeying His Messengers,

(And set for him a light whereby he can walk amongst men.) for he became guided to where he should go and how to remain on the correct path. The light mentioned here is the Qur'an, according to Ibn `Abbas, as Al-`Awfi and Ibn Abi Talhah reported from him. As-Suddi said that the light mentioned here is Islam. Both meanings are correct.

(Like him who is in the darkness) of ignorance, desires and various types of deviation,

(From which he can never come out) for he is unable to find a way out from what he is in. In Musnad Ahmad, it is recorded that the Prophet said;

»إِنَّ اللهَ خَلَقَ خَلْقَهُ فِي ظُلْمَةٍ، ثُمَّ رَشَّ عَلَيْهِمْ مِنْ نُورِهِ، فَمَنْ أَصَابَهُ ذَلِكَ النُّورُ اهْتَدَى، وَمَنْ أَخْطَأَهُ ضَلَّ«

(Allah created creation in darkness, then He showered His Light upon them. Whoever was struck by that light is guided, whoever it missed is astray.) Allah said in other Ayat,

(Allah is the Guardian of those who believe. He brings them out from darkness into light. But as for those who disbelieve, their friends are Taghut, they bring them out from light into darkness. Those are the dwellers of the Fire, and they will abide therein forever.) (2:257), and

(Is he who walks prone on his face, more rightly guided, or he who walks upright on the straight way) (67:22), and

(The parable of the two parties is as the blind and the deaf and the seer and the hearer. Are they equal when compared Will you not then take heed) (11:24), and,

(Not alike are the blind and the seeing. Nor are darkness and light. Nor are the shade and the sun's heat. Nor are the living and the dead. Verily, Allah makes whom He wills to hear, but you cannot make hear those who are in the graves. You are only a warner.) (35:19-23) There are many other Ayat on this subject. We explained before why Allah mentioned the light in the singular sense and the darkness in the plural sense when we explained the Ayah at the beginning of the Surah,

(And originated the darknesses and the light.) (6:1) Allah's statement,

(Thus it is made fair seeming to the disbelievers that which they used to do.) means, We made their ignorance and misguidance appear fair to them, as Allah decreed out of His wisdom, there is no deity worthy of worship except Him alone without partners.

Surah: 6 Ayah: 123 & Ayah: 124

﴿ وَكَذَلِكَ جَعَلْنَا فِى كُلِّ قَرْيَةٍ أَكَـٰبِرَ مُجْرِمِيهَا لِيَمْكُرُواْ فِيهَا وَمَا يَمْكُرُونَ إِلَّا بِأَنفُسِهِمْ وَمَا يَشْعُرُونَ ۝ ﴾

123. And thus We have set up in every town great ones of its wicked people to plot therein. But they plot not except against their own selves, and they perceive (it) not.

﴿ وَإِذَا جَآءَتْهُمْ ءَايَةٌ قَالُواْ لَن نُّؤْمِنَ حَتَّىٰ نُؤْتَىٰ مِثْلَ مَآ أُوتِىَ رُسُلُ ٱللَّهِ ٱللَّهُ أَعْلَمُ حَيْثُ يَجْعَلُ رِسَالَتَهُ سَيُصِيبُ ٱلَّذِينَ أَجْرَمُواْ صَغَارٌ عِندَ ٱللَّهِ وَعَذَابٌ شَدِيدٌ بِمَا كَانُواْ يَمْكُرُونَ ۝ ﴾

124. And when there comes to them a sign (from Allâh) they say: "We shall not believe until we receive the like of that which the Messengers of Allâh had received." Allâh knows best with whom to place His Message. Humiliation and disgrace from Allâh and a severe torment will overtake the criminals (polytheists, sinners) for that which they used to plot.

Transliteration

123. Wakathalika jaAAalna fee kulli qaryatin akabira mujrimeeha liyamkuroo feeha wama yamkuroona illa bi-anfusihim wama yashAAuroona   124. Wa-itha jaat-hum ayatun qaloo lan nu/mina hatta nu/ta mithla ma ootiya rusulu Allahi Allahu aAAlamu haythu yajAAalu risalatahu sayuseebu allatheena ajramoo sagharun AAinda Allahi waAAathabun shadeedun bima kanoo yamkuroona

Tafsir Ibn Kathir:

Evil Plots of the Leaders of the Criminals and their Subsequent Demise

Allah says: Just as We appointed chiefs and leaders for the criminals who call to disbelief, hinder from the path of Allah, and oppose and defy you in your town, O Muhammad. Such was also the case with the Messengers before you, who were tested with the same. But the good end was always theirs.' Allah said in other Ayat,

Chapter 6: Al-An'am (Cattle, Livestock), Verses 111-165

(Thus have We made for every Prophet an enemy among the criminals.) (25:31) Allah said,

(And when We decide to destroy a town, We send a definite order to those among them who lead a life of luxury, and they transgress therein.) (17:16) meaning, We command them to obey Us, but they defy the command and as a consequence, We destroy them. It was also said that, "We send a definite order", in the last Ayah means, "We decree for them," as Allah stated here

(to plot therein.) Ibn Abi Talhah reported that Ibn `Abbas explained the Ayah

(...great ones of its wicked people to plot therein.) "We give the leadership to these wicked ones and they commit evil in it. When they do this, We destroy them with Our torment." Mujahid and Qatadah said that in the Ayah,

(great ones) refers to leaders. I say that this is also the meaning of Allah's statements,

(And We did not send a warner to a township, but those who were given the worldly wealth and luxuries among them, said: "We believe not in what you have been sent with." And they say: "We have too much wealth and too many children and we are not going to suffer punishment.") (34:34-35) And,

(And similarly, We sent not a warner before you to any town but the luxurious ones among them said: "We found our fathers following a certain way and religion, and we will indeed follow their footsteps.") (43:23) `Plot' in the Ayah (6:123) refers to beautified speech and various actions with which the evil ones call to misguidance. Allah said about the people of Prophet Nuh, peace be upon him,

(And they have plotted a mighty plot.) (71:22) Allah said,

(But if you could see when the wrongdoers will be made to stand before their Lord, how they will cast the (blaming) word one to another! Those who were deemed weak will say to those who were arrogant: "Had it not been for you, we should certainly have been believers." And those who were arrogant will say to those who were deemed weak: "Did we keep you back from guidance after it had come to you Nay, but you were criminals." Those who were deemed weak will say to those who were arrogant: "Nay, but it was your plotting by night and day, when you ordered us to disbelieve in Allah and set up rivals for Him!") (34:31-33). Ibn Abi Hatim reported that Ibn Abi `Umar said that Sufyan said, "Every `plot' mentioned in the Qur'an refers to actions." Allah's statement,

(But they plot not except against themselves, and they perceive (it) not.) means, the harm of their wicked plots, as well as misguiding those whom they lead astray, will only strike them. Allah said in other Ayat,

(And verily, they shall bear their own loads, and other loads besides their own.) (29:13) and,

(And also of the burdens of those whom they misled without knowledge. Evil indeed is that which they shall bear!) (16:25). Allah said;

(And when there comes to them a sign they say: "We shall not believe until we receive the like of that which the Messengers of Allah received.") When there comes to them a sign they say,

("We shall not believe until we receive the like of that which the Messengers of Allah received.") until the angels bring us the Message from Allah, just as they brought it to the Messengers. In another Ayah, Allah said,

(And those who expect not a meeting with Us said: "Why are not the angels sent down to us, or why do we not see our Lord") (25:21). Allah's statement,

(Allah knows best with whom to entrust His Message.) means, He knows best with whom His Message should be given and which of His creatures are suitable for it. Allah said in other Ayat,

(And they say: "Why is not this Qur'an sent down to some great man of the two towns" Is it they who would portion out the mercy of your Lord) (43:31-32). They said, why was not this Qur'an revealed to a mighty, respectable leader, honored by us,

(...from one of the two towns) Of Makkah and At-Ta'if. This is because they, may Allah curse them, belittled the Messenger out of envy, transgression, rebellion and defiance. Allah described them,

(And when they see you, they only mock: "Is this the one whom Allah has sent as a Messenger") (25:41) and

(And when those who disbelieved see you, they only mock at you: "Is this the one who talks about your gods" While they disbelieve at the mention of the Most Gracious (Allah).) (21:36), and,

(Indeed Messengers were mocked before, but the scoffers were surrounded by that, whereat they used to mock.) (21:41)

The Disbelievers Admit to the Prophet's Nobility of Lineage

The disbelievers did all of this although they admitted to the Prophet's virtue, honorable lineage, respectable ancestry and purity of household and upbringing, may Allah, His angels, and the believers send blessings upon him. The disbelievers used to call the Prophet , before he received revelation, `Al-Amin' -- the Truthful. The leader of the Quraysh disbelievers, Abu Sufyan, had to admit to this fact when Heraclius, emperor of Rome, asked him, "How honorable is his (the Prophet's) ancestral lineage among you" Abu Sufyan answered, "His ancestry is highly regarded among us." Heraclius asked, "Do you find that he lied, before he started his mission" Abu Sufyan replied, "No." The emperor of Rome relied on the honor and purity of the Prophet to recognize the truth of his prophethood and what he came with. Imam Ahmad recorded that Wathilah bin Al-Asqa` said that the Messenger of Allah said,

Chapter 6: Al-An'am (Cattle, Livestock), Verses 111-165

«إِنَّ اللَّهَ اصْطَفَى مِنْ وَلَدِ إِبْرَاهِيمَ إِسْمَاعِيلَ، وَاصْطَفَى مِنْ بَنِي إِسْمَاعِيلَ بَنِي كِنَانَةَ وَاصْطَفَى مِنْ بَنِي كِنَانَةَ قُرَيْشًا وَاصْطَفَى مِنْ قُرَيْشٍ بَنِي هَاشِمٍ وَاصْطَفَانِي مِنْ بَنِي هَاشِمٍ»

(Verily, Allah has chosen Isma`il from the offspring of Ibrahim, Bani Kinanah from the offspring of Isma`il, Quraysh from Bani Kinanah, Bani Hashim from Quraysh and, He has chosen me from Bani Hashim.) Muslim recorded this Hadith. Al-Bukhari recorded that Abu Hurayrah said that the Messenger of Allah said,

«بُعِثْتُ مِنْ خَيْرِ قُرُونِ بَنِي آدَمَ قَرْنًا فَقَرْنًا، حَتَّى بُعِثْتُ مِنَ الْقَرْنِ الَّذِي كُنْتُ فِيه»

(I was chosen from a succession of the best generations of the Children of Adam, until the generation I was sent in.) Allah's said,

(Humiliation and disgrace from Allah and a severe torment will overtake the criminals...) This is a stern threat and sure promise from Allah for those who arrogantly refrain from obeying His Messengers and adhering to what they came with. On the Day of Resurrection, they will suffer humiliation and eternal disgrace before Allah, because they were arrogant in the worldly life. This is why it is befitting that they earn disgrace on the Day of Resurrection. Allah said in another Ayah,

(Verily, those who scorn My worship, they will surely enter Hell in humiliation!) (40:60) disgrace and dishonor. Allah said next,

(and a severe torment for that which they used to plot.) Since plotting usually takes place in secret and involves treachery and deceit, the disbelievers were recompensed with severe torment from Allah on the Day of Resurrection, as a just reckoning,

(And your Lord treats no one with injustice) (18:49) Allah said in another Ayah,

(The Day when all the secrets will be examined.) (86:9) Meaning, the secrets, hidden thoughts and intentions will be exposed. In the Two Sahihs, it is recorded that the Messenger of Allah said,

«يُنْصَبُ لِكُلِّ غَادِرٍ لِوَاءٌ عِنْدَ اسْتِهِ يَوْمَ الْقِيَامَةِ، فَيُقَالُ: هَذِهِ غَدْرَةُ فُلَانِ بْنِ فُلَانِ بْنِ فُلَان»

(A banner will be raised for every deceitful person from his anus on the Day of Resurrection, and it will say; `This is the treacherous plot of so-and-so, son of so-and-so, son of so-and-so.,) The wisdom in this is that since a plot occurs in secret, and people are usually unaware of it, then on the Day of Resurrection the plot itself will become public news testifying to the actions of those who committed it.

Surah: 6 Ayah: 125

﴿ فَمَن يُرِدِ ٱللَّهُ أَن يَهۡدِيَهُۥ يَشۡرَحۡ صَدۡرَهُۥ لِلۡإِسۡلَٰمِۖ وَمَن يُرِدۡ أَن يُضِلَّهُۥ يَجۡعَلۡ صَدۡرَهُۥ ضَيِّقًا حَرَجٗا كَأَنَّمَا يَصَّعَّدُ فِي ٱلسَّمَآءِۚ كَذَٰلِكَ يَجۡعَلُ ٱللَّهُ ٱلرِّجۡسَ عَلَى ٱلَّذِينَ لَا يُؤۡمِنُونَ ﴾

125. And whomsoever Allâh wills to guide, He opens his breast to Islâm; and whomsoever He wills to send astray, He makes his breast closed and constricted, as if he is climbing up to the sky. Thus Allâh puts the wrath on those who believe not.

Transliteration

125. Faman yuridi Allahu an yahdiyahu yashrah sadrahu lil-islami waman yurid an yudillahu yajAAal sadrahu dayyiqan harajan kaannama yassaAAAAadu fee alssama-i kathalika yajAAalu Allahu alrrijsa AAala allatheena la yu/minoona

Tafsir Ibn Kathir:

Allah said,

(And whomsoever Allah wills to guide, He opens his breast to Islam;) He makes Islam easy for him and strengthens his resolve to embrace it, and these are good signs. Allah said in other Ayat,

(Is he whose breast Allah has opened to Islam, so that he is in light from His Lord (as he who is a non-Muslim)) (39:22) and,

(But Allah has endeared the faith to you and has beautified it in your hearts, and has made disbelief, wickedness and disobedience hated by you. Such are they who are the rightly guided.) (49:7) Ibn `Abbas commented on Allah's statement,

(And whomsoever Allah wills to guide, He opens his breast to Islam;), "Allah says that He will open his heart to Tawhid and faith in Him." This is the same as was reported from Abu Malik and several others, and it is sound. Allah's statement,

(and whomsoever He wills to send astray, He makes his breast closed and constricted,) refers to inability to accept guidance, thus being deprived of beneficial faith.

(...as if he is climbing up to the sky.) because of the heaviness of faith on him. Sa`id bin Jubayr commented that in this case, "(Islam) finds every path in his heart impassable." Al-Hakam bin Aban said that `Ikrimah narrated from Ibn `Abbas that he commented on:

(...as if he is climbing up to the sky), "Just as the Son of Adam cannot climb up to the sky, Tawhid and faith will not be able to enter his heart, until Allah decides to allow it into his heart." Imam Abu Ja`far bin Jarir commented: "This is a parable that Allah has given for the heart of the disbeliever, which is completely impassable and closed to faith. Allah says, the example of the disbeliever's inability to accept faith in his heart and that it is too small to accommodate it, is the example of his inability to climb up to the sky, which is beyond his capability and power." He also commented on Allah's statement,

(Thus Allah puts the Rijs (wrath) on those who believe not.) "Allah says that just as He makes the heart of whomever He decides to misguide, closed and constricted, He also appoints Shaytan for him and for his likes, those who refused to believe in Allah and His Messenger. Consequently, Shaytan lures and hinders them from the path of Allah." `Ali bin Abi Talhah reported that Ibn `Abbas said that, Rijs, refers to Shaytan, while Mujahid said that it refers to all that does not contain goodness. `Abdur-Rahman bin Zayd bin Aslam said that, Rijs, means, `torment'.

Surah: 6 Ayah: 126 & Ayah: 127

﴿ وَهَـذَا صِرَاطُ رَبِّكَ مُسْتَقِيمًا قَدْ فَصَّلْنَا ٱلْأَيَـٰتِ لِقَوْمٍ يَذَّكَّرُونَ ۝ ﴾

126. And this is the Path of your Lord (the Qur'ân and Islâm) leading Straight. We have detailed Our Revelations for a people who take heed.

﴿ ۞ لَهُمْ دَارُ ٱلسَّلَـٰمِ عِندَ رَبِّهِمْ وَهُوَ وَلِيُّهُم بِمَا كَانُواْ يَعْمَلُونَ ۝ ﴾

127. For them will be the home of peace (Paradise) with their Lord. And He will be their Walî (Helper and Protector) because of what they used to do.

Transliteration

126. Wahatha siratu rabbika mustaqeeman qad fassalna al-ayati liqawmin yaththakkaroona   127. Lahum daru alssalami AAinda rabbihim wahuwa waliyyuhum bima kanoo yaAAmaloona

Tafsir Ibn Kathir:

After Allah mentioned the way of those who were themselves led to stray from His path and who hindered others from it, He emphasized the honor of the guidance and religion of truth that He sent His Messenger with. Allah said next,

(And this is the path of your Lord leading straight.) that is, Islam, that We have legislated for you, O Muhammad, by revealing this Qur'an to you, is Allah's straight path.

(We have detailed Our Ayat...) We have explained the Ayat and made them clear and plain, (for a people who take heed) those who have sound comprehension and understand what Allah and His Messenger convey to them,

(For them will be the abode of peace) Paradise,

(with their Lord.) on the Day of Resurrection. Allah described Paradise as `the abode of peace', because its residents are safe due to their access to the straight path, which conforms to the way of the Prophets. And just as their way was not wicked, they earned the abode of peace (which is free from all wickedness).

(And He will be their Wali) Protector, Supporter and Helper,

(because of what they used to do,) As reward for their good deeds, Allah has favored them and been generous with them, and awarded them Paradise.

Surah: 6 Ayah: 128

﴿ وَيَوْمَ يَحْشُرُهُمْ جَمِيعًا يَـٰمَعْشَرَ ٱلْجِنِّ قَدِ ٱسْتَكْثَرْتُم مِّنَ ٱلْإِنسِ وَقَالَ أَوْلِيَآؤُهُم مِّنَ ٱلْإِنسِ رَبَّنَا ٱسْتَمْتَعَ بَعْضُنَا بِبَعْضٍ وَبَلَغْنَآ أَجَلَنَا ٱلَّذِىٓ أَجَّلْتَ لَنَا ۚ قَالَ ٱلنَّارُ مَثْوَىٰكُمْ خَـٰلِدِينَ فِيهَآ إِلَّا مَا شَآءَ ٱللَّهُ ۗ إِنَّ رَبَّكَ حَكِيمٌ عَلِيمٌ ۝ ﴾

128. And on the Day when He will gather them (all) together (and say): "O you assembly of jinn! Many did you mislead of men," and their Auliyâ' (friends and helpers) amongst men will say: "Our Lord! We benefited one from the other, but now we have reached our appointed term which You did appoint for us." He will say: "The Fire be your dwelling-place, you will dwell therein forever, except as Allâh may will. Certainly your Lord is All-Wise, All-Knowing."

Transliteration

128. Wayawma yahshuruhum jameeAAan ya maAAshara aljinni qadi istakthartum mina al-insi waqala awliyaohum mina al-insi rabbana istamtaAAa baAAduna bibaAAdin wabalaghna ajalana allathee ajjalta lana qala alnnaru mathwakum khalideena feeha illa ma shaa Allahu inna rabbaka hakeemun AAaleemun

Tafsir Ibn Kathir:

Allah says, `Mention, O Muhammad, in what you convey and warn,' that,

(on the Day when He will gather them (all) together.) gather the Jinns and their loyal supporters from mankind who used to worship them in this life, seek refuge with them, obey them and inspire each other with adorned, deceitful speech. Allah will proclaim then,

(O you assembly of Jinn! Many did you mislead of men,) So the Ayah;

(Many did you mislead of men) refers to their misguiding and leading them astray. Allah also said;

Chapter 6: Al-An'am (Cattle, Livestock), Verses 111-165

(Did I not command you, O Children of Adam, that you should not worship Shaytan. Verily, he is a plain enemy to you. And that you should worship Me. That is the straight path. And indeed he (Shaytan) did lead astray a great multitude of you. Did you not, then, understand) (36:60-62), and

(and their friends among the people will say: "Our Lord! We benefited one from the other...") The friends of the Jinns among humanity will give this answer to Allah, after Allah chastises them for being misguided by the Jinns. Al-Hasan commented, "They benefited from each other when the Jinns merely commanded and mankind obeyed." Ibn Jurayj said, "During the time of Jahiliyyah, a man would reach a land and proclaim, `I seek refuge with the master (Jinn) of this valley,' and this is how they benefited from each other. They used this as an excuse for them on the Day of Resurrection." Therefore, the Jinns benefit from humans since humans revere the Jinns by invoking them for help. The Jinns would then proclaim, "We became the masters of both mankind and the Jinns."

(but now we have reached our appointed term which You did appoint for us.) meaning, death, according to As-Suddi.

(He (Allah) will say: "The Fire be your dwelling place...") where you will reside and live, you and your friends,

(you will dwell therein forever.) and will never depart except what Allah may will.

Surah: 6 Ayah: 129

﴿ وَكَذَٰلِكَ نُوَلِّى بَعْضَ ٱلظَّٰلِمِينَ بَعْضًۢا بِمَا كَانُوا۟ يَكْسِبُونَ ۝ ﴾

129. And thus We do make the Zâlimûn (polytheists and wrong-doers) Auliyâ' (supporters and helpers) of one another (in committing crimes), because of that which they used to earn.

Transliteration

129. Wakathalika nuwallee baAAda alththalimeena baAAdan bima kanoo yaksiboona

Tafsir Ibn Kathir:

The Wrongdoers Are the Supporters of Each other

Ma`mar said that Qatadah commented on this Ayah, "Allah makes the wrongdoers supporters for each other in the Fire by following one another into it." `Abdur-Rahman bin Zayd bin Aslam commented on Allah's statement,

(And thus We do make the wrongdoers supporters of one another.) "It refers to the wrongdoers of the Jinns and mankind." He then recited,

(And whosoever turns away blindly from the remembrance of the Most Gracious (Allah), We appoint for him Shaytan to be a companion to him.)(43:36) He said next -- concerning the meaning of the Ayah; "We appoint the wrongdoer of the Jinns over the wrongdoer of mankind." A poet once said, "There is no hand, but Allah's Hand is above it, and no wrongdoer but will be tested by another wrongdoer." The meaning of this honorable Ayah thus becomes: `Just as We made this losing group of mankind supporters of the Jinns that misguided them, We also appoint the wrongdoers over one another, destroy them by the hands of one another, and take revenge from them with one another. This is the just recompense for their injustice and transgression.'

Surah: 6 Ayah: 130

﴿ يَـٰمَعْشَرَ ٱلْجِنِّ وَٱلْإِنسِ أَلَمْ يَأْتِكُمْ رُسُلٌ مِّنكُمْ يَقُصُّونَ عَلَيْكُمْ ءَايَـٰتِى وَيُنذِرُونَكُمْ لِقَآءَ يَوْمِكُمْ هَـٰذَا قَالُوا۟ شَهِدْنَا عَلَىٰٓ أَنفُسِنَا وَغَرَّتْهُمُ ٱلْحَيَوٰةُ ٱلدُّنْيَا وَشَهِدُوا۟ عَلَىٰٓ أَنفُسِهِمْ أَنَّهُمْ كَانُوا۟ كَـٰفِرِينَ ﴾

130. O you assembly of jinn and mankind! "Did not there come to you Messengers from amongst you, reciting unto you My Verses and warning you of the meeting of this Day of yours?" They will say: "We bear witness against ourselves." It was the life of this world that deceived them. And they will bear witness against themselves that they were disbelievers.

Transliteration

130. Ya maAAshara aljinni waal-insi alam ya/tikum rusulun minkum yaqussoona AAalaykum ayatee wayunthiroonakum liqaa yawmikum hatha qaloo shahidna AAala anfusina wagharrat-humu alhayatu aldunya washahidoo AAala anfusihim annahum kanoo kafireena

Tafsir Ibn Kathir:

Chastising the Jinns and Humans after their Admission that Allah Sent Messengers to Them

Allah will chastise the disbelieving Jinns and humans on the Day of Resurrection, when He asks them, while having better knowledge, if the Messengers delivered His Messages to them,

("O you assembly of Jinn and humans! Did not there come to you Messengers from among you") We should note here that the Messengers are from among mankind only, not vice versa, as Mujahid, Ibn Jurayj and others from the Imams of Salaf and later generations have stated. The proof for this is that Allah said,

(Verily, We have sent the revelation to you as We sent the revelation to Nuh and the Prophets after him.) (4:163), until,

(Messengers as bearers of good news as well as of warning in order that mankind should have no plea against Allah after the (coming of) Messengers.) (4:165) Allah said, concerning the Prophet Ibrahim,

(And We ordained among his offspring prophethood and the Book) (29: 27), thus sending the prophethood and the Book exclusively through the offspring of the

Prophet Ibrahim. No one has claimed that there were Prophets from among the Jinns before the time of Ibrahim, but not after that. Allah said,

(And We never sent before you any of the Messengers but verily, they ate food and walked in the markets.) (25:20), and,

(And We sent not before you any but men unto whom We revealed, from among the people of townships.) (12:109) Therefore, concerning prophethood, the Jinns follow mankind in this regard and this is why Allah said about them,

(And (remember) when We sent towards you a group of the Jinn, listening to the Qur'an. When they stood in the presence thereof, they said: "Listen in silence!" And when it was finished, they returned to their people, as warners. They said: "O our people! Verily, we have heard a Book sent down after Musa, confirming what came before it, it guides to the truth and to the straight way. O our people! Respond to Allah's caller, and believe in him. He (Allah) will forgive you your sins, and will save you from a painful torment (i.e. Hell-fire). And whosoever does not respond to Allah's caller, he cannot escape on earth, and there will be no helpers for him besides Allah. Those are in manifest error.) (46:29-32) A Hadith collected by At-Tirmidhi stated that the Messenger of Allah recited Surat Ar-Rahman, to these Jinns, in which Allah said,

(We shall attend to you, O you two classes (Jinn and men)! Then which of the blessings of your Lord will you both (Jinn and men) deny) (55:31-32) Allah said in this honorable Ayah,

(O you assembly of Jinn and humans! "Did not there come to you Messengers from amongst you, reciting unto you My verses and warning you of the meeting of this Day of yours" They will say: "We bear witness against ourselves.") meaning, we affirm that the Messengers have conveyed Your Messages to us and warned us about the meeting with You, and that this Day will certainly occur. Allah said next,

(It was the life of this world that deceived them.) and they wasted their lives and brought destruction to themselves by rejecting the Messengers and denying their miracles. This is because they were deceived by the beauty, adornment and lusts of this life.

(And they will bear witness against themselves) on the Day of Resurrection,

(that they were disbelievers...) in this worldly life, rejecting what the Messengers, may Allah's peace and blessings be on them, brought them.

Surah: 6 Ayah: 131 & Ayah: 132

﴿ ذَٰلِكَ أَن لَّمْ يَكُن رَّبُّكَ مُهْلِكَ ٱلْقُرَىٰ بِظُلْمٍ وَأَهْلُهَا غَٰفِلُونَ ۝ ﴾

131. This is because your Lord would not destroy the (populations of) towns for their wrong-doing (i.e. associating others in worship along with Allâh) while their people were unaware (so the Messengers were sent).

﴿ وَلِكُلٍّ دَرَجَتٌ مِّمَّا عَمِلُواْ وَمَا رَبُّكَ بِغَفِلٍ عَمَّا يَعْمَلُونَ ﴾

132. For all there will be degrees (or ranks) according to what they did. And your Lord is not unaware of what they do.

Transliteration

131. Thalika an lam yakun rabbuka muhlika alqura bithulmin waahluha ghafiloona
132. Walikullin darajatun mimma AAamiloo wama rabbuka bighafilin AAamma yaAAmaloona

Tafsir Ibn Kathir:

Allah said,

(This is because your Lord would not destroy the (populations of) towns for their wrongdoing while their people were unaware.) meaning: `We sent the Messengers and revealed the Books to the Jinns and mankind, so that no one has an excuse that he is being punished for his wrongs although he did not receive Allah's Message. Therefore, We did not punish any of the nations, except after sending Messengers to them, so that they have no excuse.' Allah said in other Ayat,

(And there never was a nation but a warner had passed among them.) (35:24), and

(And verily, We have sent among every Ummah a Messenger (proclaiming): "Worship Allah, and stay away from At-Taghut (all false deities).") (16:36), and

(And We never punish until We have sent a Messenger.) (17:15), and,

(Every time a group is cast therein, its keeper will ask: "Did no warner come to you" They will say: "Yes, indeed a warner did come to us, but we belied him.") (67:8-9) There are many other Ayat on this subject. At-Tabari said, "Allah's statement,

(For all there will be degrees according to what they did.) means, every person who obeys Allah or behaves disobediently, has grades and ranks according to their works, which Allah gives them as recompense, good for good and evil for evil." I say, it is possible that Allah's statement,

(For all there will be degrees according to what they did.) refers to the disbelievers of the Jinns and mankind who will earn a place in the Fire according to their evil deeds. Allah said,

(He will say: "For each one there is double (torment).")(7:38), and,

(Those who disbelieved and hinder (others) from the path of Allah, for them We will add torment to the torment because they used to spread corruption.) (16:88) Allah said next,

(And your Lord is not unaware of what they do.) Ibn Jarir commented, "All these deeds that they did, O Muhammad, they did while your Lord is aware of them, and He collects and records these deeds with Him, so that He recompenses them when they meet Him and return to Him.

Surah: 6 Ayah: 133, Ayah: 134 & Ayah: 135

﴿ وَرَبُّكَ ٱلْغَنِيُّ ذُو ٱلرَّحْمَةِ إِن يَشَأْ يُذْهِبْكُمْ وَيَسْتَخْلِفْ مِنۢ بَعْدِكُم مَّا يَشَآءُ كَمَآ أَنشَأَكُم مِّن ذُرِّيَّةِ قَوْمٍ ءَاخَرِينَ ۝ ﴾

133. And your Lord is Rich (Free of all wants), full of Mercy; if He wills, He can destroy you, and in your place make whom He wills as your successors, as He raised you from the seed of other people.

﴿ إِنَّ مَا تُوعَدُونَ لَآتٍ وَمَآ أَنتُم بِمُعْجِزِينَ ۝ ﴾

134. Surely, that which you are promised will verily come to pass, and you cannot escape (from the Punishment of Allâh).

﴿ قُلْ يَـٰقَوْمِ ٱعْمَلُوا۟ عَلَىٰ مَكَانَتِكُمْ إِنِّى عَامِلٌ ۖ فَسَوْفَ تَعْلَمُونَ مَن تَكُونُ لَهُۥ عَـٰقِبَةُ ٱلدَّارِ ۗ إِنَّهُۥ لَا يُفْلِحُ ٱلظَّـٰلِمُونَ ۝ ﴾

135. Say (O Muhammad (peace be upon him)) "O my people! Work according to your way, surely, I too am working (in my way), and you will come to know for which of us will be the (happy) end in the Hereafter. Certainly the Zâlimûn (polytheists and wrong-doers) will not be successful."

Transliteration

133. Warabbuka alghaniyyu thoo alrrahmati in yasha/ yuthhibkum wayastakhlif min baAAdikum ma yashao kama anshaakum min thurriyyati qawmin akhareena   134. Inna ma tooAAadoona laatin wama antum bimuAAjizeena   135. Qul ya qawmi iAAmaloo AAala makanatikum innee AAamilun fasawfa taAAlamoona man takoonu lahu AAaqibatu alddari innahu la yuflihu alththalimoona

Tafsir Ibn Kathir:

If They Disobey, They Will Perish

Allah said,

(And your Lord...), O Muhammad,

(is Al-Ghani) Rich, free from needing His creatures in any way or form, while they stand in need of Him in all situations,

(full of mercy;) towards creation. Allah said in another Ayah,

(Truly, Allah is full of kindness, the Most Merciful towards mankind.) (2:143)

(if He wills, He can destroy you.) if you defy His commandments,

(And in your place make whom He wills as your successors,) who behave obediently,

(As He raised you from the seed of other people.) and surely, He is able to do this, and it is easy for Him. And just as Allah has destroyed the earlier nations and brought their successors, He is able to do away with these generations and bring other people in their place. Allah has also said;

(If He wills, He can take you away, O people, and bring others. And Allah is Ever Capable over that.) (4:133),

(O mankind! It is you who stand in need of Allah. But Allah is Rich (free of all needs), Worthy of all praise. If He willed, He could destroy you and bring about a new creation. And that is not hard for Allah.) (35:15-17), and,

(But Allah is Rich (free of all needs), and you are poor. And if you turn away, He will exchange you for some other people and they will not be your likes.) (47:38). Muhammad bin Ishaq said that Ya`qub bin `Utbah said that he heard Aban bin `Uthman saying about this Ayah,

(As He raised you from the seed of other people.) "`The seed' means the offspring and the children." Allah's statement,

(Surely, that which you are promised, will verily, come to pass and you cannot escape.) means, tell them, O Muhammad, that what they have been promised of Resurrection will surely occur,

(and you cannot escape.) from Allah. Rather, He is able to resurrect you even after you become dust and bones. Certainly, Allah is able to do all things and nothing ever escapes His power. Allah said;

(Say: "O my people! Work according to your way, surely, I too am working and you will come to know.") This contains a stern warning and a sure promise, saying; remain on your way, if you think that you are rightly guided, for I will remain on mine. Allah said in another Ayah,

(And say to those who do not believe: "Act according to Makanatikum, We are acting (in our way). And you wait! We (too) are waiting.") (11:121-122). `Ali bin Abi Talhah reported that Ibn `Abbas said that,

(according to Makanatikum...) means, your way.

(And you will come to know for which of us will be the (happy) end in the Hereafter. Certainly the wrongdoers will not be successful) (6:135), You will come to know if the happy end will be mine (Muhammad's) or yours (the disbelievers). Allah has indeed kept His promise and allowed Muhammad to prevail in the land and rise above those who defied him. He conquered Makkah for him and made him triumphant over his people who rejected and showed enmity towards him. The Prophet's rule soon spread over the Arabian Peninsula, Yemen and Bahrain, and all this occurred during his

Chapter 6: Al-An'am (Cattle, Livestock), Verses 111-165

lifetime. After his death, the various lands and provinces were conquered during the time of his successors, may Allah be pleased with them all. Allah also said,

(Allah has decreed: "Verily, it is I and My Messengers who shall be the victorious." Verily, Allah is All-Powerful, Almighty.) (58:21)

(Verily, We will indeed make victorious Our Messengers and those who believe in this world's life and on the Day when the witnesses will stand forth. The Day when their excuses will be of no profit to the wrongdoers. Theirs will be the curse, and theirs will be the evil abode.) (40:51-52) and,

(And indeed We have written in the Zabur after the Dhikr that My righteous servants shall inherit the land.) (21:105)

Surah: 6 Ayah: 136

﴿ وَجَعَلُواْ لِلَّهِ مِمَّا ذَرَأَ مِنَ ٱلْحَرْثِ وَٱلْأَنْعَمِ نَصِيبًا فَقَالُواْ هَذَا لِلَّهِ بِزَعْمِهِمْ وَهَذَا لِشُرَكَآئِنَا فَمَا كَانَ لِشُرَكَآئِهِمْ فَلَا يَصِلُ إِلَى ٱللَّهِ وَمَا كَانَ لِلَّهِ فَهُوَ يَصِلُ إِلَىٰ شُرَكَآئِهِمْ سَآءَ مَا يَحْكُمُونَ ﴾

136. And they assign to Allâh a share of the tilth and cattle which He has created, and they say: "This is for Allâh according to their claim, and this is for our (Allâh's so-called) partners." But the share of their (Allâh's so-called) "partners" reaches not Allâh, while the share of Allâh reaches their (Allâh's so-called) "partners"! Evil is the way they judge!

Transliteration

136. WajaAAaloo lillahi mimma tharaa mina alharthi waal-anAAami naseeban faqaloo hatha lillahi bizaAAmihim wahatha lishuraka-ina fama kana lishuraka-ihim fala yasilu ila Allahi wama kana lillahi fahuwa yasilu ila shuraka-ihim saa ma yahkumoona

Tafsir Ibn Kathir:

Some Acts of Shirk

Allah chastises and criticizes the idolators who invented innovations, Kufr and Shirk, and called on partners and rivals with Allah among His creation, although He created every thing, all praise is due to Him. This is why Allah said,

(And they assign to Allah from that which He has created,)

(of the tilth) meaning, fruits and produce,

(and of the cattle a share) meaning a part and a section.

(and they say: "This is for Allah," according to their claim, "and this is for our partners.") Allah said next,

(But the share of their "partners" reaches not Allah, while the share of Allah reaches their "partners"!) `Ali bin Abi Talhah and Al-`Awfi narrated that Ibn `Abbas said; "When they, the enemies of Allah, would cultivate the land or collect produce, they would assign a part of it to Allah and another part to the idol. They would keep the share for the idol, whether land, produce or anything else, and preserve its division to such an extent that they would collect anything that accidentally falls from the share they assigned to Allah and add it to the share of the idol. If the water that they assigned for the idol irrigated something (a section of land, for instance) that they assigned for Allah, they would add whatever this water irrigated to the idol's share! If the land or produce that they assigned for Allah was accidentally mixed with the share that they assigned for the idol, they would say that the idol is poor. Therefore, they would add it to the share they assigned for the idol and would not return it to the share they assigned for Allah. If the water that they assigned for Allah irrigated what they assigned for the idol they would leave it (the produce) for the idol. They also made some of their other property sacred, like the Bahirah, Sa'ibah, Wasilah and Ham, assigning them to the idols, claiming that they do so as way of seeking a means of approach to Allah. Allah said,

(And they assign to Allah a share of the tilth and cattle which He has created...)." Similar was said by Mujahid, Qatadah, As-Suddi and others. `Abdur-Rahman bin Zayd bin Aslam commented; "Every type of slaughter that they would assign for Allah, would never be eaten unless they mentioned the names of their idols when slaughtering it. Yet for what they sacrificed in the names of the idols, they would not mention Allah's Name when slaughtering it." He then recited the Ayah (6:136) until he reached,

(Evil is the way they judge!) This Ayah means, evil is that which they determined, for they committed error in the division. Certainly, Allah is the Lord, Owner and Creator of all things and His is the dominion. All things are His property and under His supreme control, will and decree. There is no deity worthy of worship, or Lord, except Him. And even when the polytheists made this evil division, they did not preserve it, but cheated in it. Allah said in other Ayat,

(And they assign daughters unto Allah -- glory be to Him -- and unto themselves what they desire.) (16:57), and

(Yet, they assign to some of His servants a share with Him. Verily, man is indeed a manifest ingrate!) (43:15), and,

(Is it for you the males and for Him the females That indeed is a division most unfair!) (53:21-22).

Surah: 6 Ayah: 137

﴿ وَكَذَٰلِكَ زَيَّنَ لِكَثِيرٍ مِّنَ ٱلْمُشْرِكِينَ قَتْلَ أَوْلَٰدِهِمْ شُرَكَآؤُهُمْ لِيُرْدُوهُمْ وَلِيَلْبِسُوا۟ عَلَيْهِمْ دِينَهُمْ ۖ وَلَوْ شَآءَ ٱللَّهُ مَا فَعَلُوهُ ۖ فَذَرْهُمْ وَمَا يَفْتَرُونَ ﴾

137. And so to many of the Mushrikûn (polytheists - see V.2:105) their (Allâh's so-called) "partners" have made fair-seeming the killing of their children, in order to lead them to their own destruction and cause confusion in their religion. And if Allâh had willed they would not have done so. So leave them alone with their fabrications.

Transliteration

137. Wakathalika zayyana likatheerin mina almushrikeena qatla awladihim shurakaohum liyurdoohum waliyalbisoo AAalayhim deenahum walaw shaa Allahu ma faAAaloohu fatharhum wama yaftaroona

Tafsir Ibn Kathir:

Shaytan Lured the Idolators to Kill Their Children

Allah says, just as the Shayatin lured the idolators to assign a share for Allah from what He created of agriculture and cattle - and a share for the idols, they also made it seem fair for them to kill their children, for fear of poverty, and burying their daughters alive, for fear of dishonor. `Ali bin Abi Talhah reported from Ibn `Abbas that he commented;

(And so to many of the idolators, their "partners" have made fair seeming the killing of their children...) "They make killing their children attractive to them." Mujahid said, "Idolators' partners among the devils ordered them to bury their children for fear of poverty." As-Suddi said, "The devils commanded them to kill their daughters so that they,

(lead them to their own destruction), and to,

(cause confusion in their religion.)" Allah said,

(And if Allah had willed, they would not have done so.) meaning, all this occurred by Allah's leave, will and decree, but He dislikes these practices, and He has the perfect wisdom in every decree. He is never questioned about what He does, but they all will be questioned.

(So leave them alone with their fabrications.) meaning, avoid and abandon them and what they do, for Allah will judge between you and them.

Surah: 6 Ayah: 138

﴿ وَقَالُواْ هَـذِهِ أَنْعَـمٌ وَحَرْثٌ حِجْرٌ لاَّ يَطْعَمُهَا إِلاَّ مَن نَّشَآءُ بِزَعْمِهِمْ وَأَنْعَـمٌ حُرِّمَتْ ظُهُورُهَا وَأَنْعَـمٌ لاَّ يَذْكُرُونَ اسْمَ اللَّهِ عَلَيْهَا افْتِرَآءً عَلَيْهِ سَيَجْزِيهِم بِمَا كَانُواْ يَفْتَرُونَ ﴾

138. And according to their claim, they say that such and such cattle and crops are forbidden, and none should eat of them except those whom we allow. And (they say) there are cattle forbidden to be used for burden or any other work, and cattle on which (at slaughtering) the Name of Allâh is not pronounced; lying against Him (Allâh). He will recompense them for what they used to fabricate.

Transliteration

138. Waqaloo hathihi anAAamun waharthun hijrun la yatAAamuha illa man nashao bizaAAmihim waanAAamun hurrimat thuhooruha waanAAamun la yathkuroona isma Allahi AAalayha iftiraan AAalayhi sayajzeehim bima kanoo yaftaroona

Tafsir Ibn Kathir:

The Idolators Forbade Certain Types of Cattle

`Ali bin Abi Talhah reported that Ibn `Abbas said, "Hijr refers to what they forbade, such as the Wasilah, and the like." Similar was said by Mujahid, Ad-Dahhak, As-Suddi, Qatadah, `Abdur-Rahman bin Zayd bin Aslam and others. Qatadah commented on,

(They say that such and such cattle and crops are Hijr,) "It is a prohibition that the Shayatin appointed for their wealth, and a type of exaggeration and extremism that did not come from Allah." (`Abdur-Rahman) Ibn Zayd bin Aslam said that, d

(Hijr,) refers to what the idolators designated for their deities. As-Suddi said that the Ayah,

(And none should eat of them except those whom we allow, they claimed...) means, "They said, only those whom we choose can eat of them., and the rest are prohibited from eating them." Similar to this honorable Ayah, Allah said,

(Say: "Tell me, what provision Allah has sent down to you! And you have made of it lawful and unlawful." Say: "Has Allah permitted you (to do so), or do you invent a lie against Allah") (10:59), and,

(Allah has not instituted things like Bahirah or a Sa'ibah or a Wasilah or a Ham. But those who disbelieve invent lies against Allah, and most of them have no understanding.) (5:103) As-Suddi said that cattle forbidden to be used for burden were the Bahirah, Sa'ibah, Wasilah and Ham, as well as cattle for which the idolators did not mention Allah's Name when slaughtering them nor when they were born. Abu Bakr bin `Ayyash said that `Asim bin Abi An-Najud said, "Abu Wa'il said to me, `Do you know the meaning of the Ayah,

Chapter 6: Al-An'am (Cattle, Livestock), Verses 111-165

(And (they say) there are cattle forbidden to be used for burden, and cattle on which the Name of Allah is not pronounced.) I said, `No.' He said, `It is the Bahirah, which they would not use to for Hajj (either by riding it or carrying things on it).'" Mujahid also said that they were some of the camels belonging to idolators on which Allah's Name was not mentioned when riding, milking, carrying things, copulation or any other action.

(lying against Him.) against Allah. The idolators indeed lied when they attributed this evil to Allah's religion and Law; He did not allow them to do that nor did He approve of it,

(He will recompense them for what they used to fabricate.) against Him, and falsely attribute to Him.

Surah: 6 Ayah: 139

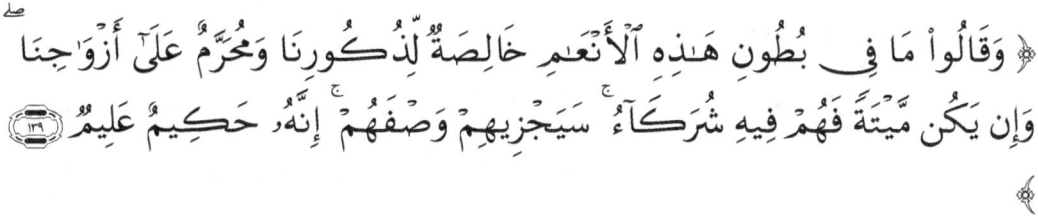

139. And they say: "What is in the bellies of such and such cattle (milk or fetus) is for our males alone, and forbidden to our females (girls and women), but if it is born dead, then all have shares therein." He will punish them for their attribution (of such false orders to Allâh). Verily, He is All-Wise, All-Knower. (Tafsir At-Tabarî).

Transliteration

139. Waqaloo ma fee butooni hathihi al-anAAami khalisatun lithukoorina wamuharramun AAala azwajina wa-in yakun maytatan fahum feehi shurakao sayajzeehim wasfahum innahu hakeemun AAaleemun

Tafsir Ibn Kathir:

Abu Ishaq As-Subay`i narrated that `Abdullah bin Abi Al-Hudhayl reported that Ibn `Abbas said that,

(And they say: "What is in the bellies of such and such cattle is for our males alone...") refers to milk. `Awfi said that Ibn `Abbas said about this Ayah,

(And they say: "What is in the bellies of such and such cattle is for our males alone...") "It is about milk, which they prohibited for their females and allowed only their males to drink. When a sheep would give birth to a male sheep, they would slaughter it and feed it to their males, but not to their females. If the newly born lamb was a female, they would not slaughter it, but if it was stillborn, they would share in it (with their females)! Allah forbade this practice." Similar was said by As-Suddi. Ash-Sha`bi said, "The Bahirah's milk was only given to the men. But if any cattle from the Bahirah died, both men and women would share in eating it." Similar was said by `Ikrimah, Qatadah and `Abdur-Rahman bin Zayd bin Aslam. Mujahid commented;

(And they say: "What is in the bellies of such and such cattle is for our males alone, and forbidden to our females...") "It refers to the Sa'ibah and the Bahirah." Abu Al-`Aliyah, Mujahid and Qatadah said that Allah's statement,

(He will punish them for their attribution.) means, uttering such falsehood. This is explained by Allah's statement,

(And say not concerning that which your tongues falsely utter: "This is lawful and this is forbidden." so as to invent lies against Allah. Verily, those who invent lies against Allah will never prosper.) (16:116) Allah said,

(Verily, He is All-Wise.) in His actions, statements, Law and decree,

(All-Knower), in the actions of His servants, whether good or evil, and He will recompense them for these deeds completely.

Surah: 6 Ayah: 140

﴿ قَدْ خَسِرَ ٱلَّذِينَ قَتَلُوٓا۟ أَوْلَٰدَهُمْ سَفَهًۢا بِغَيْرِ عِلْمٍ وَحَرَّمُوا۟ مَا رَزَقَهُمُ ٱللَّهُ ٱفْتِرَآءً عَلَى ٱللَّهِ قَدْ ضَلُّوا۟ وَمَا كَانُوا۟ مُهْتَدِينَ ۝ ﴾

140. Indeed lost are they who have killed their children, from folly, without knowledge, and have forbidden that which Allâh has provided for them, inventing a lie against Allâh. They have indeed gone astray and were not guided.

Transliteration

140. Qad khasira allatheena qataloo awladahum safahan bighayri AAilmin waharramoo ma razaqahumu Allahu iftiraan AAala Allahi qad dalloo wama kanoo muhtadeena

Tafsir Ibn Kathir:

Allah says that those who committed these evil acts have earned the loss of this life and the Hereafter.

As for this life, they lost when they killed their children and made it difficult for themselves by prohibiting some types of their wealth, as an act of innovation that they invented on their own. As for the Hereafter, they will end up in the worst dwellings, because they used to lie about Allah and invent falsehood about Him. Allah also said,

(Say: "Verily, those who invent a lie against Allah will never be successful." (A brief) enjoyment in this world! And then unto Us will be their return, then We shall make them taste the severest torment because they used to disbelieve.) (10:69-70) Al-Hafiz Abu Bakr bin Marduwyah recorded that Ibn `Abbas commented, "If it pleases you to know how ignorant the Arabs used to be, then recite the Ayat beyond Ayah one hundred and thirty in Surat Al-An`am,

(Indeed lost are they who have killed their children, foolishly, without knowledge, and (they) have forbidden that which Allah has provided for them, inventing a lie against Allah. They have indeed gone astray and were not guided.)" Al-Bukhari also recorded this in the section of his Sahih on the virtues of the Quraysh.

Surah: 6 Ayah: 141 & Ayah: 142

﴿ ۞ وَهُوَ ٱلَّذِىٓ أَنشَأَ جَنَّـٰتٍ مَّعْرُوشَـٰتٍ وَغَيْرَ مَعْرُوشَـٰتٍ وَٱلنَّخْلَ وَٱلزَّرْعَ مُخْتَلِفًا أُكُلُهُۥ وَٱلزَّيْتُونَ وَٱلرُّمَّانَ مُتَشَـٰبِهًا وَغَيْرَ مُتَشَـٰبِهٍ ۚ كُلُوا۟ مِن ثَمَرِهِۦٓ إِذَآ أَثْمَرَ وَءَاتُوا۟ حَقَّهُۥ يَوْمَ حَصَادِهِۦ ۖ وَلَا تُسْرِفُوٓا۟ ۚ إِنَّهُۥ لَا يُحِبُّ ٱلْمُسْرِفِينَ ﴿١٤١﴾ ﴾

141. And it is He Who produces gardens trellised and untrellised, and date-palms, and crops of different shape and taste (their fruits and their seeds) and olives, and pomegranates, similar (in kind) and different (in taste). Eat of their fruit when they ripen, but pay the due thereof (its Zakât, according to Allâh's Orders 1/10th or 1/20th) on the day of its harvest, and waste not by extravagance. Verily, He likes not Al-Musrifûn (those who waste by extravagance),

﴿ وَمِنَ ٱلْأَنْعَـٰمِ حَمُولَةً وَفَرْشًا ۚ كُلُوا۟ مِمَّا رَزَقَكُمُ ٱللَّهُ وَلَا تَتَّبِعُوا۟ خُطُوَٰتِ ٱلشَّيْطَـٰنِ ۚ إِنَّهُۥ لَكُمْ عَدُوٌّ مُّبِينٌ ﴿١٤٢﴾ ﴾

142. And of the cattle (are some) for burden (like camels) and (some are) small (unable to carry burden like sheep and goats - for food, meat, milk and wool). Eat of what Allâh has provided for you, and follow not the footsteps of Shaitân (Satan). Surely he is to you an open enemy.

Transliteration

141. Wahuwa allathee anshaa jannatin maAArooshatin waghayra maAArooshatin waalnnakhla waalzzarAAa mukhtalifan okuluhu waalzzaytoona waalrrummana mutashabihan waghayra mutashabihin kuloo min thamarihi itha athmara waatoo haqqahu yawma hasadihi wala tusrifoo innahu la yuhibbu almusrifeena 142. Wamina al-anAAami hamoolatan wafarshan kuloo mimma razaqakumu Allahu wala tattabiAAoo khutuwati alshshaytani innahu lakum AAaduwwun mubeenun

Tafsir Ibn Kathir:

Allah Created the Produce, Seed Grains and Cattle

Allah states that He created everything, including the produce, fruits and cattle that the idolators mishandled by their misguided ideas, dividing them into various designated parts, allowing some and prohibiting some. Allah said,

(And it is He Who produces gardens Ma`rushat and not Ma`rushat,) `Ali bin Abi Talhah reported that Ibn `Abbas commented, "Ma`rushat refers to what the people trellise, while `not Ma`rushat' refers to fruits (and produce) that grow wild inland and on mountains." `Ata' Al-Khurasani said that Ibn `Abbas said, "Ma`rushat are the grapevines that are trellised, while `not Ma`rushat' refers to grapevines that are not trellised." As-Suddi said similarly. As for these fruits being similar, yet different, Ibn Jurayj said, "They are similar in shape, but different in taste." Muhammad bin Ka`b said that the Ayah,

(Eat of their fruit when they ripen,) means, "(Eat) from the dates and grapes they produce." Allah said next,

(but pay the due thereof on the day of their harvest,) Mujahid commented, "When the poor people are present (on the day of harvest), give them some of the produce." `Abdur-Razzaq recorded that Mujahid commented on the Ayah,

(but pay the due thereof on the day of their harvest.) "When planting, one gives away handfuls (of seed grains) and on harvest, he gives away handfuls and allows them to pick whatever is left on the ground of the harvest." Ath-Thawri said that Hammad narrated that Ibrahim An-Nakha`i said, "One gives away some of the hay." Ibn Al-Mubarak said that Shurayk said that Salim said that Sa`id bin Jubayr commented;

(but pay the due thereof on the day of their harvest,) "This ruling, giving the poor the handfuls (of seed grains) and some of the hay as food for their animals, was before Zakah became obligatory." Allah has chastised those who harvest, without giving away a part of it as charity. Allah mentioned the story of the owners of the garden in Surat Nun,

(When they swore to pluck the fruits of the (garden) in the morning. Without saying: "If Allah wills." Then there passed by on the (garden) a visitation (fire) from your Lord at night, burning it while they were asleep. So the (garden) became black by the morning, like a pitch dark night (in complete ruins). Then they called out one to another as soon as the morning broke. Saying: "Go to your tilth in the morning, if you would pluck the fruits." So they departed, conversing in secret low tones (saying). "No poor person shall enter upon you into it today." And they went in the morning with strong intention, thinking that they have power (to prevent the poor taking anything of the fruits therefrom). But when they saw the (garden), they said: "Verily, we have gone astray." (Then they said): "Nay! Indeed we are deprived of (the fruits)!" The best among them said: "Did I not tell you, why say you not: `If Allah wills'." They said: "Glory to Our Lord! Verily, we have been wrongdoers." Then they turned one against another, blaming. They said: "Woe to us! We have transgressed. We hope that our Lord will give us in exchange a better (garden) than this. Truly, we turn to our Lord." Such is the punishment (in this life), but truly, the punishment of the Hereafter is greater if they but knew.) (68:18-33).

Prohibiting Extravagance

Allah said,

(And waste not by extravagance. Verily, He likes not the wasteful.) It was said that the extravagance prohibited here refers to excessive charity beyond normal amounts. Ibn Jurayj said, "This Ayah was revealed concerning Thabit bin Qays bin Shammas, who plucked the fruits of his date palms. Then he said to himself, `This day, every person who comes to me, I will feed him from it.' So he kept feeding (them) until the evening came and he ended up with no dates. Allah sent down,

(And waste not by extravagance. Verily, He likes not the wasteful.)'' Ibn Jarir recorded this statement from Ibn Jurayj. However, thhe apparent meaning of this Ayah, and Allah knows best, is that;

(Eat of their fruit when they ripen, but pay the due thereof on the day of their harvest, and waste not...) refers to eating, meaning, do not waste in eating because this spoils the mind and the body. Allah said in another Ayah,

(And eat and drink but waste not by extravagance.) (7: 31) In his Sahih, Al-Bukhari recorded a Hadith without a chain of narration; a

(Eat, drink and clothe yourselves without extravagance or arrogance.) Therefore, these Ayat have the same meaning as this Hadith. and Allah knows best.

Benefits of Cattle

Allah's statement,

(And of the cattle (are some) for burden and (some smaller) for Farsh.) means, He created cattle for you, some of which are suitable for burden, such as camels, and some are Farsh. Ath-Thawri narrated that Abu Ishaq said that Abu Al-Ahwas said that `Abdullah said that `animals for burden' are the camels that are used for carrying things, while, `Farsh', refers to small camels. Al-Hakim recorded it and said, "Its chain is Sahih and they did not record it." `Abdur-Rahman bin Zayd bin Aslam said that `animals for burden' refers to the animals that people ride, while, `Farsh' is that they eat (its meat) and milk it. The sheep is not able to carry things, so you eat its meat and use its wool for covers and mats (or clothes). This statement of `Abdur-Rahman is sound, and the following Ayat testify to it,

(Do they not see that We have created for them of what Our Hands have created, the cattle, so that they are their owners. And We have subdued them unto them so that some of them they have for riding and some they eat.) (36:71-72), and,

(And verily, in the cattle, there is a lesson for you. We give you to drink of that which is in their bellies, from between excretions and blood, pure milk; palatable to the drinkers.) (16:66), until,

(And of their wool, fur and hair, furnishings and articles of convenience, comfort for a while.) (16:80).

Eat the Meat of These Cattle, But Do Not Follow Shaytan's Law Concerning Them

Allah said,

(Eat of what Allah has provided for you,) of fruits, produce and cattle. Allah created all these and provided you with them as provision.

(and follow not the footsteps of Shaytan.) meaning, his way and orders, just as the idolators followed him and prohibited fruits and produce that Allah provided for them, claiming that this falsehood came from Allah.

(Surely, he is to you) meaning; Shaytan, O people, is to you,

(an open enemy) and his enmity to you is clear and apparent. Allah said in other Ayat,

(Surely, Shaytan is an enemy to you, so take (treat) him as an enemy. He only invites his Hizb (followers) that they may become the dwellers of the blazing Fire.) (35:6) and,

(O Children of Adam! Let not Shaytan deceive you, as he got your parents out of Paradise, stripping them of their raiment, to show them their private parts.) (7:27) and,

(Will you then take him (Iblis) and his offspring as protectors and helpers rather than Me while they are enemies to you What an evil is the exchange for the wrongdoers.)(18:50) There are many other Ayat on this subject.

Surah: 6 Ayah: 143 & Ayah: 144

﴿ ثَمَـٰنِيَةَ أَزْوَٰجٍ مِّنَ ٱلضَّأْنِ ٱثْنَيْنِ وَمِنَ ٱلْمَعْزِ ٱثْنَيْنِ قُلْ ءَآلذَّكَرَيْنِ حَرَّمَ أَمِ ٱلْأُنثَيَيْنِ أَمَّا ٱشْتَمَلَتْ عَلَيْهِ أَرْحَامُ ٱلْأُنثَيَيْنِ نَبِّـُٔونِى بِعِلْمٍ إِن كُنتُمْ صَـٰدِقِينَ ﴾

143. Eight pairs; of the sheep two (male and female), and of the goats two (male and female). Say: "Has He forbidden the two males or the two females, or (the young) which the wombs of the two females enclose? Inform me with knowledge if you are truthful."

﴿ وَمِنَ ٱلْإِبِلِ ٱثْنَيْنِ وَمِنَ ٱلْبَقَرِ ٱثْنَيْنِ قُلْ ءَآلذَّكَرَيْنِ حَرَّمَ أَمِ ٱلْأُنثَيَيْنِ أَمَّا ٱشْتَمَلَتْ عَلَيْهِ أَرْحَامُ ٱلْأُنثَيَيْنِ أَمْ كُنتُمْ شُهَدَآءَ إِذْ وَصَّىٰكُمُ ٱللَّهُ بِهَـٰذَا فَمَنْ أَظْلَمُ مِمَّنِ ٱفْتَرَىٰ عَلَى ٱللَّهِ كَذِبًا لِّيُضِلَّ ٱلنَّاسَ بِغَيْرِ عِلْمٍ إِنَّ ٱللَّهَ لَا يَهْدِى ٱلْقَوْمَ ٱلظَّـٰلِمِينَ ﴾

144. And of the camels two (male and female), and of oxen two (male and female). Say: "Has He forbidden the two males or the two females or (the young) which the wombs of the two females enclose? Or were you present when Allâh ordered you such a thing? Then who does more wrong than one who invents a lie against Allâh, to lead mankind astray without knowledge. Certainly Allâh guides not the people who are Zâlimûn (polytheists and wrong-doers)."

Chapter 6: Al-An'am (Cattle, Livestock), Verses 111-165

Transliteration

143. Thamaniyata azwajin mina aldda/ni ithnayni wamina almaAAzi ithnayni qul alththakarayni harrama ami alonthayayni amma ishtamalat AAalayhi arhamu alonthayayni nabbi-oonee biAAilmin in kuntum sadiqeena   144. Wamina al-ibili ithnayni wamina albaqari ithnayni qul alththakarayni harrama ami alonthayayni amma ishtamalat AAalayhi arhamu alonthayayni am kuntum shuhadaa ith wassakumu Allahu bihatha faman athlamu mimmani iftara AAala Allahi kathiban liyudilla alnnasa bighayri AAilmin inna Allaha la yahdee alqawma alththalimeena

Tafsir Ibn Kathir:

These Ayat demonstrate the ignorance of the Arabs before Islam.

They used to prohibit the usage of some of their cattle and designate them as Bahirah, Sa'ibah, Wasilah and Ham etc. These were some of the innovations they invented for cattle, fruits and produce. Allah stated that He has created gardens, trellised and untrellised, and cattle, as animals of burden and as Farsh. Allah next mentioned various kinds of cattle, male and female, such as sheep and goats. He also created male and female camels and the same with cows. Allah did not prohibit any of these cattle or their offspring. Rather, they all were created for the sons of Adam as a source for food, transportation, work, milk, and other benefits, which are many. Allah said,

(And He has sent down for you of cattle eight pairs...) (39:6) Allah said;

(...or (the young) which the wombs of the two females enclose...) This refutes the idolators' statement,

(What is in the bellies of such and such cattle is for our males alone, and forbidden to our females.) (6:139) Allah said,

(Inform me with knowledge if you are truthful.) meaning, tell me with sure knowledge, how and when did Allah prohibit what you claimed is prohibited, such as the Bahirah, Sa'ibah, Wasilah and Ham etc. Al-`Awfi said that Ibn `Abbas said, "Allah's statement,

(Eight pairs: of the sheep two, and of the goats two...) these are four pairs,

(Say: "Has He forbidden the two males or the two females...") I (Allah) did not prohibit any of these.

(or (the young) which the wombs of the two females enclose) and does the womb produce but males and females So why do you prohibit some and allow some others

(Inform me with knowledge if you are truthful.) Allah is saying that all of this is allowed." Allah said,

(Or, were you present when Allah ordered you such a thing) mocking the idolators' innovations, and their lies that Allah made sacred what they have prohibited.

(Then who does more wrong than one who invents a lie against Allah, to lead mankind astray without knowledge.) Therefore, no one is more unjust than the people described here and

(Certainly, Allah guides not the people who are wrongdoers.) The person most worthy of this condemnation is `Amr bin Luhay bin Qum`ah. He was the first person to change the religion of the Prophets and designate the Sa'ibah, Wasilah and Ham, as mentioned in the Sahih.

Surah: 6 Ayah: 145

﴿ قُل لَّآ أَجِدُ فِى مَآ أُوحِىَ إِلَىَّ مُحَرَّمًا عَلَىٰ طَاعِمٍ يَطْعَمُهُ إِلَّآ أَن يَكُونَ مَيْتَةً أَوْ دَمًا مَّسْفُوحًا أَوْ لَحْمَ خِنزِيرٍ فَإِنَّهُ رِجْسٌ أَوْ فِسْقًا أُهِلَّ لِغَيْرِ ٱللَّهِ بِهِۦ فَمَنِ ٱضْطُرَّ غَيْرَ بَاغٍ وَلَا عَادٍ فَإِنَّ رَبَّكَ غَفُورٌ رَّحِيمٌ ﴾

145. Say (O Muhammad (peace be upon him)) "I find not in that which has been revealed to me anything forbidden to be eaten by one who wishes to eat it, unless it be Maitah (a dead animal) or blood poured forth (by slaughtering or the like), or the flesh of swine (pork); for that surely is impure or impious (unlawful) meat (of an animal) which is slaughtered as a sacrifice for others than Allâh (or has been slaughtered for idols, or on which Allâh's Name has not been mentioned while slaughtering). But whosoever is forced by necessity without willful disobedience, nor transgressing due limits; (for him) certainly, your Lord is Oft-Forgiving, Most Merciful."

Transliteration

145. Qul la ajidu feema oohiya ilayya muharraman AAala taAAimin yatAAamuhu illa an yakoona maytatan aw daman masfoohan aw lahma khinzeerin fa-innahu rijsun aw fisqan ohilla lighayri Allahi bihi famani idturra ghayra baghin wala AAadin fa-inna rabbaka ghafoorun raheemun

Tafsir Ibn Kathir:

Forbidden Things

Allah commands His servant and Messenger, Muhammad ,

(Say) O Muhammad to those who prohibited what Allah has provided them, claiming this falsehood to be from Allah,

(I find not in that which has been revealed to me anything forbidden to be eaten by one who wishes to eat it,) This Ayah means, I do not find any animals that are prohibited, except these mentioned here. We should mention here that the prohibited things mentioned in Surat Al-Ma'idah and the Hadiths on this subject amend the meaning of this Ayah.

(or blood poured.) Qatadah commented, "Poured blood was prohibited, but the meat that still has some blood in it is allowed." Al-Humaydi said that Sufyan narrated to us that `Amr bin Dinar narrated to us, "I said to Jabir bin `Abdullah, `They claim that the Messenger of Allah prohibited the meat of donkeys during (the day of) Khaybar.' He said, `Al-Hakam bin `Amr narrated that from the Messenger of Allah . That scholar - refering to Ibn `Abbas - denied it, reciting the Ayah;

(Say: "I find not in that which has been revealed to me anything forbidden to be eaten by one who wishes to eat it...")"' Al-Bukhari and Abu Dawud collected it. Abu Bakr bin Marduwyah and Al-Hakim, in his Mustadrak, recorded that Ibn `Abbas said, "During the time of Jahiliyyah, the people used to eat some things and avoid some other things, because they disliked them. Later on, Allah sent His Prophet , revealed His Book, allowed what He allowed, and prohibited what He prohibited. Therefore, whatever Allah allowed is lawful and whatever He prohibited is unlawful. Whatever He did not mention, there is no sin in it." He then recited the Ayah,

(Say: "I find not in that which has been revealed to me anything forbidden to be eaten by one who wishes to eat it...") This is the wording with Ibn Marduwyah. Abu Dawud also recorded this statement, and Al-Hakim said, "Its chain is Sahih and they did not record it." Imam Ahmad recorded that Ibn `Abbas said, "A sheep belonging to Sawdah bint Zam`ah died and she said, `O Allah's Messenger! So-and-so (sheep) has died.' He said,

«فَلِمَ لَا أَخَذْتُمْ مَسْكَهَا؟»

(Why did you not use its skin) She said, `Should we use the skin of a sheep that has died' Allah's Messenger said,

«إِنَّمَا قَالَ اللهُ:

(قُل لاَ أَجِدُ فِى مَا أُوْحِىَ إِلَىَّ مُحَرَّمًا عَلَى طَاعِمٍ يَطْعَمُهُ إِلاَّ أَن يَكُونَ مَيْتَةً أَوْ دَمًا مَّسْفُوحًا أَوْ لَحْمَ خِنزِيرٍ)

وَإِنَّكُمْ لَا تَطْعَمُونَهُ أَنْ تَدْبَغُوهُ فَتَنْتَفِعُوا بِهِ»

(Allah only said, (Say: "I find not in that which has been revealed to me anything forbidden to be eaten by one who wishes to eat it, except Maytah (a dead animal) or blood poured forth, or the flesh of swine....) You will not be eating it if you tan its skin and benefit from it.) So she had the sheep skinned, the skin was tanned and made into a water skin that she kept until it wore out." Al-Bukhari and an-Nasa'i collected a similar Hadith. Allah said,

(But whosoever is forced by necessity without willful disobedience, nor transgressing due limits;) Therefore, whoever is forced by necessity to eat anything that Allah has forbidden in this honorable Ayah, without transgressing his limits, then for him,

(certainly, your Lord is Oft-Forgiving, Most Merciful.) We mentioned the explanation of this Ayah in Surat Al-Baqarah. This honorable Ayah contradicts the idolators' innovated prohibitions for certain kinds of wealth, relying merely on their misguided ideas, such as the Bahirah, Sa'ibah, Wasilah and Ham. Allah commanded His Messenger to inform them that he does not find that such types of animals are prohibited in what Allah revealed to him. In this Ayah, Allah only prohibited dead animals, poured blood, the flesh of swine and what has been slaughtered for something other than Allah. Other things were not prohibited here, but rather treated as that which does not have a ruling, i.e., permissible. Therefore, how do you -- idolators -- claim that such items are prohibited, and why did you prohibit them when Allah did not prohibit them

Surah: 6 Ayah: 146

﴿ وَعَلَى ٱلَّذِينَ هَادُواْ حَرَّمْنَا كُلَّ ذِى ظُفُرٍ ۖ وَمِنَ ٱلْبَقَرِ وَٱلْغَنَمِ حَرَّمْنَا عَلَيْهِمْ شُحُومَهُمَآ إِلَّا مَا حَمَلَتْ ظُهُورُهُمَآ أَوِ ٱلْحَوَايَآ أَوْ مَا ٱخْتَلَطَ بِعَظْمٍ ۚ ذَٰلِكَ جَزَيْنَـٰهُم بِبَغْيِهِمْ ۖ وَإِنَّا لَصَـٰدِقُونَ ﴾

146. And unto those who are Jews, We forbade every (animal) with undivided hoof, and We forbade them the fat of the ox and the sheep except what adheres to their backs or their entrails, or is mixed up with a bone. Thus We recompensed them for their rebellion (committing crimes like murdering the Prophets and eating of Ribâ (usury)) And verily, We are Truthful.

Transliteration

146. WaAAala allatheena hadoo harramna kulla thee thufurin wamina albaqari waalghanami harramna AAalayhim shuhoomahuma illa ma hamalat thuhooruhuma awi alhawaya aw ma ikhtalata biAAathmin thalika jazaynahum bibaghyihim wa-inna lasadiqoona

Tafsir Ibn Kathir:

Foods that were Prohibited for the Jews Because of their Transgression

Allah says, We forbade for the Jews every bird and animal with undivided hoof, such as the camel, ostrich, duck and goose. Allah said here,

(and We forbade them the fat of the ox and the sheep...) The Jews used to forbid these types of foods saying that Isra'il, or Ya`qub, used to forbid them for himself so they too forbid them. This was mentioned by As-Suddi. `Ali bin Abi Talhah reported that Ibn `Abbas said that, (except what adheres to their backs) refers to the fat that clings to their backs. Allah said next,

(or their Hawaya) that is, the entrails, according to Abu Ja`far bin Jarir. He also said, "The meaning here is, `And from ox and sheep, We forbade their fat for the Jews, except the fat on their backs and what the entrails carry." `Ali bin Abi Talhah said that, Ibn `Abbas said that the, Hawaya, are the entrails. Similar was reported from Mujahid, Sa`id bin Jubayr and Ad-Dahhak. Allah's statement,

(....or is mixed up with a bone.) means, We allowed the Jews the fat that is mixed with bones. Ibn Jurayj commented, "The fat on the rump that is mixed with the tailbone was allowed for them, and also the fat on the legs, head, eyes and what adheres to the bones." As-Suddi said similarly. Allah said,

(Thus We recompensed them for their rebellion.) meaning, We imposed this restriction on them as recompense for their rebellion and defying Our commandments. Allah said in another Ayah,

(For the wrongdoing of the Jews, We made unlawful for them certain good foods which had been lawful for them -- and for their hindering many from Allah's way) (4:160). Allah's statement,

(And verily, We are Truthful.) means, We were justified in the penalty We gave them. Ibn Jarir commented, "We are Truthful in what We informed you of, O Muhammad; Our forbidding these foods for them, not as they claimed, that Israel merely forbade these things for himself (so they imitated him, they claimed)."

The Tricks of the Jews, and Allah's Curse

`Abdullah bin `Abbas narrated, "When `Umar bin Al-Khattab was told that Samurah sold liquor, he commented, `May Allah fight Samurah! Did he not know that the Messenger of Allah said,

$$\langle\langle\text{لَعَنَ اللهُ الْيَهُودَ حُرِّمَتْ عَلَيْهِمُ الشُّحُومُ فَجَمَلُوهَا فَبَاعُوهَا}\rangle\rangle$$

(May Allah curse the Jews! The fats were forbidden for them, so they melted the fat and sold it.)" This Hadith is recorded in the Two Sahihs. Jabir bin `Abdullah said, "In the year of the victory of Makkah, I heard Allah's Messenger saying;

$$\langle\langle\text{إِنَّ اللهَ وَرَسُولَهُ حَرَّمَ بَيْعَ الْخَمْرِ وَالْمَيْتَةِ وَالْخِنْزِيرِ وَالْأَصْنَامِ}\rangle\rangle$$

(Allah and His Messenger have forbidden selling alcoholic drinks (intoxicants), dead animals, swine and idols.) He was asked, `What about the fat of dead animals They are used to dye skins, paint ships and are used as light by the people.' He said,

$$\langle\langle\text{لَا هُوَ حَرَامٌ}\rangle\rangle$$

(No, it is still unlawful.) He then said,

«قَاتَلَ اللَّهُ الْيَهُودَ إِنَّ اللَّهَ لَمَّا حَرَّمَ عَلَيْهِمْ شُحُومَهَا جَمَلُوهُ ثُمَّ بَاعُوهُ وَأَكَلُوا ثَمَنَهُ»

(May Allah fight the Jews! When Allah forbade them the fats of animals, they melted the fat, sold it and ate its price.)" The Group recorded this Hadith.

Surah: 6 Ayah: 147

﴿ فَإِن كَذَّبُوكَ فَقُل رَّبُّكُمْ ذُو رَحْمَةٍ وَاسِعَةٍ وَلَا يُرَدُّ بَأْسُهُ عَنِ ٱلْقَوْمِ ٱلْمُجْرِمِينَ ۝ ﴾

147. If they (Jews) belie you (Muhammad (peace be upon him)) say: "Your Lord is the Owner of Vast Mercy, and never will His Wrath be turned back from the people who are Mujrimûn (criminals, polytheists or sinners)."

Transliteration

147. Fa-in kaththabooka faqul rabbukum thoo rahmatin wasiAAatin wala yuraddu ba/suhu AAani alqawmi almujrimeena

Tafsir Ibn Kathir:

Allah says, if your opponents among the idolators, Jews and their likes reject you, O Muhammad,

(Say: "Your Lord is the Owner of vast mercy...") encouraging them to seek Allah's vast mercy and follow His Messenger ,

(and never will His wrath be turned back from the people who are criminals.) discouraging them from defying the Messenger, the Final Prophet, Muhammad . Allah often joins encouragement with threats in the Qur'an. Allah said at the end of this Surah:

(Surely, your Lord is swift in retribution, and certainly He is Oft-Forgiving, Most Merciful.) (6:165) Allah also said,

(But verily, your Lord is full of forgiveness for mankind in spite of their wrongdoing. And verily, your Lord is (also) severe in punishment.) (13:6), and

(Declare unto My servants, that truly, I am the Oft-Forgiving, the Most Merciful. And that My torment is indeed the most painful torment.) (15:49-50), and

(The Forgiver of sin, the Acceptor of repentance, the Severe in punishment.) (40:3) and,

(Verily, the punishment of your Lord is severe and painful. Verily, He it is Who begins and repeats. And He is Oft-Forgiving, full of love.)(85:12-14). There are many other Ayat on this subject.

Surah: 6 Ayah: 148, Surah: 6 Ayah: 149 & Ayah: 150

﴿ سَيَقُولُ ٱلَّذِينَ أَشْرَكُواْ لَوْ شَآءَ ٱللَّهُ مَآ أَشْرَكْنَا وَلَآ ءَابَآؤُنَا وَلَا حَرَّمْنَا مِن شَىْءٍ ۚ كَذَٰلِكَ كَذَّبَ ٱلَّذِينَ مِن قَبْلِهِم حَتَّىٰ ذَاقُواْ بَأْسَنَا ۗ قُلْ هَلْ عِندَكُم مِّنْ عِلْمٍ فَتُخْرِجُوهُ لَنَآ ۖ إِن تَتَّبِعُونَ إِلَّا ٱلظَّنَّ وَإِنْ أَنتُمْ إِلَّا تَخْرُصُونَ ۝١٤٨ ﴾

148. Those who took partners (in worship) with Allâh will say: "If Allâh had willed, we would not have taken partners (in worship) with Him, nor would our fathers, and we would not have forbidden anything (against His Will)." Likewise belied those who were before them, (they argued falsely with Allâh's Messengers), till they tasted of Our Wrath. Say: "Have you any knowledge (proof) that you can produce before us? Verily, you follow nothing but guess and you do nothing but lie."

﴿ قُلْ فَلِلَّهِ ٱلْحُجَّةُ ٱلْبَٰلِغَةُ ۖ فَلَوْ شَآءَ لَهَدَىٰكُمْ أَجْمَعِينَ ۝١٤٩ ﴾

149. Say: "With Allâh is the perfect proof and argument, (i.e. the Oneness of Allâh, the sending of His Messengers and His Holy Books to mankind); had He so willed, He would indeed have guided you all."

﴿ قُلْ هَلُمَّ شُهَدَآءَكُمُ ٱلَّذِينَ يَشْهَدُونَ أَنَّ ٱللَّهَ حَرَّمَ هَٰذَا ۖ فَإِن شَهِدُواْ فَلَا تَشْهَدْ مَعَهُمْ ۚ وَلَا تَتَّبِعْ أَهْوَآءَ ٱلَّذِينَ كَذَّبُواْ بِـَٔايَٰتِنَا وَٱلَّذِينَ لَا يُؤْمِنُونَ بِٱلْءَاخِرَةِ وَهُم بِرَبِّهِمْ يَعْدِلُونَ ۝١٥٠ ﴾

150. Say: "Bring forward your witnesses, who can testify that Allâh has forbidden this. Then if they testify, testify not you (O Muhammad (peace be upon him)) with them. And you should not follow the vain desires of such as treat Our Ayât (proofs, evidences, verses, lessons, signs, revelations, etc.) as falsehoods, and such as believe not in the Hereafter, and they hold others as equal (in worship) with their Lord."

Transliteration

148. Sayaqoolu allatheena ashrakoo law shaa Allahu ma ashrakna wala abaona wala harramna min shay-in kathalika kaththaba allatheena min qablihim hatta thaqoo ba/sana qul hal AAindakum min AAilmin fatukhrijoohu lana in tattabiAAoona illa alththanna wa-in antum illa takhrusoona   149. Qul falillahi alhujjatu albalighatu falaw shaa lahadakum ajmaAAeena   150. Qul halumma shuhadaakumu allatheena yashhadoona anna Allaha harrama hatha fa-in shahidoo fala tashhad maAAahum wala

tattabiAA ahwaa allatheena kaththaboo bi-ayatina waallatheena la yu/minoona bial-akhirati wahum birabbihim yaAAdiloona

Tafsir Ibn Kathir:

A False Notion and its Rebuttal

Here Allah mentioned a debate with the idolators, refuting a false notion they have over their Shirk and the things that they prohibited. They said, surely, Allah has full knowledge of the Shirk we indulge in, and that we forbid some kinds of wealth. Allah is able to change this Shirk by directing us to the faith, - they claimed - and prevent us from falling into disbelief, but He did not do that. Therefore - they said Allah indicated that He willed, decided and agreed that we do all this. They said,

("If Allah had willed, we would not have taken partners (in worship) with Him, nor would our fathers, and we would not have forbidden anything.") Allah said in another Ayah,

(And they said: "If it had been the will of the Most Gracious (Allah), we should not have worshipped them (false deities)") (43:20). Similar is mentioned in Surat An-Nahl. Allah said next,

(Likewise belied those who were before them,) for by using and relying on this understanding, the misguided ones before them were led astray. This notion is false and ungrounded, for had it been true, Allah would not have harmed them, destroyed them, aided His honorable Messengers over them, and made them taste His painful punishment.

(Say: "Have you any knowledge...") that Allah is pleased with you and with your ways,

(that you can produce before us.) and make it plain, apparent and clear for us. However,

(Verily, you only follow the Zann) doubts and wishful thinking,

(and you do nothing but lie) about Allah in the false claims that you utter. Allah said next,

(Say: "With Allah is the perfect proof and argument; had He so willed, He would indeed have guided you all.") Allah said to His Prophet

(Say) O Muhammad, to them,

("With Allah is the perfect proof and argument. ..") the perfect wisdom and unequivocal proof to guide whom He wills and misguide whom He wills.

(had He so willed, He would indeed have guided you all.) All of this happens accordng to His decree, His will, and His choice. So in this way, He is pleased with the believers, and angry with the disbelievers. Allah said in other Ayat,

(And had Allah willed, He could have gathered them together (all) on true guidance,) (6:35) and

(And had your Lord willed, those on earth would have believed, all of them together.) (10:99) and,

(And if your Lord had so willed, He could surely have made mankind one Ummah, but they will not cease to disagree. Except him on whom your Lord has bestowed His mercy and for that did He create them. And the Word of your Lord has been fulfilled: "Surely, I shall fill Hell with Jinns and men all together.") (11:118-119) Ad-Dahhak said, "No one has an excuse if he disobeys Allah. Surely, Allah has the perfect proof established against His servants." Allah said,

(Bring forward your witnesses,) produce your witnesses,

(who can testify that Allah has forbidden this.) which you have forbidden and lied and invented about Allah in this regard,

(Then if they testify, do not testify with them.) because in this case, their testimony is false and untrue,

(And do not follow the vain desires of those who belie Our Ayat, and such as believe not in the Hereafter, and they hold others as equal with their Lord.) by associating others with Allah in worship and treating them as equals to Him.

Surah: 6 Ayah: 151

﴿ ۞ قُلْ تَعَالَوْاْ أَتْلُ مَا حَرَّمَ رَبُّكُمْ عَلَيْكُمْ أَلَّا تُشْرِكُواْ بِهِ شَيْئًا وَبِٱلْوَٰلِدَيْنِ إِحْسَٰنًا وَلَا تَقْتُلُوٓاْ أَوْلَٰدَكُم مِّنْ إِمْلَٰقٍ نَّحْنُ نَرْزُقُكُمْ وَإِيَّاهُمْ وَلَا تَقْرَبُواْ ٱلْفَوَٰحِشَ مَا ظَهَرَ مِنْهَا وَمَا بَطَنَ وَلَا تَقْتُلُواْ ٱلنَّفْسَ ٱلَّتِى حَرَّمَ ٱللَّهُ إِلَّا بِٱلْحَقِّ ذَٰلِكُمْ وَصَّىٰكُم بِهِۦ لَعَلَّكُمْ تَعْقِلُونَ ۝

151. Say (O Muhammad (peace be upon him)) "Come, I will recite what your Lord has prohibited you from: Join not anything in worship with Him; be good and dutiful to your parents; kill not your children because of poverty - We provide sustenance for you and for them; come not near to Al-Fawâhish (shameful sins, illegal sexual intercourse) whether committed openly or secretly; and kill not anyone whom Allâh has forbidden, except for a just cause (according to Islâmic law). This He has commanded you that you may understand.

Transliteration

151. Qul taAAalaw atlu ma harrama rabbukum AAalaykum alla tushrikoo bihi shay-an wabialwalidayni ihsanan wala taqtuloo awladakum min imlaqin nahnu narzuqukum

wa-iyyahum wala taqraboo alfawahisha ma thahara minha wama batana wala taqtuloo alnnafsa allatee harrama Allahu illa bialhaqqi thalikum wassakum bihi laAAallakum taAAqiloona

Tafsir Ibn Kathir:

Ten Commandments

Dawud Al-Awdy narrated that, Ash-Sha`bi said that, `Alqamah said that Ibn Mas`ud said, "Whoever wishes to read the will and testament of the Messenger of Allah on which he placed his seal, let him read these Ayat,

(Say: "Come, I will recite what your Lord has prohibited you from: Join not anything in worship with Him...") until,

(...so that you may have Taqwa) (6:153)." In his Mustadrak, Al-Hakim recorded that Ibn `Abbas said, "In Surah Al-An`am (6), there are clear Ayat, and they are the Mother of the Book (the Qur'an)." He then recited,

(Say: "Come, I will recite what your Lord has prohibited you from...") Al-Hakim said, "Its chain is Sahih, and they did not record it." In his Mustadrak Al-Hakim also recorded that `Ubadah bin As-Samit said, "The Messenger of Allah said,

«أَيُّكُمْ يُبَايِعُنِي عَلَى ثَلَاثٍ»

(Who among you will give me his pledge to do three things) He then recited the Ayah,

(قُلْ تَعَالَوْا أَتْلُ مَا حَرَّمَ رَبُّكُمْ عَلَيْكُمْ)

(Say: "Come, I will recite what your Lord has prohibited you from...") until the end of the Ayat. He then said,

«فَمَنْ وَفَى فَأَجْرُهُ عَلَى اللهِ وَمَنِ انْتَقَصَ مِنْهُنَّ شَيْئًا فَأَدْرَكَهُ اللهُ بِهِ فِي الدُّنْيَا كَانَتْ عُقُوبَتَهُ، وَمَنْ أَخَّرَ إِلَى الْآخِرَةِ فَأَمْرُهُ إِلَى اللهِ إِنْ شَاءَ عَذَّبَهُ وَإِنْ شَاءَ عَفَا عَنْهُ»

(Whoever fulfills (this pledge), then his reward will be with Allah, but whoever fell into shortcomings and Allah punishes him for it in this life, then that will be his recompense. Whoever Allah delays (his reckoning) until the Hereafter, then his matter is with Allah. If He wills, He will punish him, and if He wills, He will forgive him.)" Al-Hakim said, "Its chain is Sahih and they did not record it." As for the explanation of this Ayah, Allah said to His Prophet and Messenger Muhammad : Say, O Muhammad,

Chapter 6: Al-An'am (Cattle, Livestock), Verses 111-165

to those idolators who worshipped other than Allah, forbade what Allah provided them with and killed their children, following their opinions and the lures of the devils,'

(Say) to them

(Come) come here, come close

(I will recite what your Lord has prohibited you from.) meaning, I will inform you about what your Lord has forbidden for you in truth, not guessing or wishful thinking. Rather, it is revelation and an order from Him.

Shirk is Forbidden

(Join not anything in worship with Him;) this Allah has ordained, for He said at the end of the Ayah,

(This He has commanded you that you may understand.) In the the Two Sahihs, it is recorded that Abu Dharr said that the Messenger of Allah said,

«أَتَانِي جِبْرِيلُ فَبَشَّرَنِي أَنَّهُ مَنْ مَاتَ لَا يُشْرِكُ بِاللهِ شَيْئًا مِنْ أُمَّتِكَ دَخَلَ الْجَنَّةَ، قُلْتُ وَإِنْ زَنَى وَإِنْ سَرَقَ؟ قَالَ: وَإِنْ زَنَى وَإِنْ سَرَقَ، قُلْتُ: وَإِنْ زَنَى وَإِنْ سَرَقَ؟ قَالَ: وَإِنْ زَنَى وَإِنْ سَرَقَ، قُلْت: وَإِنْ زَنَى وَإِنْ سَرَقَ؟ قَالَ: وَإِنْ زَنَى وَإِنْ سَرَقَ وَإِنْ شَرِبَ الْخَمْر»

(Jibril came to me and conveyed the good news that, "Whoever among your followers dies, worshipping none along with Allah, will enter Paradise." I said, "Even if he stole or committed illegal sexual intercourse" He said, "Even if he stole or committed illegal sexual intercourse." I said, "Even if he stole or committed illegal sexual intercourse" He said, "Even if he stole or committed illegal sexual intercourse." I said, "Even if he stole or committed illegal sexual intercourse" He said, "Even if he stole or committed illegal sexual intercourse or even if drank alcohol.") Some of the Musnad and Sunan compilers recorded that Abu Dharr said that the Messenger of Allah said,

«يَقُولُ تَعَالَى: يَا ابْنَ آدَمَ إِنَّكَ مَا دَعَوْتَنِي وَرَجَوْتَنِي فَإِنِّي أَغْفِرُ لَكَ عَلَى مَا كَانَ مِنْكَ وَلَا أُبَالِي، وَلَوْ أَتَيْتَنِي بِقُرَابِ الْأَرْضِ خَطِيئَةً أَتَيْتُكَ بِقُرَابِهَا مَغْفِرَةً مَا لَمْ تُشْرِكْ بِي شَيْئًا، وَإِنْ أَخْطَأْتَ حَتَّى تَبْلُغَ خَطَايَاكَ عَنَانَ السَّمَاءِ ثُمَّ اسْتَغْفَرْتَنِي غَفَرْتُ لَك»

(Allah said, `O Son of Adam! As long as you supplicate to Me and hope of Me, I will forgive whatever you committed, and it will be easy for Me to do that. And even if you brought the earth's fill of sins to Me, I will bring forth its fill of forgiveness, as long as you do not associate anything or anyone in worship with Me. And even if you err and your errors accumulate until they reach the boundaries of the sky and you then ask Me for forgiveness, I will forgive you.') This subject is also mentioned in the Qur'an, for Allah said,

(Verily, Allah forgives not (the sin of) setting up partners (in worship) with Him, but He forgives whom He wills, sins other than that.) (4:116) Muslim recorded a Hadith in the Sahih that reads,

«مَنْ مَاتَ لَا يُشْرِكُ بِاللهِ شَيْئًا دَخَلَ الْجَنَّةَ»

(Whoever dies associating none with Allah will enter Paradise.) There are many Ayat and Hadiths on this subject.

The Order for Kindness to Parents

Allah said next,

(be kind and dutiful to your parents;) meaning, Allah has commanded and ordered you to be kind to your parents. Allah said in another Ayah,

(And your Lord has decreed that you worship none but Him. And that you be dutiful to your parents.) (17:23) Allah often mentions obeying Him and being dutiful to parents together. Allah said,

(Give thanks to Me and to your parents. Unto Me is the final destination. But if they (both) strive with you to make you join in worship with Me others that of which you have no knowledge, then obey them not; but behave with them in this world kindly, and follow the path of him who turns to Me in repentance and in obedience. Then to Me will be your return, and I shall tell you what you used to do.) (31:14-15) Therefore, Allah ordered children to be dutiful and kind to their parents, even if they were idolators. Allah also said,

(And (remember) when We took a covenant from the Children of Israel, (saying): Worship none but Allah and be dutiful and kind to parents.) (2:83) There are several Ayat on this subject. It is recorded in the Two Sahihs that Ibn Mas`ud said, "I asked Allah's Messenger about which deed is the best. He said,

«الصَّلَاةُ عَلَى وَقْتِهَا»

(The prayer, when it is performed on time.) I said, `Then' He said,

«بِرُّ الْوَالِدَيْنِ»

(Being dutiful to parents.) I asked, `Then' He said,

$$\text{«الْجِهَادُ فِي سَبِيلِ اللهِ»}$$

(Jihad in Allah's cause.) Ibn Mas`ud said, "The Messenger of Allah said these words to me, and had I asked him for more, he would have said more."

Killing Children is Forbidden

Allah said,

(Kill not your children because of poverty, We shall provide sustenance for you and for them.) After Allah commanded kindness to parents and grandparents, He next ordered kindness to children and grandchildren. Allah said,

(kill not your children because of poverty,) because the idolators used to kill their children, obeying the lures of the devils. They used to bury their daughters alive for fear of shame, and sometimes kill their sons for fear of poverty. It is recorded in the Two Sahihs that `Abdullah bin Mas`ud said, "I asked the Messenger of Allah , `Which sin is the biggest' He said,

$$\text{«أَنْ تَجْعَلَ لِلَّهِ نِدًّا وَهُوَ خَلَقَكَ»}$$

(To call a rival for Allah, while He Alone created you.) I said, `Then what' He said,

$$\text{«أَنْ تَقْتُلَ وَلَدَكَ خَشْيَةَ أَنْ يَطْعَمَ مَعَكَ»}$$

(To kill your son for fear that he might share your food.') I said, `Then what' He said,

$$\text{«أَنْ تُزَانِيَ حَلِيلَةَ جَارِكَ»}$$

(To commit adultery with your neighbor's wife.) Then the Messenger of Allah recited the Ayah,

(And those who invoke not any other god along with Allah, nor kill such person as Allah has forbidden, except for just cause, nor commit illegal sexual intercourse...) (25:68)." Allah's statement,

(Because of Imlaq) refers to poverty, according to Ibn `Abbas, Qatadah, As-Suddi and others. The Ayah means, do not kill your children because you are poor. Allah said in Surat Al-Isra',

(And do not kill your children for fear from Imlaq.) (17:31), that is, do not kill your children for fear that you might become poor in the future. This is why Allah said,

(We shall provide sustenance for them and for you) (17:31), thus mentioning the provision of the children first, meaning, do not fear poverty because of feeding your children. Certainly, their provision is provided by Allah. Allah said,

(We provide sustenance for you and for them,) thus starting with parents, because this is the appropriate subject here and Allah knows. Allah said next,

(Come not near Al-Fawahish (immoral sins) whether committed openly or secretly) Allah said in a similar Ayah,

(Say: "(But) the things that my Lord has indeed forbidden are Al-Fawahish (immoral sins) whether committed openly or secretly, sins (of all kinds), unrighteous oppression, joining partners (in worship) with Allah for which He has given no authority, and saying things about Allah of which you have no knowledge.") (7:33) We also explained this meaning in the explanation of the Ayah,

(Leave sin, open and secret) (6:120). The Two Sahihs recorded that Ibn Mas`ud said that the Messenger of Allah said,

«لَا أَحَدٌ أَغْيَرُ مِنَ اللهِ، مِنْ أَجْلِ ذَلِكَ حَرَّمَ الْفَوَاحِشَ مَا ظَهَرَ مِنْهَا وَمَا بَطَن»

(None is more jealous than Allah. This is why He has forbidden the immoral sins committed openly or secretly.) `Abdul-Malik bin `Umayr said that Warrad narrated that Al-Mughirah said that Sa`d bin `Ubadah said, "If I see a man with my wife (committing adultery), I will kill him with the sword." When the matter came to the Messenger of Allah, he said,

«أَتَعْجَبُونَ مِنْ غَيْرَةِ سَعْدٍ؟ فَوَاللهِ لَأَنَا أَغْيَرُ مِنْ سَعْدٍ، وَاللهُ أَغْيَرُ مِنِّي، مِنْ أَجْلِ ذَلِكَ حَرَّمَ الْفَوَاحِشَ مَا ظَهَرَ مِنْهَا وَمَا بَطَن»

(Do you wonder at Sa`d's jealousy By Allah, I am more jealous than Sa`d, and Allah is more jealous than I. This is why He has forbidden the immoral sins committed openly and in secret.) This Hadith is in the Two Sahihs).

The Prohibition of Unjustified Killing

Allah said,

(And kill not anyone whom Allah has forbidden, except for a just cause (according to Islamic law).) This part of the Ayah emphasizes this prohibition in specific, although it is included in the immoral sins committed openly and in secret. In the Two Sahihs, it is recorded that Ibn Mas`ud said that the Messenger of Allah said,

«لَا يَحِلُّ دَمُ امْرِئٍ مُسْلِمٍ يَشْهَدُ أَنْ لَا إِلَهَ إِلَّا اللهُ وَأَنِّي رَسُولُ اللهِ، إِلَّا بِإِحْدَى ثَلَاثٍ: الثَّيِّبُ الزَّانِي، وَالنَّفْسُ بِالنَّفْسِ، وَالتَّارِكُ لِدِينِهِ الْمُفَارِقُ لِلْجَمَاعَة»

(The blood of a Muslim person who testifies that there is no deity worthy of worship except Allah and that I am the Messenger of Allah is prohibited, except for three offenses: a married person who commits illegal sexual intercourse, life for life, and whoever reverts from the religion and abandons the Jama`ah (the community of faithful believers).) There is a prohibition, a warning and a threat against killing the Mu`ahid, i.e., non-Muslims who have a treaty of peace with Muslims. Al-Bukhari recorded that `Abdullah bin `Amr said that the Prophet said,

«مَنْ قَتَلَ مُعَاهِدًا لَمْ يَرَحْ رَائِحَةَ الْجَنَّةِ، وَإِنَّ رِيحَهَا لَيُوجَدُ مِنْ مَسِيرَةِ أَرْبَعِينَ عَامًا»

(Whoever killed a person having a treaty of protection with Muslims, shall not smell the scent of Paradise, though its scent is perceived from a distance of forty years.) Abu Hurayrah narrated that the Prophet said,

«مَنْ قَتَلَ مُعَاهِدًا لَهُ ذِمَّةُ اللهِ وَذِمَّةُ رَسُولِهِ فَقَدْ أَخْفَرَ بِذِمَّةِ اللهِ، فَلَا يَرَحْ رَائِحَةَ الْجَنَّةِ، وَإِنَّ رِيحَهَا لَيُوجَدُ مِنْ مَسِيرَةِ سَبْعِينَ خَرِيفًا»

(Whoever killed a person having a treaty of protection with the Muslims, and who enjoys the guarantee of Allah and His Messenger, he will have spoiled the guarantee of Allah (for him). He shall not smell the scent of Paradise though its smell is perceived from a distance of seventy years.) Ibn Majah and At-Tirmidhi recorded this Hadith, and At-Tirmidhi said, "Hasan Sahih." Allah's statement,

(This He has commanded you that you may understand.) means, this is what He has commanded you that you may comprehend His commandments and prohibitions.

Surah: 6 Ayah: 152

﴿وَلَا تَقْرَبُوا مَالَ ٱلْيَتِيمِ إِلَّا بِٱلَّتِى هِىَ أَحْسَنُ حَتَّىٰ يَبْلُغَ أَشُدَّهُۥ وَأَوْفُوا۟ ٱلْكَيْلَ وَٱلْمِيزَانَ بِٱلْقِسْطِ لَا نُكَلِّفُ نَفْسًا إِلَّا وُسْعَهَا وَإِذَا قُلْتُمْ فَٱعْدِلُوا۟ وَلَوْ كَانَ ذَا قُرْبَىٰ وَبِعَهْدِ ٱللَّهِ أَوْفُوا۟ ذَٰلِكُمْ وَصَّىٰكُم بِهِۦ لَعَلَّكُمْ تَذَكَّرُونَ ۝﴾

152. "And come not near to the orphan's property, except to improve it, until he (or she) attains the age of full strength; and give full measure and full weight with justice. We burden not any person, but that which he can bear. And whenever you give your word (i.e. judge between men or give evidence), say the truth even if a near relative is concerned, and fulfill the Covenant of Allâh, This He commands you, that you may remember.

Transliteration

152. Wala taqraboo mala alyateemi illa biallatee hiya ahsanu hatta yablugha ashuddahu waawfoo alkayla waalmeezana bialqisti la nukallifu nafsan illa wusAAaha wa-itha qultum faiAAdiloo walaw kana tha qurba wabiAAahdi Allahi awfoo thalikum wassakum bihi laAAallakum tathakkaroona

Tafsir Ibn Kathir:

The Prohibition of Consuming the Orphan's Property

`Ata' bin As-Sa'ib said that Sa`id bin Jubayr said that Ibn `Abbas said, "When Allah revealed,

(And come not near to the orphan's property, except to improve it.) and,

(Verily, those who unjustly eat up the property of orphans.) those who were guardians of orphans separated their food from the orphans' food and their drink from their drink. When any of that food or drink remained, they used to keep it for the orphan until he or she ate it or it spoiled. This became difficult for the companions and they talked about it to the Messenger of Allah, and Allah sent down the Ayah,

(And they ask you about orphans. Say: "The best thing is to work honestly in their property, and if you mix your affairs with theirs, then they are your brothers.") (2:220) Thereafter, they mixed their food and drink with food and drink of the orphans." Abu Dawud collected this statement. Allah's statement,

(until he (or she) attains the age of full strength;), refers to reaching the age of adolescence, according to Ash-Sha`bi, Malik and several others among the Salaf.

The Command to Give Full Measure and Full Weight with Justice

Allah's statement,

(and give full measure and full weight with justice.) is a command to establish justice while giving and taking. Allah has also warned against abandoning this commandment, when He said,

(Woe to Al-Mutaffifin. Those who, when they have to receive by measure from men, demand full measure. And when they have to give by measure or weight to (other) men, give less than due. Do they not think that they will be resurrected (for reckoning). On a Great Day The Day when (all) mankind will stand before the Lord of all that exists) (83:1-6). Allah destroyed an entire nation that was accustomed to giving less in weights and measures. Allah said next,

(We burden not any person, but that which he can bear.) that is, whoever strives while pursuing his rights and giving other peoples' full rights, then there is no sin on him if he commits an honest mistake after trying his best and striving to do what is right.

The Order for Just Testimony

Allah said;

(And whenever you give your word, say the truth even if a near relative is concerned.) This is similar to His statement,

(O you who believe! Stand out firmly for Allah as just witnesses.) (5:8) And there is a similar Ayah in Surat An-Nisa'. So Allah commands justice in action and statement, with both near relatives and distant relatives. Indeed, Allah orders justice for everyone at all times and in all situations.

Fulfilling the Covenant of Allah is an Obligation

Allah said next,

(and fulfill the Covenant of Allah.) Ibn Jarir commented, "Allah commands: Fulfill Allah's commandments that He has ordered you. You will do so when you obey Him in what He commanded, refrain from what He prohibited and abide by His Book and the Sunnah of His Messenger . This constitutes fulfilling the covenant of Allah,

(...This He commands you, that you may remember.) Allah says here, that this is what He has ordered and commanded, and He stressed its importance for you,

(...that you may remember.), that you may be advised and thus refrain from what you used to do before this."

Surah: 6 Ayah: 153

﴿ وَأَنَّ هَـٰذَا صِرَٰطِى مُسْتَقِيمًا فَٱتَّبِعُوهُ ۖ وَلَا تَتَّبِعُواْ ٱلسُّبُلَ فَتَفَرَّقَ بِكُمْ عَن سَبِيلِهِ ۚ ذَٰلِكُمْ وَصَّىٰكُم بِهِۦ لَعَلَّكُمْ تَتَّقُونَ ﴿١٥٣﴾ ﴾

153. "And verily, this (i.e. Allâh's Commandments mentioned in the above two Verses 151 and 152) is my Straight Path, so follow it, and follow not (other) paths, for they will separate you away from His Path. This He has ordained for you that you may become Al-Muttaqûn (the pious - see V.2:2)."

Transliteration

153. Waanna hatha siratee mustaqeeman faittabiAAoohu wala tattabiAAoo alssubula fatafarraqa bikum AAan sabeelihi thalikum wassakum bihi laAAallakum tattaqoona

Tafsir Ibn Kathir:

The Command to Follow Allah's Straight Path and to Avoid All Other Paths

`Ali bin Abi Talhah reported that Ibn `Abbas commented on Allah's statements,

(And follow not (other) paths, for they will separate you away from His path.), and,

((Saying) that you should establish religion and make no divisions in it.) (42:13), and similar Ayat in the Qur'an, "Allah commanded the believers to adhere to the Jama`ah and forbade them from causing divisions and disputes. He informed them that those before them were destroyed because of divisions and disputes in the religion of Allah." Similar was said by Mujahid and several others. Imam Ahmad bin Hanbal recorded that `Abdullah bin Mas`ud said, "The Messenger of Allah drew a line with his hand (in the sand) and said,

《هَذَا سَبِيلُ اللهِ مُسْتَقِيمًا》

(This is Allah's path, leading straight.) He then drew lines to the right and left of that line and said,

《هَذِهِ السُّبُلُ لَيْسَ مِنْهَا سَبِيلٌ إِلَّا عَلَيْهِ شَيْطَانٌ يَدْعُو إِلَيْهِ》

(These are the other paths, on each path there is a devil who calls to it.) He then recited,

(وَأَنَّ هَذَا صِرَطِي مُسْتَقِيمًا فَاتَّبِعُوهُ وَلاَ تَتَّبِعُواْ السُّبُلَ فَتَفَرَّقَ بِكُمْ عَن سَبِيلِهِ)

(And verily, this is My straight path, so follow it, and follow not (other) paths, for they will separate you away from His path.)(6:153)" Al-Hakim also recorded this Hadith and said; "Its chain is Sahih, but they did not record it." Imam Ahmad and `Abd bin Humayd recorded (and this is the wording of Ahmad) that Jabir said; "We were sitting with the Prophet when he drew a line in front of him and said,

《هَذَا سَبِيلُ الله》

(This is Allah's path.) He also drew two lines to its right and two lines to its left and said,

《هَذِهِ سُبُلُ الشَّيْطَان》

(These are the paths of Shaytan.) He then placed his hand on the middle path and recited this Ayah;

Chapter 6: Al-An'am (Cattle, Livestock), Verses 111-165

(وَأَنَّ هَـٰذَا صِرَٰطِى مُسْتَقِيمًا فَٱتَّبِعُوهُ وَلَا تَتَّبِعُوا۟ ٱلسُّبُلَ فَتَفَرَّقَ بِكُمْ عَن سَبِيلِهِ ذَٰلِكُمْ وَصَّىٰكُم بِهِ لَعَلَّكُمْ تَتَّقُونَ)

(And verily, this is My straight path, so follow it, and follow not (other) paths, for they will separate you away from His path. This He has ordained for you that you may have Taqwa.) Imam Ahmad, Ibn Majah, in the Book of the Sunnah in his Sunan, and Al-Bazzar collected this Hadith. Ibn Jarir recorded that a man asked Ibn Mas`ud, "What is As-Sirat Al-Mustaqim (the straight path)" Ibn Mas`ud replied, "Muhammad left us at its lower end and its other end is in Paradise. To the right of this Path are other paths, and to the left of it are other paths, and there are men (on these paths) calling those who pass by them. Whoever goes on the other paths will end up in the Fire. Whoever takes the Straight Path, will end up in Paradise." Ibn Mas`ud then recited the Ayah;

(وَأَنَّ هَـٰذَا صِرَٰطِى مُسْتَقِيمًا فَٱتَّبِعُوهُ وَلَا تَتَّبِعُوا۟ ٱلسُّبُلَ فَتَفَرَّقَ بِكُمْ عَن سَبِيلِهِ)

(And verily, this is My straight path, so follow it, and follow not (other) paths, for they will separate you away from His path.)'" Imam Ahmad recorded that, An-Nawwas bin Sam`an said that the Messenger of Allah said,

«ضَرَبَ اللهُ مَثَلًا صِرَاطًا مُسْتَقِيمًا، وَعَنْ جَنْبَيِ الصِّرَاطِ سُورَانِ فِيهِمَا أَبْوَابٌ مُفَتَّحَةٌ، وَعَلَى الْأَبْوَابِ سُتُورٌ مُرْخَاةٌ وَعَلَى بَابِ الصِّرَاطِ دَاعٍ يَدْعُو: يَا أَيُّهَا النَّاسُ هَلُمُّوا ادْخُلُوا الصِّرَاطَ الْمُسْتَقِيمَ جَمِيعًا وَلَا تَفَرَّقُوا وَدَاعٍ يَدْعُو مِنْ فَوْقِ الصِّرَاطِ فَإِذَا أَرَادَ الْإِنْسَانُ أَنْ يَفْتَحَ شَيْئًا مِنْ تِلْكَ الْأَبْوَابِ قَالَ وَيْحَكَ لَا تَفْتَحْهُ فَإِنَّكَ إِنْ فَتَحْتَهُ تَلِجْهُ فَالصِّرَاطُ الْإِسْلَامُ وَالسُّورَانِ حُدُودُ اللهِ وَالْأَبْوَابُ الْمُفَتَّحَةُ مَحَارِمُ اللهِ وَذَلِكَ الدَّاعِي عَلَى رَأْسِ الصِّرَاطِ كِتَابُ اللهِ، وَالدَّاعِي مِنْ فَوْقِ الصِّرَاطِ وَاعِظُ اللهِ فِي قَلْبِ كُلِّ مُسْلِمٍ»

(Allah has given a parable of the straight path, and on the two sides of this path, there are two walls containing door ways. On these door ways, there are curtains that are lowered down. on the gate of this path there is a caller heralding, `O people! come and enter the straight path all together and do not divide. ' There is also another caller that heralds from above the path, who says when a person wants to remove the curtain on any of these doors, `Woe to you! Do not open this door, for if you open it, you will enter it. The (straight) path is Islam, the two walls are Allah's set limits, the open doors lead to Allah's prohibitions, the caller on the gate of the path is Allah's Book (the Qur'an), while the caller from above the path is Allah's admonition in the heart of every Muslim.) At-Tirmidhi and An-Nasa'i also recorded this Hadith, and At-Tirmidhi said, "Hasan Gharib." Allah's statement,

(so follow it, and follow not (other) paths...) describes Allah's path in the singular sense, because truth is one. Allah describes the other paths in the plural, because they are many and are divided. Allah said in another Ayah,

(Allah is the Wali (Protector or Guardian) of those who believe. He brings them out from darknesses into light. But as for those who disbelieve, their supporters are Taghut (false deities), they bring them out from light into darknesses. Those are the dwellers of the Fire, and they will abide therein forever.) (2:257)

Surah: 6 Ayah: 154 & Ayah: 155

﴿ ثُمَّ ءَاتَيْنَا مُوسَى ٱلْكِتَـٰبَ تَمَامًا عَلَى ٱلَّذِىٓ أَحْسَنَ وَتَفْصِيلًا لِّكُلِّ شَىْءٍ وَهُدًى وَرَحْمَةً لَّعَلَّهُم بِلِقَآءِ رَبِّهِمْ يُؤْمِنُونَ ۝ ﴾

154. Then, We gave Mûsâ (Moses) the Book (the Taurât (Torah)) to complete (Our Favor) upon those who would do right, and explaining all things in detail and a guidance and a mercy that they might believe in the meeting with their Lord.

﴿ وَهَـٰذَا كِتَـٰبٌ أَنزَلْنَـٰهُ مُبَارَكٌ فَٱتَّبِعُوهُ وَٱتَّقُوا۟ لَعَلَّكُمْ تُرْحَمُونَ ۝ ﴾

155. And this is a blessed Book (the Qur'ân) which We have sent down, so follow it and fear Allâh (i.e. do not disobey His Orders), that you may receive mercy (i.e. be saved from the torment of Hell).

Transliteration

154. Thumma atayna moosa alkitaba tamaman AAala allathee ahsana watafseelan likulli shay-in wahudan warahmatan laAAallahum biliqa-i rabbihim yu/minoona 155. Wahatha kitabun anzalnahu mubarakun faittabiAAoohu waittaqoo laAAallakum turhamoona

Tafsir Ibn Kathir:

Praising the Tawrah and the Qur'an

After Allah described the Qur'an by saying,

(And verily, this is My straight path, so follow it...) He then praised the Tawrah and its Messenger,

(Then, We gave Musa the Book...) Allah often mentions the Qur'an and the Tawrah together. Allah said,

(And before this was the Scripture of Musa as a guide and a mercy. And this is a confirming Book in the Arabic language.) (46:12). Allah said in the beginning of this Surah,

(Say: "Who then sent down the Book which Musa brought, a light and a guidance to mankind which you have made into paper sheets, disclosing (some of it) and concealing (much)") (6:91), and

(And this is a blessed Book which we have sent down. ..) (6:92) Allah said about the idolators,

(But when the truth has come to them from Us, they say: "Why is he not given the like of what was given to Musa") (28:48). Allah replied,

("Did they not disbelieve in that which was given to Musa of old" They say: "Two kinds of magic (the Tawrah and the Qur'an), each helping the other!" And they say: "Verily, in both we are disbelievers.") (28:48) Allah said about the Jinns that they said,

("O our people! Verily, we have heard a Book sent down after Musa, confirming what came before it, it guides to the truth.") (46:30) Allah's statement,

(...complete for that which is best, and explaining all things in detail...") means; `We made the Book that We revealed to Musa, a complete and comprehensive Book, sufficient for what he needs to complete his Law.' Similarly, Allah said in another Ayah,

(And We wrote for him on the Tablets the lesson to be drawn from all things.) (7:145) Allah's statement,

(for that which is best,) means: `as a reward for his doing right and obeying Our commands and orders.' Allah said in other Ayat,

(Is there any reward for good other than what is best)(55:60),

(And (remember) when the Lord of Ibrahim tried him with (certain) commands, which he fulfilled. He (Allah) said (to him), "Verily, I am going to make you an Imam for mankind.") (2:124) and,

y(And We made from among them (Children of Israel), leaders, giving guidance under Our command, when they were patient and believed with certainty in Our Ayat.) (32:24) Allah said;

(and explaining all things in detail and a guidance and a mercy) praising the Book that Allah sent down to Musa, while,

(. ..that they might believe in the meeting with their Lord. And this is a blessed Book (the Qur'an) which We have sent down, so follow it and have Taqwa so that you may receive mercy.) This calls to following the Qur'an. Allah encourages His servants to follow His Book (the Qur'an) and orders them to understand it, adhere to it and call to it. He also describes it as being blessed, for those who follow and implement it in this life and the Hereafter, because it is the Firm Rope of Allah.

Surah: 6 Ayah: 156 & Ayah: 157

﴿ أَن تَقُولُوٓاْ إِنَّمَآ أُنزِلَ ٱلْكِتَٰبُ عَلَىٰ طَآئِفَتَيْنِ مِن قَبْلِنَا وَإِن كُنَّا عَن دِرَاسَتِهِمْ لَغَٰفِلِينَ ۝ ﴾

156. Lest you (pagan Arabs) should say: "The Book was only sent down to two sects before us (the Jews and the Christians), and for our part, we were in fact unaware of what they studied."

﴿ أَوْ تَقُولُواْ لَوْ أَنَّآ أُنزِلَ عَلَيْنَا ٱلْكِتَٰبُ لَكُنَّآ أَهْدَىٰ مِنْهُمْ ۚ فَقَدْ جَآءَكُم بَيِّنَةٌ مِّن رَّبِّكُمْ وَهُدًى وَرَحْمَةٌ ۚ فَمَنْ أَظْلَمُ مِمَّن كَذَّبَ بِـَٔايَٰتِ ٱللَّهِ وَصَدَفَ عَنْهَا ۗ سَنَجْزِى ٱلَّذِينَ يَصْدِفُونَ عَنْ ءَايَٰتِنَا سُوٓءَ ٱلْعَذَابِ بِمَا كَانُواْ يَصْدِفُونَ ۝ ﴾

157. Or lest you (pagan Arabs) should say: "If only the Book had been sent down to us, we would surely have been better guided than they (Jews and Christians)." So now has come unto you a clear proof (the Qur'ân) from your Lord, and a guidance and a mercy. Who then does more wrong than one who rejects the Ayât (proofs, evidences, verses, lessons, signs, revelations, etc.) of Allâh and turns away therefrom? We shall requite those who turn away from Our Ayât with an evil torment, because of their turning away (from them). (Tafsir At-Tabari)

Transliteration

156. An taqooloo innama onzila alkitabu AAala ta-ifatayni min qablina wa-in kunna AAan dirasatihim laghafileena   157. Aw taqooloo law anna onzila AAalayna alkitabu lakunna ahda minhum faqad jaakum bayyinatun min rabbikum wahudan warahmatun faman athlamu mimman kaththaba bi-ayati Allahi wasadafa AAanha sanajzee allatheena yasdifoona AAan ayatina soo-a alAAathabi bima kanoo yasdifoona

Tafsir Ibn Kathir:

The Qur'an is Allah's Proof Against His Creation

Ibn Jarir commented on the Ayah, "The Ayah means, this is a Book that We sent down, so that you do not say,

("The Book was sent down only to two sects before us.") This way, you will have no excuse. Allah said in another Ayah,

(Otherwise, they would have suffered a calamity because of what their hands sent forth, and said: "Our Lord! Why did You not send us a Messenger We would then have followed Your Ayat.")(28:47)." The Ayah,

(to two sects before us) refers to the Jews and Christians, according to `Ali bin Abi Talhah who narrated it from Ibn `Abbas. Similar was reported from Mujahid, As-Suddi, Qatadah and several others. Allah's statement, ("...and for our part, we were in fact unaware of what they studied.") meaning: `we did not understand what they said because the revelation was not in our tongue. We, indeed, were busy and unaware of their message,' so they said. Allah said next,

(Or lest you should say: "If only the Book had been sent down to us, we would surely, have been better guided than they.") meaning: We also refuted this excuse, had you used it, lest you say, "If a Book was revealed to us, just as they received a Book, we would have been better guided than they are." Allah also said. (And they swore by Allah their most binding oath that if a warner came to them, they would be more guided than any of the nations (before them).) (35:42) Allah replied here,

(So now has come unto you a clear proof from your Lord, and a guidance and a mercy.) Allah says, there has come to you from Allah a Glorious Qur'an revealed to Muhammad , the Arab Prophet. In it is the explanation of the lawful and unlawful matters, guidance for the hearts and mercy from Allah to His servants who follow and implement it. Allah said;

(Who then does more wrong than one who rejects the Ayat of Allah and Sadafa away therefrom) This refers to the one who neither benefited from what the Messenger brought, nor followed what he was sent with by abandoning all other ways. Rather, he Sadafa from following the Ayat of Allah, meaning, he discouraged and hindered people from following it. This is the explanation of As-Suddi for Sadafa, while Ibn `Abbas, Mujahid and Qatadah said that Sadafa means, he turned away from it.

Surah: 6 Ayah: 158

﴿ هَلْ يَنظُرُونَ إِلَّا أَن تَأْتِيَهُمُ ٱلْمَلَٰٓئِكَةُ أَوْ يَأْتِىَ رَبُّكَ أَوْ يَأْتِىَ بَعْضُ ءَايَٰتِ رَبِّكَ يَوْمَ يَأْتِى بَعْضُ ءَايَٰتِ رَبِّكَ لَا يَنفَعُ نَفْسًا إِيمَٰنُهَا لَمْ تَكُنْ ءَامَنَتْ مِن قَبْلُ أَوْ كَسَبَتْ فِىٓ إِيمَٰنِهَا خَيْرًا قُلِ ٱنتَظِرُوٓاْ إِنَّا مُنتَظِرُونَ ﴾

158. Do they then wait for anything other than that the angels should come to them, or that your Lord (Allah) should come, or that some of the Signs of your Lord should come (i.e. portents of the Hour e.g., arising of the sun from the west)! The day that some of the Signs of your Lord do come, no good will it do to a person to believe then, if he believed not before, nor earned good (by performing deeds of righteousness) through his Faith. Say: "Wait you! we (too) are waiting."

Transliteration

158. Hal yanthuroona illa an ta/tiyahumu almala-ikatu aw ya/tiya rabbuka aw ya/tiya baAAdu ayati rabbika yawma ya/tee baAAdu ayati rabbika la yanfaAAu nafsan eemanuha lam takun amanat min qablu aw kasabat fee eemaniha khayran quli intathiroo inna muntathiroona

Tafsir Ibn Kathir:

The Disbelievers Await the Commencement of the Hereafter, or Some of its Portents

Allah sternly threatens the disbelievers, those who defy His Messengers, deny His Ayat and hinder from His path,

(Do they then wait for anything other than that the angels should come to them, or that your Lord (Allah) should come...) on the Day of Resurrection,

(or that some of the signs of your Lord should come! The day that some of the signs of your Lord do come no good will it do to a person to believe then.) Before the commencement of the Day of Resurrection, there will come signs and portents of the Last Hour that will be witnessed by the people living at that time. In a section explaining this Ayah, Al-Bukhari recorded that Abu Hurayrah said that the Messenger of Allah said,

(The Last Hour will not commence until the sun rises from the west. When the people witness that, they will all believe. This is when.

(no good will it do to a person to believe then, if he believed not before.)) Ibn Jarir recorded that Abu Hurayrah said that the Messenger of Allah said,

«ثَلَاثٌ إِذَا خَرَجْنَ لَا يَنْفَعُ نَفْسًا إِيمَانُهَا لَمْ تَكُنْ آمَنَتْ مِنْ قَبْلُ أَوْ كَسَبَتْ فِي إِيمَانِهَا خَيْرًا، طُلُوعُ الشَّمْسِ مِنْ مَغْرِبِهَا وَالدَّجَّالُ وَدَابَّةُ الْأَرْضِ»

(Three, if they appear, then a soul will not benefit from its faith, if it had not believed before or earned good in its faith: when the sun rises from the west, Ad-Dajjal and the Beast of the earth.) Ahmad also recorded this Hadith, and in his narration, the Prophet mentioned the Smoke. Imam Ahmad recorded that `Amr bin Jarir said, "Three Muslim men sat with Marwan in Al-Madinah and they heard him talking about the signs (of the Last Hour). He said that the first sign will be the appearance of Ad-Dajjal. So these men went to `Abdullah bin `Amr and told him what they heard from Marwan about the signs. Ibn `Amr said, Marwan said nothing. I remember that I heard the Messenger of Allah saying,

> «إِنَّ أَوَّلَ الْآيَاتِ خُرُوجًا طُلُوعُ الشَّمْسِ مِنْ مَغْرِبِهَا وَخُرُوجُ الدَّابَّةِ ضُحًى فَأَيَّتُهُمَا كَانَتْ قَبْلَ صَاحِبَتِهَا فَالْأُخْرَى عَلَى أَثَرِهَا»

(The first of the signs to appear are the sun rising from the west and the Beast that appears in the early morning. Whichever comes before the other, then the second sign will appear soon after it.") Then `Abdullah said - and he used to read the Scriptures - "And I think the first of them is the sun rising from the west. That is because when it sets it comes under the Throne, prostrates and seeks permission to return. So it is permitted to return until Allah wants it to rise from the west. So it does as it normally would, it comes beneath the Throne, it prostrates and seeks permission to return. But it will get no response. Then it will seek permission to return (again), but it will get no response, until what Allah wills of the night to pass goes by, and it realizes that if it is permitted to return it would not (be able to) reach the east. It says; `My Lord! The east is so far, what good would I be to the people' Until the horizons appear as a (lightless) ring, it seeks permission to return and is told; `Rise from your place,' so it rises upon the people from where it set." Then he recited,

(no good will it do to a person to believe then, if he believed not before,) This was also recorded by Muslim in his Sahih, and Abu Dawud and Ibn Majah in their Sunans. Allah's statement,

(no good will it do to a person to believe then, if he believed not before,) means, when the disbeliever believes then, it will not be accepted from him. As for those who were believers before, if they earned righteous deeds, they will have earned a great deal of good. If they had not done good nor repented before then, it will not be accepted from them, according to the Hadiths that we mentioned. This is also the meaning of Allah's statement,

(...nor earned good through his faith.) meaning, one's good deeds will not be accepted from him unless he performed good deeds before. Allah said next,

(Say: "Wait you! We (too) are waiting.") This is a stern threat to the disbelievers and a sure promise for those who delay embracing the faith and repenting until a time when faith or repentance shall not avail. This will occur when the sun rises from the west because the Last Hour will then be imminent and its major signs will have begun to appear. Allah said in other Ayat, (Do they then await (anything) other than the Hour, that it should come upon them suddenly But some of its portents have already come; and when it is upon them, how can they benefit then by their reminder) (47:18), and,

(So when they saw Our punishment, they said: "We believe in Allah alone and reject (all) that we used to associate with Him as partners." Then their faith could not avail them when they saw Our punishment.) (40:84-85)

Surah: 6 Ayah: 159

﴿ إِنَّ ٱلَّذِينَ فَرَّقُوا۟ دِينَهُمْ وَكَانُوا۟ شِيَعًا لَّسْتَ مِنْهُمْ فِى شَىْءٍ ۚ إِنَّمَآ أَمْرُهُمْ إِلَى ٱللَّهِ ثُمَّ يُنَبِّئُهُم بِمَا كَانُوا۟ يَفْعَلُونَ ﴾

159. Verily, those who divide their religion and break up into sects (all kinds of religious sects), you (O Muhammad (peace be upon him)) have no concern in them in the least. Their affair is only with Allâh, Who then will tell them what they used to do.

Transliteration

159. Inna allatheena farraqoo deenahum wakanoo shiyaAAan lasta minhum fee shay-in innama amruhum ila Allahi thumma yunabbi-ohum bima kanoo yafAAaloona

Tafsir Ibn Kathir:

Criticizing Division in the Religion

Mujahid, Qatadah, Ad-Dahhak and As-Suddi said that this Ayah was revealed about the Jews and Christians. Al-`Awfi said that Ibn `Abbas commented,

(Verily, those who divide their religion and break up into sects...) "Before Muhammad was sent, the Jews and Christians disputed and divided into sects. When Muhammad was sent, Allah revealed to him,

(Verily, those who divide their religion and break up into sects, you have no concern with them in the least.) It is apparent that this Ayah refers to all those who defy the religion of Allah, or revert from it. Allah sent His Messenger with guidance and the religion of truth so that He makes it victorious and dominant above all religions. His Law is one and does not contain any contradiction or incongruity. Therefore, those who dispute in the religion,

(...and break up into sects,) religious sects, just like those who follow the various sects, desires and misguidance - then Allah has purified His Messenger from their ways. In a similar Ayah, Allah said,

(He (Allah) has ordained for you the same religion which He ordained for Nuh, and that which We have revealed to you.)(42:13) A Hadith reads,

«نَحْنُ مَعَاشِرُ الْأَنْبِيَاءِ أَوْلَادُ عَلَّاتٍ دِينُنَا وَاحِدٌ»

(We, the Prophets, are half brothers but have one religion.) This, indeed, is the straight path which the Messengers have brought and which commands worshipping Allah alone without partners and adhering to the Law of the last Messenger whom Allah sent. All other paths are types of misguidance, ignorance, sheer opinion and desires; and as such, the Messengers are free from them. Allah said here,

Chapter 6: Al-An'am (Cattle, Livestock), Verses 111-165

(You have no concern with them in the least...) (6:159). Allah's statement,

(Their affair is only with Allah, Who then will tell them what they used to do.) is similar to His statement,

(Verily, those who believe, and those who are Jews, and the Sabians, and the Christians, and the Majus, and those who worship others besides Allah; truly, Allah will judge between them on the Day of Resurrection.) (22:17) eAllah then mentioned His kindness in His decisions and His justice on the Day of Resurrection, when He said,

Surah: 6 Ayah: 160

﴿ مَن جَآءَ بِٱلْحَسَنَةِ فَلَهُ عَشْرُ أَمْثَالِهَا ۖ وَمَن جَآءَ بِٱلسَّيِّئَةِ فَلَا يُجْزَىٰٓ إِلَّا مِثْلَهَا وَهُمْ لَا يُظْلَمُونَ ﴾

160. Whoever brings a good deed (Islâmic Monotheism and deeds of obedience to Allâh and His Messenger (peace be upon him)) shall have ten times the like thereof to his credit, and whoever brings an evil deed (polytheism, disbelief, hypocrisy, and deeds of disobedience to Allâh and His Messenger (peace be upon him)) shall have only the recompense of the like thereof, and they will not be wronged.

Transliteration

160. Man jaa bialhasanati falahu AAashru amthaliha waman jaa bialssayyi-ati fala yujza illa mithlaha wahum la yuthlamoona

Tafsir Ibn Kathir:

The Good Deed is Multiplied Tenfold, While the Sin is Recompensed with the Same

This Ayah explains the general Ayah;

(Whoever comes with good, then he will receive better than that.)(28:84) There are several Hadiths that are in agreement with the apparent wording of this honorable Ayah. Imam Ahmad bin Hanbal recorded that Ibn `Abbas said that the Messenger of Allah said about his Lord,

«إِنَّ رَبَّكُمْ عَزَّ وَجَلَّ رَحِيمٌ مَنْ هَمَّ بِحَسَنَةٍ فَلَمْ يَعْمَلْهَا كُتِبَتْ لَهُ حَسَنَةً فَإِنْ عَمِلَهَا كُتِبَتْ لَهُ عَشْرًا إِلَى سَبْعِمِائَةٍ إِلَى أَضْعَافٍ كَثِيرَةٍ. وَمَنْ هَمَّ بِسَيِّئَةٍ فَلَمْ

يَعْمَلْهَا كُتِبَتْ لَهُ حَسَنَةً فَإِنْ عَمِلَهَا كُتِبَتْ لَهُ وَاحِدَةً أَوْ يَمْحُوهَا اللهُ عَزَّ وَجَلَّ وَلَا يَهْلِكُ عَلَى اللهِ إِلَّا هَالِكٌ»

(Your Lord is Most Merciful. Whoever intends to perform a good deed and does not do it, it will be written for him as a good deed. If he performs it, it will be written for him as ten deeds, to seven hundred, to multifold. Whoever intends to commit an evil deed, but does not do it, it will be written for him as a good deed. If he commits it, it will be written for him as a sin, unless Allah erases it. Only those who deserve destruction will be destroyed by Allah.) Al-Bukhari, Muslim and An-Nasa'i also recorded this Hadith. Ahmad also recorded that Abu Dharr said that the Messenger of Allah said,

«يَقُولُ اللهُ عَزَّ وَجَلَّ: مَنْ عَمِلَ حَسَنَةً فَلَهُ عَشْرُ أَمْثَالِهَا وَأَزِيدُ وَمَنْ عَمِلَ سَيِّئَةً فَجَزَاؤُهَا مِثْلُهَا أَوْ أَغْفِرُ وَمَنْ عَمِلَ قُرَابَ الْأَرْضِ خَطِيئَةً ثُمَّ لَقِيَنِي لَا يُشْرِكُ بِي شَيْئًا جَعَلْتُ لَهُ مِثْلَهَا مَغْفِرَةً، وَمَنِ اقْتَرَبَ إِلَيَّ شِبْرًا اقْتَرَبْتُ إِلَيْهِ ذِرَاعًا وَمَنِ اقْتَرَبَ إِلَيَّ ذِرَاعًا اقْتَرَبْتُ إِلَيْهِ بَاعًا وَمَنْ أَتَانِي يَمْشِي أَتَيْتُهُ هَرْوَلَةً»

(Allah says, `Whoever performs a good deed, will have tenfold for it and more. Whoever commits a sin, then his recompense will be the same, unless I forgive. Whoever commits the earth's fill of sins and then meets Me while associating none with Me, I will give him its fill of forgiveness. Whoever draws closer to Me by a hand's span, I will draw closer to him by a forearm's length. Whoever draws closer to Me by a forearm's length, I will draw closer to him by an arm's length. And whoever comes to Me walking, I will come to him running.') Muslim also collected this Hadith. Know that there are three types of people who refrain from committing a sin that they intended. There are those who refrain from committing the sin because they fear Allah, and thus will have written for them a good deed as a reward. This type contains both a good intention and a good deed. In some narrations of the Sahih, Allah says about this type, "He has left the sin for My sake." Another type does not commit the sin because of forgetfulness or being busy attending to other affairs. This type of person will neither earn a sin, nor a reward. The reason being that, this person did not intend to do good, nor commit evil. Some people abandon the sin because they were unable to commit it or due to laziness, after trying to commit it and seeking the means that help commit it. This person is just like the person who commits the sin. There is an authentic Hadith that states,

«إِذَا الْتَقَى الْمُسْلِمَانِ بِسَيْفَيْهِمَا فَالْقَاتِلُ وَالْمَقْتُولُ فِي النَّارِ»

Chapter 6: Al-An'am (Cattle, Livestock), Verses 111-165

(When two Muslims meet with their swords, then the killer and the killed will be in the Fire.) They said, "O Allah's Messenger! We know about the killer, so what about the killed" He said,

《إِنَّهُ كَانَ حَرِيصًا عَلَى قَتْلِ صَاحِبِهِ》

(He was eager to kill his companion.) Al-Hafiz Abu Al-Qasim At-Tabarani said that Abu Malik Al-Ash`ari said that the Messenger of Allah said,

《الجُمُعَةُ كَفَّارَةٌ لِمَا بَيْنَهَا وَبَيْنَ الجُمُعَةِ الَّتِي تَلِيهَا وَزِيَادَةُ ثَلَاثَةِ أَيَّامٍ، وَذَلِكَ لِأَنَّ اللهَ تَعَالَى قَالَ:

(مَن جَآءَ بِالْحَسَنَةِ فَلَهُ عَشْرُ أَمْثَالِهَا)》

(Friday (prayer) to the next Friday (preayer), plus three more days, erase whatever was committed (of sins) between them. This is because Allah says: Whoever brings a good deed shall have ten times the like thereof to his credit) Abu Dharr narrated that the Messenger of Allah said,

《مَنْ صَامَ ثَلَاثَةَ أَيَّامٍ مِنْ كُلِّ شَهْرٍ فَقَدْ صَامَ الدَّهْرَ كُلَّهُ》

(Whoever fasts three days every month, will have fasted all the time.) Ahmad, An-Nasa'i, and Ibn Majah recorded this Hadith, and this is Ahmad's wording. At-Tirmidhi also recorded it with this addition;

《فأنزل الله تصديق ذلك في كتابه》

(So Allah sent down affirmation of this statement in His Book,)

[مَن جَآءَ بِالْحَسَنَةِ فَلَهُ عَشْرُ أَمْثَالِهَا]

(Whoever brings a good deed shall have ten times the like thereof to his credit,)

《اليوم بعشرة أيام》

(Therefore, a day earns ten days.) At-Tirmidhi said; "This Hadith is Hasan". There are many other Hadiths and statements on this subject, but what we mentioned should be sufficient, Allah willing, and our trust is in Him.

Surah: 6 Ayah: 161, Ayah: 162 & Ayah: 163

﴿ قُلْ إِنَّنِى هَدَىٰنِى رَبِّى إِلَىٰ صِرَٰطٍ مُّسْتَقِيمٍ دِينًا قِيَمًا مِّلَّةَ إِبْرَٰهِيمَ حَنِيفًا ۚ وَمَا كَانَ مِنَ ٱلْمُشْرِكِينَ ﴿١٦١﴾ ﴾

161. Say (O Muhammad (peace be upon him)) "Truly, my Lord has guided me to a Straight Path, a right religion, the religion of Ibrâhîm (Abraham), Hanîfa (i.e. the true Islâmic Monotheism - to believe in One God (Allâh i.e. to worship none but Allâh, Alone)) and he was not of Al-Mushrikûn (see V.2:105)."

﴿ قُلْ إِنَّ صَلَاتِى وَنُسُكِى وَمَحْيَاىَ وَمَمَاتِى لِلَّهِ رَبِّ ٱلْعَٰلَمِينَ ﴿١٦٢﴾ ﴾

162. Say (O Muhammad (peace be upon him)) "Verily, my Salât (prayer), my sacrifice, my living, and my dying are for Allâh, the Lord of the 'Alamîn (mankind, jinn and all that exists).

﴿ لَا شَرِيكَ لَهُ ۖ وَبِذَٰلِكَ أُمِرْتُ وَأَنَا۠ أَوَّلُ ٱلْمُسْلِمِينَ ﴿١٦٣﴾ ﴾

163. "He has no partner. And of this I have been commanded, and I am the first of the Muslims."

Transliteration

161. Qul innanee hadanee rabbee ila siratin mustaqeemin deenan qiyaman millata ibraheema haneefan wama kana mina almushrikeena   162. Qul inna salatee wanusukee wamahyaya wamamatee lillahi rabbi alAAalameena   163. La shareeka lahu wabithalika omirtu waana awwalu almuslimeena

Tafsir Ibn Kathir:

Islam is the Straight Path

Allah commands His Prophet , the chief of the Messengers, to convey the news of being guided to Allah's straight path. This path is neither wicked, nor deviant,

(a right religion...) that is, established on firm grounds,

(The religion of Ibrahim, Hanifan and he was not of the Mushrikin.) Allah said in similar Ayat,

(And who turns away from the religion of Ibrahim except him who deludes himself) (2:130), and,

(And strive hard in Allah's cause as you ought to strive. He has chosen you, and has not laid upon you in religion any hardship: it is the religion of your father Ibrahim.) (22:78), and,

(Verily, Ibrahim was an Ummah (or a nation), obedient to Allah, a Hanif, and he was not one of the Mushrikin. (He was) thankful for His (Allah's) favors. He (Allah) chose him (as an intimate friend) and guided him to a straight path. And We gave him good in this world, and in the Hereafter he shall be of the righteous. Then, We have sent the revelation to you (saying): "Follow the religion of Ibrahim, (he was a) Hanif, and he was not of the Mushrikin") (16:120-123). Ordering the Prophet to follow the religion of Ibrahim, the Hanifiyyah, does not mean that Prophet Ibrahim reached more perfection in it than our Prophet . Rather, our Prophet perfectly established the religion and it was completed for him; and none before him reached this level of perfection. This is why he is the Final Prophet, the chief of all the Children of Adam who holds the station of praise and glory, the honor of intercession on the Day of Resurrection. All creation (on that Day) will seek him, even Ibrahim the friend of Allah, peace be upon him (to request the beginning of Judgement). Imam Ahmad recorded that Ibn `Abbas said, "The Messenger of Allah was asked, `Which religion is the best with Allah, the Exalted' He said,

«الْحَنِيفِيَّةُ السَّمْحَة»

(Al-Hanifiyyah As-Samhah (the easy monotheism))"

The Command for Sincerity in Worship

Allah said next,

(Say: "Verily, my Salah, my sacrifice, my living, and my dying are for Allah, the Lord of the all that exists.") Allah commands the Prophet to inform the idolators who worship other than Allah and sacrifice to something other than Him, that he opposes them in all this, for his prayer is for Allah, and his rituals are in His Name alone, without partners. Allah said in a similar statement,

(Therefore turn in prayer to your Lord and sacrifice.) (108:2), meaning, make your prayer and sacrifice for Allah alone. As for the idolators, they used to worship the idols and sacrifice to them, so Allah commanded the Prophet to defy them and contradict their practices. Allah, the Exalted, commanded him to dedicate his intention and heart to being sincere for Him alone. Mujahid commented,

(Verily, my prayer and my Nusuk...) refers to sacrificing during Hajj and `Umrah.

Islam is the Religion of all Prophets

The Ayah,

(and I am the first of the Muslims.) means, from this Ummah, according to Qatadah. This is a sound meaning, because all Prophets before our Prophet were calling to Islam, which commands worshipping Allah alone without partners. Allah said in another Ayah,

(And We did not send any Messenger before you but We revealed to him (saying): "None has the right to be worshipped but I, so worship Me.") (21:25) Allah informed us that Nuh said to his people,

(But if you turn away, then no reward have I asked of you, my reward is only from Allah, and I have been commanded to be of the Muslims.) (10:72) Allah said,

(And who turns away from the religion of Ibrahim except him who deludes himself Truly, We chose him in this world and verily, in the Hereafter he will be among the righteous. When his Lord said to him, "Submit (i.e. be a Muslim)!" He said, "I have submitted myself (as a Muslim) to the Lord of the all that exists." And this was enjoined by Ibrahim upon his sons and by Ya`qub (saying), "O my sons! Allah has chosen for you the (true) religion, then die not except as Muslims.")(2:130-132). Yusuf, peace be upon him, said,

(My Lord! You have indeed bestowed on me of the sovereignty, and taught me something of the interpretation of dreams -- the (Only) Creator of the heavens and the earth! You are my Wali (Protector) in this world and in the Hereafter. Cause me to die as a Muslim, and join me with the righteous.) (12:101) Musa said,

(And Musa said: "O my people! If you have believed in Allah, then put your trust in Him if you are Muslims." They said: "In Allah we put our trust. Our Lord! Make us not a trial for the folk who are wrongdoers. And save us by your mercy from the disbelieving folk") (10:84-86) Allah said,

(Verily, We did send down the Tawrah, therein was guidance and light, by which the Prophets, who submitted themselves to Allah's will, judged for the Jews. And the rabbis and the priests (did also).) (5:44), and,

(And when I (Allah) inspired Al-Hawariyyun (the disciples) (of `Isa) to believe in Me and My Messenger, they said: "We believe. And bear witness that we are Muslims.") (5:111) Therefore, Allah states that He sent all His Messengers with the religion of Islam, although their respective laws differed from each other, and some of them abrogated others. Later on, the Law sent with Muhammad abrogated all previous laws and nothing will ever abrogate it, forever. Certainly, Muhammad's Law will always be apparent and its flags raised high, until the Day of Resurrection. The Prophet said,

«نَحْنُ مَعَاشِرُ الْأَنْبِيَاءِ أَوْلَادُ عَلَّاتٍ دِينُنَا وَاحِدٌ»

(We, the Prophets, are half brothers, but our religion is one.) Half brothers, mentioned in the Hadith, refers to the brothers to one father, but different mothers. Therefore, the religion, representing the one father, is one; worshipping Allah alone without partners, even though the laws which are like the different mothers in this parable, are different. Allah the Most High knows best. Imam Ahmad recorded that `Ali said that when the Messenger of Allah used to start the prayer with Takbir (saying, "Allahu Akbar" (Allah is the Great)) he would then supplicate,

«وَجَّهْتُ وَجْهِيَ لِلَّذِي فَطَرَ السَّمَوَاتِ وَالْأَرْضَ حَنِيفًا وَمَا أَنَا مِنَ الْمُشْرِكِينَ،
إِنَّ صَلَاتِي وَنُسُكِي وَمَحْيَايَ وَمَمَاتِي لِلهِ رَبِّ الْعَالَمِينَ»

Chapter 6: Al-An'am (Cattle, Livestock), Verses 111-165

(I have directed my face towards He Who has created the heavens and earth, Hanifan and I am not among the Mushrikin. Certainly, my prayer, sacrifice, living and dying are all for Allah, Lord of the worlds.)

«اللَّهُمَّ أَنْتَ الْمَلِكُ لَا إِلَهَ إِلَّا أَنْتَ، أَنْتَ رَبِّي وَأَنَا عَبْدُكَ ظَلَمْتُ نَفْسِي وَاعْتَرَفْتُ بِذَنْبِي فَاغْفِرْ لِي ذُنُوبِي جَمِيعًا لَا يَغْفِرُ الذُّنُوبَ إِلَّا أَنْتَ، وَاهْدِنِي لِأَحْسَنِ الْأَخْلَاقِ لَا يَهْدِي لِأَحْسَنِهَا إِلَّا أَنْتَ، وَاصْرِفْ عَنِّي سَيِّئَهَا لَا يَصْرِفُ عَنِّي سَيِّئَهَا إِلَّا أَنْتَ، تَبَارَكْتَ وَتَعَالَيْتَ، أَسْتَغْفِرُكَ وَأَتُوبُ إِلَيْكَ»

(O Allah! You are the King, there is no deity worthy of worship except You. You are my Lord and I am Your servant. I have committed wrong against myself and admitted to my error, so forgive me all my sins. Verily, You, only You forgive the sins. (O Allah!) Direct me to the best conduct, for none except You directs to the best conduct. Divert me from the worst conduct, for only You divert from the worst conduct. Glorified and Exalted You are. I seek Your forgiveness and repent to You.) This Hadith, which was also recorded by Muslim in the Sahih, continues and mentions the Prophet's supplication in his bowing, prostrating and final sitting positions.

Surah: 6 Ayah: 164

﴿ قُلْ أَغَيْرَ اللَّهِ أَبْغِي رَبًّا وَهُوَ رَبُّ كُلِّ شَيْءٍ ۚ وَلَا تَكْسِبُ كُلُّ نَفْسٍ إِلَّا عَلَيْهَا ۚ وَلَا تَزِرُ وَازِرَةٌ وِزْرَ أُخْرَىٰ ۚ ثُمَّ إِلَىٰ رَبِّكُمْ مَرْجِعُكُمْ فَيُنَبِّئُكُمْ بِمَا كُنْتُمْ فِيهِ تَخْتَلِفُونَ ﴾

164. Say: "Shall I seek a lord other than Allâh, while He is the Lord of all things? No person earns any (sin) except against himself (only), and no bearer of burdens shall bear the burden of another. Then unto your Lord is your return, so He will tell you that wherein you have been differing."

Transliteration

164. Qul aghayra Allahi abghee rabban wahuwa rabbu kulli shay-in wala taksibu kullu nafsin illa AAalayha wala taziru waziratun wizra okhra thumma ila rabbikum marjiAAukum fayunabbi-okum bima kuntum feehi takhtalifoona

Tafsir Ibn Kathir:

The Command to Sincerely Trust in Allah

Allah said,

(Say), O Muhammad, to those idolators, about worshipping Allah alone and trusting in Him,

(Shall I seek a lord other than Allah...) (6:164),

(while He is the Lord of all things) and Who protects and saves me and governs all my affairs But, I only trust in Him and go back to Him, because He is the Lord of everything, Owner of all things and His is the creation and the decision. This Ayah commands sincerely trusting Allah, while the Ayah before it commands sincerely worshipping Allah alone without partners. These two meanings are often mentioned together in the Qur'an. Allah directs His servants to proclaim,

(You (alone) we worship, and You (alone) we ask for help (for each and every thing).) (1:5) Allah said,

(So worship Him and put your trust in Him.) (11:123), and

(Say: "He is the Most Gracious (Allah), in Him we believe, and in Him we put our trust".) (67:29), and,

(Lord of the east and the west; none has the right to be worshipped but He. So take Him a guardian.) (73:9) There are similar Ayat on this subject.

Every Person Carries His Own Burden

Allah said,

(No person earns any (sin) except against himself (only), and no bearer of burdens shall bear the burden of another.) thus emphasizing Allah's reckoning, decision and justice that will occur on the Day of Resurrection. The souls will only be recompensed for their deeds, good for good and evil for evil. No person shall carry the burden of another person, a fact that indicates Allah's perfect justice. Allah said in other Ayat,

(And if one heavily laden calls another to (bear) his load, nothing of it will be lifted even though he be near of kin.) (35:18), and,

(Then he will have no fear of injustice, nor of any curtailment (of his reward).) (20:112) Scholars of Tafsir commented, "No person will be wronged by carrying the evil deeds of another person, nor will his own good deeds be curtailed or decreased." Allah also said;

(Every person is a pledge for what he has earned. Except those on the Right.) (74:38-39), meaning, every person will be tied to his evil deeds. But, for those on the right -- the believers -- the blessing of their good works will benefit their offspring and relatives, as well. Allah said in Surat At-Tur,

(And those who believe and whose offspring follow them in faith, to them shall We join their offspring, and We shall not decrease the reward of their deeds in anything.) (52:21), meaning, We shall elevate their offspring to their high grades in Paradise, even though the deeds of the offspring were less righteous, since they shared faith with them in its general form. Allah says, We did not decrease the grades of these righteous believers so that those (their offspring and relatives) who have lesser grades, can share the same grades as them. Rather Allah elevated the lesser believers to the grades of their parents by the blessing of their parents' good works, by His favor and bounty. Allah said next (in Surat At-Tur),

(Every person is a pledge for that which he has earned.) (52:21), meaning, of evil. Allah's statement here,

(Then unto your Lord is your return, so He will tell you that wherein you have been differing.) means, work you (disbelievers), and we will also work. Surely, both you and us will be gathered to Allah and He will inform us of our deeds and your deeds and the decision on what we used to dispute about in the life of this world. Allah said in other Ayat,

(Say: "You will not be asked about our sins, nor shall we be asked of what you do." Say: "Our Lord will assemble us all together, then He will judge between us with truth. And He is the Just Judge, the All-Knower of the true state of affairs.") (34:25-26).

Surah: 6 Ayah: 165

﴿ وَهُوَ ٱلَّذِى جَعَلَكُمْ خَلَٰٓئِفَ ٱلْأَرْضِ وَرَفَعَ بَعْضَكُمْ فَوْقَ بَعْضٍ دَرَجَٰتٍ لِّيَبْلُوَكُمْ فِى مَآ ءَاتَىٰكُمْ إِنَّ رَبَّكَ سَرِيعُ ٱلْعِقَابِ وَإِنَّهُۥ لَغَفُورٌ رَّحِيمٌ ۝ ﴾

165. And it is He Who has made you generations coming after generations, replacing each other on the earth. And He has raised you in ranks, some above others that He may try you in that which He has bestowed on you. Surely your Lord is Swift in retribution, and certainly He is Oft-Forgiving, Most Merciful.

Transliteration

165. Wahuwa allathee jaAAalakum khala-ifa al-ardi warafaAAa baAAdakum fawqa baAAdin darajatin liyabluwakum fee ma atakum inna rabbaka sareeAAu alAAiqabi wa-innahu laghafoorun raheemun

Tafsir Ibn Kathir:

Allah Made Mankind Dwellers on the earth, Generation After Generation, of Various Grades, in order to Test Them

Allah said,

(And it is He Who has made you generations coming after generations, replacing each other on the earth.) meaning, He made you dwell on the earth generation after generation, century after century and offspring after forefathers, according to Ibn Zayd and others. Allah also said,

(And if it were Our will, We would have made angels to replace you on the earth) (43:60), and,

(And makes you inheritors of the Earth, generations after generations.) (27:62), and

(Verily, I am going to place (mankind) generations after generations on earth.) (2:30), and,

(It may be that your Lord will destroy your enemy and make you successors on the earth, so that He may see how you act.) (7:129) Allah's statement,

(And He has raised you in ranks, some above others,) means, He has made you different from each other with regards to provision, conduct, qualities, evilness, shapes, color of skin, and so forth, and He has the perfect wisdom in all this. Allah said in other Ayat,

(It is We Who portion out between them their livelihood in this world, and We raised some of them above others in ranks, so that some may employ others in their work.) (43:32), and,

(See how We prefer one above another (in this world), and verily, the Hereafter will be greater in degrees and greater in preferment.) (17:21) Allah's statement,

(that He may try you in that which He has bestowed on you.) means, so that He tests you in what He has granted you, for Allah tries the rich concerning his wealth and will ask him about how he appreciated it. He also tries the poor concerning his poverty and will ask him about his patience with it. Muslim recorded that Abu Sa`id Al-Khudri said that the Messenger of Allah said,

«إِنَّ الدُّنْيَا حُلْوَةٌ خَضِرَةٌ وَإِنَّ اللهَ مُسْتَخْلِفُكُمْ فِيهَا فَنَاظِرٌ مَاذَا تَعْمَلُونَ، فَاتَّقُوا الدُّنْيَا وَاتَّقُوا النِّسَاءَ فَإِنَّ أَوَّلَ فِتْنَةِ بَنِي إِسْرَائِيلَ كَانَتْ فِي النِّسَاءِ»

(Verily, this life is beautiful and green, and Allah made you dwell in it generation after generation so that He sees what you will do. Therefore, beware of this life and beware of women, for the first trial that the Children of Israel suffered from was with women.) Allah's statement,

(Surely, your Lord is swift in retribution, and certainly He is Oft-Forgiving, Most Merciful.) this is both discouragement and encouragement, by reminding the believers that Allah is swift in reckoning and punishment with those who disobey Him and defy His Messengers,

(And certainly He is Oft-Forgiving, Most Merciful.) for those who take Him as protector and follow His Messengers in the news and commandments they conveyed. Allah often mentions these two attributes together in the Qur'an. Allah said, (But verily, your Lord is full of forgiveness for mankind in spite of their wrongdoing. And verily, your Lord is (also) severe in punishment) (13:6), and,

(Declare unto My servants, that truly, I am the Oft-Forgiving, the Most Merciful. And that My torment is indeed the most painful torment.) (15:49-50) There are similar Ayat that contain encouragement and discouragement. Sometimes Allah calls His servants to Him with encouragement, describing Paradise and making them eager for what He has with Him. Sometimes, He calls His servants with discouragement, mentioning the Fire and its torment and punishment, as well as, the Day of Resurrection and its horrors. Sometimes Allah mentions both so that each person is affected by it according to his or her qualities. We ask Allah that He makes us among those who obey what He has commanded, avoid what He has prohibited, and believe in Him as He has informed. Certainly, He is Near, hears and answers the supplication, and He is the Most Kind, Generous and Bestowing. Imam Ahmad recorded that Abu Hurayrah said that the Messenger of Allah said,

«لَوْ يَعْلَمُ الْمُؤْمِنُ مَا عِنْدَ اللهِ مِنَ الْعُقُوبَةِ مَا طَمِعَ بِجَنَّتِهِ أَحَدٌ، وَلَوْ يَعْلَمُ الْكَافِرُ مَا اعِنْدَ اللهِ مِنَ الرَّحْمَةِ مَا قَنَطَ أَحَدٌ مِنَ الْجَنَّةِ، خَلَقَ اللهُ مِائَةَ رَحْمَةٍ فَوَضَعَ وَاحِدَةً بَيْنَ خَلْقِهِ يَتَرَاحَمُونَ بِهَا وَعِنْدَ اللهِ تِسْعَةٌ وَتِسْعُونَ»

(If the believer knew Allah's punishment, no one will hope in entering His Paradise. And if the disbeliever knew Allah's mercy, no one will feel hopeless of acquiring Paradise. Allah created a hundred kinds of mercy. He sent down one of them to His creation, and they are merciful to each other on that account. With Allah, there remains ninety-nine kinds of mercy.) Muslim and At-Tirmidhi also recorded this Hadith, At-Tirmidhi said "Hasan". Abu Hurayrah narrated that the Messenger of Allah said,

«لَمَّا خَلَقَ اللهُ الْخَلْقَ كَتَبَ فِي كِتَابٍ فَهُوَ عِنْدَهُ فَوْقَ الْعَرْشِ إِنَّ رَحْمَتِي تَغْلِبُ غَضَبِي»

(When Allah created the creation, He wrote in a Book, and this Book is with Him above the Throne: `My mercy overcomes My anger.') This is the end of the Tafsir of Surat Al-An`am, all the thanks and appreciation for Allah.

CHAPTER (SURAH) 7: AL-ARAF (THE HEIGHTS), VERSES 001 - 087

﴿بِسْمِ ٱللَّهِ ٱلرَّحْمَٰنِ ٱلرَّحِيمِ﴾

(In the Name of Allah, the Most Gracious, the Most Merciful.)

Surah: 7 Ayah: 1, Ayah: 2 & Ayah: 3

﴿الٓمٓصٓ ۝﴾

1. Alif-Lâm-Mîm-Sâd. (These letters are one of the miracles of the Qur'ân and none but Allâh (Alone) knows their meanings).

﴿كِتَـٰبٌ أُنزِلَ إِلَيْكَ فَلَا يَكُن فِى صَدْرِكَ حَرَجٌ مِّنْهُ لِتُنذِرَ بِهِۦ وَذِكْرَىٰ لِلْمُؤْمِنِينَ ۝﴾

2. (This is the) Book (the Qur'ân) sent down unto you (O Muhammad (peace be upon him)) so let not your breast be narrow therefrom, that you warn thereby; and a reminder unto the believers.

﴿ٱتَّبِعُوا۟ مَآ أُنزِلَ إِلَيْكُم مِّن رَّبِّكُمْ وَلَا تَتَّبِعُوا۟ مِن دُونِهِۦٓ أَوْلِيَآءَ ۗ قَلِيلًا مَّا تَذَكَّرُونَ ۝﴾

3. (Say (O Muhammad (peace be upon him)) to these idolaters (pagan Arabs) of your folk:) Follow what has been sent down unto you from your Lord (the Qur'ân and Prophet Muhammad's Sunnah), and follow not any Auliyâ' (protectors and helpers who order you to associate partners in worship with Allâh), besides Him (Allâh). Little do you remember!

Transliteration

1. Alif-lam-meem-sad   2. Kitabun onzila ilayka fala yakun fee sadrika harajun minhu litunthira bihi wathikra lilmu/mineena   3. IttabiAAoo ma onzila ilaykum min rabbikum wala tattabiAAoo min doonihi awliyaa qaleelan ma tathakkaroona

Tafsir Ibn Kathir:

Which was revealed in Makkah

We mentioned before the explanation of the letters (such as, Alif-Lam, that are in the beginning of some Surahs in the Qur'an).

((This is the) Book (the Qur'an) sent down unto you (O Muhammad)), from your Lord,

(so let not your breast be narrow therefrom,) meaning, having doubt about it according to Mujahid, Qatadah and As-Suddi. It was also said that the meaning here is: `do not hesitate to convey the Qur'an and warn with it,'

(Therefore be patient as did the Messengers of strong will) (46:35). Allah said here,

(that you warn thereby) meaning, `We sent down the Qur'an so that you may warn the disbelievers with it,'

(and a reminder unto the believers). Allah then said to the world,

(Follow what has been sent down unto you from your Lord) meaning, follow and imitate the unlettered Prophet, who brought you a Book that was revealed for you, from the Lord and master of everything.

(and follow not any Awliya', besides Him (Allah)) meaning, do not disregard what the Messenger brought you and follow something else, for in this case, you will be deviating from Allah's judgment to the decision of someone else. Allah's statement,

(Little do you remember!) is similar to,

(And most of mankind will not believe even if you desire it eagerly)(12:103), and;

(And if you obey most of those on the earth, they will mislead you far away from Allah's path)(6:116), and,

(And most of them believe not in Allah except that they attribute partners unto Him)(12:106).

Surah: 7 Ayah: 4, Ayah: 5, Ayah: 6 & Ayah: 7

﴿ وَكَم مِّن قَرْيَةٍ أَهْلَكْنَٰهَا فَجَاءَهَا بَأْسُنَا بَيَٰتًا أَوْ هُم قَآئِلُونَ ۝ ﴾

4. And a great number of towns (their population) We destroyed (for their crimes). Our torment came upon them (suddenly) by night or while they were sleeping for their midday nap.

﴿ فَمَا كَانَ دَعْوَىٰهُمْ إِذْ جَاءَهُم بَأْسُنَا إِلَّا أَن قَالُوٓا۟ إِنَّا كُنَّا ظَٰلِمِينَ ۝ ﴾

5. No cry did they utter when Our Torment came upon them but this: "Verily, we were Zâlimûn (polytheists and wrong-doers)".

﴿ فَلَنَسْـَٔلَنَّ ٱلَّذِينَ أُرْسِلَ إِلَيْهِمْ وَلَنَسْـَٔلَنَّ ٱلْمُرْسَلِينَ ۝ ﴾

6. Then surely, We shall question those (people) to whom it (the Book) was sent and verily, We shall question the Messengers.

﴿ فَلَنَقُصَّنَّ عَلَيْهِم بِعِلْمٍ وَمَا كُنَّا غَآئِبِينَ ۝ ﴾

7. Then surely, We shall narrate unto them (their whole story) with knowledge, and indeed We were not absent.

Transliteration

4. Wakam min qaryatin ahlaknaha fajaaha ba/suna bayatan aw hum qa-iloona 5. Fama kana daAAwahum ith jaahum ba/suna illa an qaloo inna kunna thalimeena 6. Falanas-alanna allatheena orsila ilayhim walanas-alanna almursaleena 7. Falanaqussanna AAalayhim biAAilmin wama kunna gha-ibeena

Tafsir Ibn Kathir:

Nations that were destroyed

Allah said,

(And a great number of towns We destroyed.) for defying Our Messengers and rejecting them. This behavior led them to earn disgrace in this life, which led them to disgrace in the Hereafter. Allah said in other Ayat,

(And indeed (many) Messengers before you were mocked at, but their scoffers were surrounded by the very thing that they used to mock at) (6:10), and

(And many a township did We destroy while they were given to wrongdoing, so that it lie in ruins (up to this day), and (many) a deserted well and lofty castle!) (22:45), and,

(And how many a town have We destroyed, which was thankless for its means of livelihood And those are their dwellings, which have not been inhabited after them except a little. And verily, We have been the heirs)(28:58). Allah's saying,

(Our torment came upon them by night or while they were taking their midday nap.) means, Allah's command, torment and vengeance came over them at night or while taking a nap in the middle of the day. Both of these times are periods of rest and leisure or heedlessness and amusement. Allah also said

(Did the people of the towns then feel secure against the coming of Our punishment by night while they were asleep Or, did the people of the towns then feel secure against the coming of Our punishment in the forenoon while they were playing)(7:97-98) and,

(Do then those who devise evil plots feel secure that Allah will not sink them into the earth, or that the torment will not seize them from directions they perceive not Or that He may catch them in the midst of their going to and from, so that there be no escape for them Or that He may catch them with gradual wastage. Truly, Your Lord is indeed full of kindness, Most Merciful) (16:45-47). Allah's saying;

(No cry did they utter when Our torment came upon them but this: "Verily, we were wrongdoers.") This means, when the torment came to them, their cry was that they admitted their sins and that they deserved to be punished. Allah said in a similar Ayah,

(How many a town given to wrongdoing, have We destroyed)(21:11), until,

(Extinct)(21:15). Allah's saying.

(Then surely, We shall question those (people) to whom it (the Book) was sent) is similar to the Ayat,

(And (remember) the Day (Allah) will call them, and say: "What answer gave you to the Messengers") (28:65), and,

Chapter 7: Al-Araf (The Heights), Verses 001-087

(On the Day when Allah will gather the Messengers together and say to them: "What was the response you received" They will say: "We have no knowledge, verily, only You are the Knower of all that is unseen.") (5:109). Allah will question the nations, on the Day of Resurrection, how they responded to His Messengers and the Messages He sent them with. He will also question the Messengers if they conveyed His Messages. So, `Ali bin Abi Talhah reported from Ibn `Abbas, who said commenting on the Ayah:

(Then surely, We shall question those (people) to whom it (the Book) was sent and verily, We shall question the Messengers.) He said; "About what they conveyed." Ibn `Abbas commented on Allah's statement,

(Then surely, We shall narrate unto them (their whole story) with knowledge, and indeed We have not been absent.) "The Book will be brought forth on the Day of Resurrection and it will speak, disclosing what they used to do."

(and indeed We have not been absent) meaning, On the Day of Resurrection, Allah will inform His servants about what they said and did, whether substantial or minor. Certainly, He witnesses to everything, nothing escapes His observation, and He is never unaware of anything. Rather, He has perfect knowledge of what the eyes are deluded by and what the hearts conceal,

(Not a leaf falls, but He knows it. There is not a grain in the darkness of the earth nor anything fresh or dry, but is written in a Clear Record.)(6:59)

Surah: 7 Ayah: 8 & Ayah: 9

﴿ وَٱلْوَزْنُ يَوْمَئِذٍ ٱلْحَقُّ فَمَن ثَقُلَتْ مَوَٰزِينُهُۥ فَأُو۟لَٰٓئِكَ هُمُ ٱلْمُفْلِحُونَ ۝ ﴾

8. And the weighing on that day (Day of Resurrection) will be the true (weighing). So as for those whose scale (of good deeds) will be heavy, they will be the successful (by entering Paradise).

﴿ وَمَنْ خَفَّتْ مَوَٰزِينُهُۥ فَأُو۟لَٰٓئِكَ ٱلَّذِينَ خَسِرُوٓا۟ أَنفُسَهُم بِمَا كَانُوا۟ بِـَٔايَٰتِنَا يَظْلِمُونَ ۝ ﴾

9. And as for those whose scale will be light, they are those who will lose their own selves (by entering Hell) because they denied and rejected Our Ayât (proofs, evidences, verses, lessons, signs, revelations, etc.).

Transliteration

8. Waalwaznu yawma-ithini alhaqqu faman thaqulat mawazeenuhu faola-ika humu almuflihoona   9. Waman khaffat mawazeenuhu faola-ika allatheena khasiroo anfusahum bima kanoo bi-ayatina yathlimoona

Tafsir Ibn Kathir:

The Meaning of weighing the Deeds

Allah said,

(And the weighing), of deeds on the Day of Resurrection,

(will be the true (weighing)), for Allah will not wrong anyone. Allah said in other Ayat,

(And We shall set up the Balances of justice on the Day of Resurrection, then none will be dealt with unjustly in anything. And if there be the weight of a mustard seed, We will bring it. And Sufficient are We to take account.)(21:47),

(Surely, Allah wrongs not even the weight of a speck of dust, but if there is any good (done), He doubles it, and gives from Him a great reward.) (4:40),

(Then as for him whose scale (of good deeds) will be heavy. He will live a pleasant life (in Paradise). But as for him whose scale (of good deeds) will be light. He will have his home in Hawiyah (pit, Hell). And what will make you know what it is (It is) a fiercely blazing Fire!) (101:6-11) and,

(Then, when the Trumpet is blown, there will be no kinship among them that Day, nor will they ask of one another. Then, those whose scales (of good deeds) are heavy, they are the successful. And those whose scales (of good deeds) are light, they are those who lose themselves, in Hell will they abide) (23:101-103). As for what will be placed on the Balance on the Day of Resurrection, it has been said that the deeds will be placed on it, even though they are not material objects. Allah will give these deeds physical weight on the Day of Resurrection. Al-Baghawi said that this was reported from Ibn `Abbas. It is recorded in the Sahih that Al-Baqarah (chapter 2) and Al `Imran (chapter 3) will come on the Day of Resurrection in the shape of two clouds, or two objects that provide shade, or two lined groups of birds. It is also recorded in the Sahih that the Qur'an will come to its companion (who used to recite and preserve it) in the shape of a pale-faced young man. He will ask (the young man), "Who are you" He will reply, "I am the Qur'an, who made you stay up sleeplessly at night and caused you thirst in the day. " The Hadith that Al-Bara' narrated about the questioning in the grave states,

«فَيَأْتِي الْمُؤْمِنَ شَابٌّ حَسَنُ اللَّوْنِ طَيِّبُ الرِّيحِ فَيَقُولُ: مَنْ أَنْتَ؟ فَيَقُولُ: أَنَا عَمَلُكَ الصَّالِحُ»

(A young man with fair color and good scent will come to the believer, who will ask, `Who are you' He will reply, `I am your good deeds'). The Prophet mentioned the opposite in the case of the disbeliever and the hypocrite. It was also said that the Book of Records that contains the deeds will be weighed. A Hadith states that a man will be brought forth and ninety-nine scrolls containing errors and sins will be placed on one side of the balance each as long as the sight can reach. He will then be brought a card on which `La ilaha illallah' will be written. He will say, "O Lord! What would this card weigh against these scrolls" Allah will say, "You will not be wronged." So the card will be placed on the other side of the Balance, and as the Messenger of Allah said,

«فَطَاشَتِ السِّجِلَّاتُ وَثَقُلَتِ الْبِطَاقَة»

(Behold! The (ninety-nine) scrolls will go up, as the card becomes heavier.) At-Tirmidhi recorded similar wording for this Hadith and said that it is authentic. It was also said that the person who performed the deed will be weighed. A Hadith states,

«يُؤْتَى يَوْمَ الْقِيَامَةِ بِالرَّجُلِ السَّمِينِ فَلَا يَزِنُ عِنْدَ اللهِ جَنَاحَ بَعُوضَة»

(On the Day of Resurrection, a fat man will be brought forth, but he will not weigh with Allah equal to the wing of a mosquito). He then recited the Ayah,

(And on the Day of Resurrection, We shall assign no weight for them) (18:105). Also, the Prophet said about `Abdullah bin Mas`ud,

«أَتَعْجَبُونَ مِنْ دِقَّةِ سَاقَيْهِ وَالَّذِي نَفْسِي بِيَدِهِ لَهُمَا فِي الْمِيزَانِ أَثْقَلُ مِنْ أُحُد»

(Do you wonder at the thinness of his legs By He in Whose Hand is my soul! They are heavier on the Balance than (Mount) Uhud.) It is also possible to combine the meanings of these Ayat and Hadiths by stating that all this will truly occur, for sometimes the deeds will be weighed, sometimes the scrolls where they are recorded will be weighed, and sometimes those who performed the deeds will be weighed. Allah knows best.

Surah: 7 Ayah: 10

﴿ وَلَقَدْ مَكَّنَّـكُمْ فِى ٱلْأَرْضِ وَجَعَلْنَا لَكُمْ فِيهَا مَعَـٰيِشَ قَلِيلًا مَّا تَشْكُرُونَ ۝ ﴾

10. And surely, We gave you authority on the earth and appointed for you therein provisions (for your life). Little thanks do you give.

Transliteration

10. Walaqad makkannakum fee al-ardi wajaAAalna lakum feeha maAAayisha qaleelan ma tashkuroona

Tafsir Ibn Kathir:

All Bounties in the Heavens and Earth are for the Benefit of Mankind

Allah reminds of His favor on His servants in that He made the earth a fixed place for dwelling, placed firm mountains and rivers on it and made homes and allowed them to utilize its benefits. Allah made the clouds work for them (bringing rain) so that they may produce their sustenance from them. He also created the ways and means of earnings, commercial activities and other professions. Yet, most of them give little thanks for this. Allah said in another Ayah,

(And if you count the blessings of Allah, never will you be able to count them. Verily, man is indeed a wrongdoer, an ingrate.) (14:34)

Surah: 7 Ayah: 11

﴿ وَلَقَدْ خَلَقْنَـٰكُمْ ثُمَّ صَوَّرْنَـٰكُمْ ثُمَّ قُلْنَا لِلْمَلَـٰٓئِكَةِ ٱسْجُدُوا۟ لِأَدَمَ فَسَجَدُوٓا۟ إِلَّآ إِبْلِيسَ لَمْ يَكُن مِّنَ ٱلسَّـٰجِدِينَ ۝ ﴾

11. And surely, We created you (your father Adam) and then gave you shape (the noble shape of a human being); then We told the angels, "Prostrate yourselves to Adam", and they prostrated themselves, except Iblîs (Satan), he refused to be of those who prostrated themselves.

Transliteration

11. Walaqad khalaqnakum thumma sawwarnakum thumma qulna lilmala-ikati osjudoo li-adama fasajadoo illa ibleesa lam yakun mina alssajideena

Tafsir Ibn Kathir:

Prostration of the Angels to Adam and Shaytan's Arrogance

Allah informs the Children of Adam about the honor of their father and the enmity of Shaytan, who still has envy for them and for their father Adam. So they should beware of him and not follow in his footsteps. Allah said,

(And surely, We created you and then gave you shape; then We told the angels, "Prostrate yourselves to Adam," and they prostrated,) This is like His saying,

(And (remember) when your Lord said to the angels: "I am going to create a man from dried (sounding) clay of altered mud. So, when I have fashioned him completely and breathed into him the soul (which I created for him), then fall (you) down prostrating yourselves unto him.") (15:28-29). After Allah created Adam with His Hands from dried clay of altered mud and made him in the shape of a human being, He blew life into him and ordered the angels to prostrate before him, honoring Allah's glory and magnificence. The angels all heard, obeyed and prostrated, but Iblis did not prostrate. We explained this subject in the beginning of Surat Al-Baqarah. Therefore, the Ayah (7:11) refers to Adam, although Allah used the plural in this case, because Adam is the father of all mankind. Similarly, Allah said to the Children of Israel who lived during the time of the Prophet,

(And We shaded you with clouds and sent down on you manna and the quail,)(2:57) This refers to their forefathers who lived during the time of Moses. But, since that was a favor given to the forefathers, and they are their very source, then the offspring have also been favored by it. This is not the case in:

(And indeed We created man out of an extract of clay (water and earth.))(23:12) For this merely means that Adam was created from clay. His children were created from Nutfah (mixed male and female sexual discharge). This last Ayah is thus talking about the origin of mankind, not that they were all created from clay, and Allah knows best.

Surah: 7 Ayah: 12

﴿ قَالَ مَا مَنَعَكَ أَلَّا تَسْجُدَ إِذْ أَمَرْتُكَ ۖ قَالَ أَنَا۠ خَيْرٌ مِّنْهُ خَلَقْتَنِى مِن نَّارٍ وَخَلَقْتَهُۥ مِن طِينٍ ﴾

12. (Allâh) said: "What prevented you (O Iblîs) that you did not prostrate yourself, when I commanded you?" Iblîs said: "I am better than him (Adam), You created me from fire, and him You created from clay."

Transliteration

12. Qala ma manaAAaka alla tasjuda ith amartuka qala ana khayrun minhu khalaqtanee min narin wakhalaqtahu min teenin

Tafsir Ibn Kathir:

Allah said,

(What prevented you (O Iblis) that you did not prostrate) (7: 12) meaning, what stopped and hindered you from prostrating after I ordered you to do so, according to Ibn Jarir. This meaning is sound, and Allah knows best. Iblis, may Allah curse him, said,

(I am better than him (Adam)), and this excuse is worse than the crime itself! Shaytan said that he did not obey Allah because he who is better cannot prostrate to he who is less. Shaytan, may Allah curse him, meant that he is better than Adam, "So how can You order me to prostrate before him" Shaytan said that he is better than Adam because he was created from fire while, "You created him from clay, and fire is better." The cursed one looked at the origin of creation not at the honor bestowed, that is, Allah creating Adam with His Hand and blowing life into him. Shaytan made a false comparison when confronted by Allah's command,

("Then you fall down prostrate to him")(38:72). Therefore, Shaytan alone contradicted the angels, because he refused to prostrate. He, thus, became `Ablasa' from the mercy, meaning, lost hope in acquiring Allah's mercy. He committed this error, may Allah curse him, due to his false comparison. His claim that the fire is more honored than mud was also false, because mud has the qualities of wisdom, for - bearance, patience and assurance, mud is where plants grow, flourish, increase, and provide good. To the contrary, fire has the qualities of burning, recklessness and hastiness. Therefore, the origin of creation directed Shaytan to failure, while the origin of Adam led him to return to Allah with repentance, humbleness, obedience and submission to His command, admitting his error and seeking Allah's forgiveness and pardon for it. Muslim recorded that `Aishah said that the Messenger of Allah said,

(The angels were created from light, Shaytan from a smokeless flame of fire, while Adam was created from what was described to you).

Iblis was the First to use Qiyas (Analogical Comparison)

Ibn Jarir recorded that Al-Hasan commented on Shaytan's statement,

("You created me from fire, and him You created from clay.") "Iblis used Qiyas (analogy), and he was the first one to do so." This statement has an authentic chain of narration. Ibn Jarir recorded that Ibn Sirin said, "The first to use Qiyas was Iblis, and would the sun and moon be worshipped if it was not for Qiyas" This statement also has an authentic chain of narration.

Surah: 7 Ayah: 13, Ayah: 14 & Ayah: 15

﴿ قَالَ فَٱهْبِطْ مِنْهَا فَمَا يَكُونُ لَكَ أَن تَتَكَبَّرَ فِيهَا فَٱخْرُجْ إِنَّكَ مِنَ ٱلصَّٰغِرِينَ ۝ ﴾

13. (Allâh) said: "(O Iblîs) get down from this (Paradise), it is not for you to be arrogant here. Get out, for you are of those humiliated and disgraced."

﴿ قَالَ أَنظِرْنِىٓ إِلَىٰ يَوْمِ يُبْعَثُونَ ۝ ﴾

14. (Iblîs) said: "Allow me respite till the Day they are raised up (i.e. the Day of Resurrection)."

﴿ قَالَ إِنَّكَ مِنَ ٱلْمُنظَرِينَ ۝ ﴾

15. (Allâh) said: "You are of those respited."

Transliteration

13. Qala faihbit minha fama yakoonu laka an tatakabbara feeha faokhruj innaka mina alssaghireena 14. Qala anthirnee ila yawmi yubAAathoona 15. Qala innaka mina almunthareena

Tafsir Ibn Kathir:

Allah ordered Iblis;

(Get down from this) "because you defied My command and disobeyed Me. Get out, it is not for you to be arrogant here," in Paradise, according to the scholars of Tafsir. It could also refer to particular status which he held in the utmost highs. Allah said to Iblis,

(Get out, for you are of those humiliated and disgraced.) as just recompense for his ill intentions, by giving him the opposite of what he intended (arrogance). This is when the cursed one remembered and asked for respite until the Day of Judgment,

(Then allow me respite till the Day they are raised up. (Allah) said: "Then you are of those respited.") (15: 36-37) Allah gave Shaytan what he asked for out of His wisdom, being His decision and decree, that is never prevented or resisted. Surely, none can avert His decision, and He is swift in reckoning.

Surah: 7 Ayah: 16 & Ayah: 17

﴿ قَالَ فَبِمَآ أَغْوَيْتَنِى لَأَقْعُدَنَّ لَهُمْ صِرَاطَكَ ٱلْمُسْتَقِيمَ ۝ ﴾

16. (Iblîs) said: "Because You have sent me astray, surely I will sit in wait against them (human beings) on Your Straight Path.

﴿ ثُمَّ لَأَتِيَنَّهُم مِّنۢ بَيْنِ أَيْدِيهِمْ وَمِنْ خَلْفِهِمْ وَعَنْ أَيْمَـٰنِهِمْ وَعَن شَمَآئِلِهِمْ ۖ وَلَا تَجِدُ أَكْثَرَهُمْ شَـٰكِرِينَ ۝ ﴾

17. Then I will come to them from before them and behind them, from their right and from their left, and You will not find most of them as thankful ones (i.e. they will not be dutiful to You)."

Transliteration

16. Qala fabima aghwaytanee laaqAAudanna lahum sirataka almustaqeema 17. Thumma laatiyannahum min bayni aydeehim wamin khalfihim waAAan aymanihim waAAan shama-ilihim wala tajidu aktharahum shakireena

Tafsir Ibn Kathir:

Allah said that after He gave respite to Shaytan,

(till the Day they are raised up (resurrected)) and Iblis was sure that he got what he wanted, he went on in defiance and rebellion. He said,

("Because You have `Aghwaytani', surely, I will sit in wait against them (human beings) on Your straight path.") meaning, as You have sent me astray. Ibn `Abbas said that `Aghwaytani' means, "Misguided me." Others said, "As You caused my ruin, I will sit in wait for Your servants whom You will create from the offspring of the one you expelled me for." He went on,

(Your straight path), the path of truth and the way of safety. I (Iblis) will misguide them from this path so that they do not worship You Alone, because You sent me astray. Mujahid said that the `straight path', refers to the truth. Imam Ahmad recorded that Saburah bin Abi Al-Fakih said that he heard the Messenger of Allah saying,

«إِنَّ الشَّيْطَانَ قَعَدَ لِابْنِ آدَمَ بِطُرُقِهِ، فَقَعَدَ لَهُ بِطَرِيقِ الْإِسْلَامِ، فَقَالَ: أَتُسْلِمُ وَتَذَرُ دِينَكَ وَدِينَ آبَائِكَ؟ قَالَ: فَعَصَاهُ وَأَسْلَم»

(Shaytan sat in wait for the Son of Adam in all his paths. He sat in the path of Islam, saying, `Would you embrace Islam and abandon your religion and the religion of your forefathers' However, the Son of Adam disobeyed Shaytan and embraced Islam.

‏«قَعَدَ لَهُ بِطَرِيقِ الْهِجْرَةِ فَقَالَ: أَتُهَاجِرُ وَتَدَعُ أَرْضَكَ وَسَمَاءَكَ؟ وَإِنَّمَا مَثَلُ الْمُهَاجِرِ كَالْفَرَسِ فِي الطِّوَلِ، فَعَصَاهُ وَهَاجَرَ، ثُمَّ قَعَدَ لَهُ بِطَرِيقِ الْجِهَادِ وَهُوَ جِهَادُ النَّفْسِ وَالْمَالِ، فَقَالَ: تُقَاتِلُ فَتُقْتَلُ فَتُنْكَحُ الْمَرْأَةُ وَيُقْسَمُ الْمَالُ، قَالَ: فَعَصَاهُ وَجَاهَد»

So Shaytan sat in the path of Hijrah (migration in the cause of Allah), saying, `Would you migrate and leave your land and sky' But the parable of the Muhajir is that of a horse in his stamina So, he disobeyed Shaytan and migrated. So Shaytan sat in the path of Jihad, against one's self and with his wealth, saying, `If you fight, you will be killed, your wife will be married and your wealth divided.' So he disobeyed him and performed Jihad.

‏«فَمَنْ فَعَلَ ذَلِكَ مِنْهُمْ فَمَاتَ، كَانَ حَقًّا عَلَى اللهِ أَنْ يُدْخِلَهُ الْجَنَّةَ، وَإِنْ قُتِلَ كَانَ حَقًّا عَلَى اللهِ أَنْ يُدْخِلَهُ الْجَنَّةَ، وَإِنْ غَرِقَ كَانَ حَقًّا عَلَى اللهِ أَنْ يُدْخِلَهُ الْجَنَّةَ أَوْ وَقَصَتْهُ دَابَّةٌ كَانَ حَقًّا عَلَى اللهِ أَنْ يُدْخِلَهُ الْجَنَّة»

Therefore, whoever among them (Children of Adam) does this and dies, it will be a promise from Allah that He admits him into Paradise. If he is killed, it will be a promise from Allah that He admits him into Paradise. If he drowns, it will be a promise from Allah that He admits him into Paradise. If the animal breaks his neck, it will be a promise from Allah that He admits him into Paradise.) `Ali bin Abi Talhah reported that Ibn `Abbas commented on:

(Then I will come to them from before them) Raising doubts in them concerning their Hereafter,

(and (from) behind them), making them more eager for this life,

(from their right), causing them confusion in the religion,

(and from their left) luring them to commit sins." This is meant to cover all paths of good and evil. Shaytan discourages the people from the path of good and lures them to the path of evil. Al-Hakam bin Abban said that `Ikrimah narrated from Ibn `Abbas concerning the Ayah,

Chapter 7: Al-Araf (The Heights), Verses 001-087 95

(Then I will come to them from before them and behind them, from their right and from their left,) "He did not say that he will come from above them, because the mercy descends from above." `Ali bin Abi Talhah reported that Ibn `Abbas said,

(and You will not find most of them to be thankful.) "means, those who single Him out (in worship)." When Shaytan said this, it was a guess and an assumption on his part. Yet, the truth turned out to be the same, for Allah said,

(And indeed Iblis (Shaytan) did prove true his thought about them, and they followed him, all except a group of true believers. And he had no authority over them, except that We might test him who believes in the Hereafter, from him who is in doubt about it. And your Lord is Watchful over everything.) (34:20-21). tThis is why there is a Hadith that encourages seeking refuge with Allah from the lures of Shaytan from all directions. Imam Ahmad narrated that `Abdullah bin `Umar said, "The Messenger of Allah used to often recite this supplication in the morning and when the night falls,

»اللَّهُمَّ إِنِّي أَسْأَلُكَ الْعَافِيَةَ فِي الدُّنْيَا وَالْآخِرَةِ، اللَّهُمَّ إِنِّي أَسْأَلُكَ الْعَفْوَ وَالْعَافِيَةَ فِي دِينِي وَدُنْيَايَ وَأَهْلِي وَمَالِي، اللَّهُمَّ اسْتُرْ عَوْرَاتِي وَآمِنْ رَوْعَاتِي، اللَّهُمَّ احْفَظْنِي مِنْ بَيْنِ يَدَيَّ وَمِنْ خَلْفِي وَعَنْ يَمِينِي وَعَنْ شِمَالِي وَمِنْ فَوْقِي وَأَعُوذُ بِعَظَمَتِكَ أَنْ أُغْتَالَ مِنْ تَحْتِي«

(O Allah! I ask You for well-being in this life and the Hereafter. O Allah! I ask You for pardon and well-being in my religion, life, family and wealth. O Allah! Cover my errors and reassure me in times of difficulty. O Allah! Protect me from before me, from behind me, from my right, from my left and from above me. I seek refuge with Your greatness from being killed from below me.)" Waki` commented (about being killed from below), "This refers to earthquakes." Abu Dawud, An-Nasa'i, Ibn Majah, Ibn Hibban and Al-Hakim collected this Hadith, and Al-Hakim said, "Its chain is Sahih."

Surah: 7 Ayah: 18

﴿ قَالَ اخْرُجْ مِنْهَا مَذْءُومًا مَّدْحُورًا ۖ لَّمَن تَبِعَكَ مِنْهُمْ لَأَمْلَأَنَّ جَهَنَّمَ مِنكُمْ أَجْمَعِينَ ۝ ﴾

18. (Allâh) said (to Iblîs) "Get out from this (Paradise) disgraced and expelled. Whoever of them (mankind) will follow you, then surely I will fill Hell with you all."

Transliteration

18. Qala okhruj minha mathooman madhooran laman tabiAAaka minhum laamlaanna jahannama minkum ajmaAAeena

Tafsir Ibn Kathir:

Allah emphasized His cursing, expelling, banishing and turning Shaytan away from the uppermost heights, saying; Ibn Jarir said, "As for Madh'um, it is disgraced." And he said, "Madhur is the distanced, that is, he is banished and expelled." `Abdur-Rahman bin Zayd bin Aslam said, "We do not know of any who is Madh'uh and Madhmum except for one." Sufyan Ath-Thawri narrated from Abu Ishaq from At-Tamimi from Ibn `Abbas,

(Get out from this (Paradise), Madh'uman Madhura) "despised." `Ali bin Abi Talhah reported that Ibn `Abbas commented on,

(Get out from this (Paradise), Madh'uman Madhura) (7:18) "Belittled and despised", while As-Suddi commented, "Hateful and expelled." Qatadah commented, "Cursed and despised", while Mujahid said, "Expelled and banished." Ar-Rabi` bin Anas said that `Madh'um' means banished, while, `Madhura' means belittled. Allah said,

(Whoever of them (mankind) will follow you, then surely, I will fill Hell with you all.) This is similar to

((Allah) said: "Go, and whosoever of them follows you, surely, Hell will be the recompense of you (all) an ample recompense. And gradually delude those whom you can among them with your voice, make assaults on them with your cavalry and your infantry, share with them wealth and children, and make promises to them." But Shaytan promises them nothing but deceit. "Verily, My servants -- you have no authority over them. And All-Sufficient is your Lord as a Guardian.") (17:63-65)

Surah: 7 Ayah: 19, Ayah: 20 & Ayah: 21

﴿ وَيَـٰٓـَٔادَمُ ٱسْكُنْ أَنتَ وَزَوْجُكَ ٱلْجَنَّةَ فَكُلَا مِنْ حَيْثُ شِئْتُمَا وَلَا تَقْرَبَا هَـٰذِهِ ٱلشَّجَرَةَ فَتَكُونَا مِنَ ٱلظَّـٰلِمِينَ ۝ ﴾

19. "And O Adam! Dwell you and your wife in Paradise, and eat thereof as you both wish, but approach not this tree otherwise you both will be of the Zâlimûn (unjust and wrong-doers)."

﴿ فَوَسْوَسَ لَهُمَا ٱلشَّيْطَـٰنُ لِيُبْدِىَ لَهُمَا مَا وُۥرِىَ عَنْهُمَا مِن سَوْءَٰتِهِمَا وَقَالَ مَا نَهَىٰكُمَا رَبُّكُمَا عَنْ هَـٰذِهِ ٱلشَّجَرَةِ إِلَّآ أَن تَكُونَا مَلَكَيْنِ أَوْ تَكُونَا مِنَ ٱلْخَـٰلِدِينَ ۝ ﴾

20. Then Shaitân (Satan) whispered suggestions to them both in order to uncover that which was hidden from them of their private parts (before); he said: "Your Lord did not forbid you this tree save you should become angels or become of the immortals."

Chapter 7: Al-Araf (The Heights), Verses 001-087

﴿ وَقَاسَمَهُمَآ إِنِّى لَكُمَا لَمِنَ ٱلنَّـٰصِحِينَ ۝ ﴾

21. And he (Shaitân (Satan)) swore by Allâh to them both (saying): "Verily, I am one of the sincere well-wishers for you both."

Transliteration

19. Waya adamu oskun anta wazawjuka aljannata fakula min haythu shi/tuma wala taqraba hathihi alshshajarata fatakoona mina alththalimeena 20. Fawaswasa lahuma alshshaytanu liyubdiya lahuma ma wooriya AAanhuma min saw-atihima waqala ma nahakuma rabbukuma AAan hathihi alshshajarati illa an takoona malakayni aw takoona mina alkhalideena 21. Waqasamahuma innee lakuma lamina alnnasiheena

Tafsir Ibn Kathir:

Shaytan's Deceit with Adam and Hawwa' and Their eating from the Forbidden Tree

Allah states that He allowed Adam and his wife to dwell in Paradise and to eat from all of its fruits, except one tree. We have already discussed this in Surat Al-Baqarah. Thus, Shaytan envied them and plotted deceitfully, whispering and suggesting treachery. He wished to rid them of the various favors and nice clothes that they were enjoying.

(He (Shaytan) said) uttering lies and falsehood,

("Your Lord did not forbid you this tree save you should become angels...") meaning, so that you do not become angels or dwell here for eternity. Surely, if you eat from this tree, you will attain both, he said. In another Ayah,

(Shaytan whispered to him, saying: "O Adam! Shall I lead you to the Tree of Eternity and to a kingdom that will never waste away") (20:120). Here, the wording is similar, so it means, `so that you do not become angels' as in;

((Thus) does Allah make clear to you (His Law) lest you go astray.) (4:176) meaning, so that you do not go astray, and,

(And He has affixed into the earth mountains standing firm, lest it should shake with you;) (16:15) that is, so that the earth does not shake with you.

(And he Qasamahuma), swore to them both by Allah, saying,

("Verily, I am one of the sincere well-wishers for you both.") for I was here before you and thus have better knowledge of this place. It is a fact that the believer in Allah might sometimes become the victim of deceit. Qatadah commented on this Ayah, "Shaytan swore by Allah, saying, `I was created before you, and I have better knowledge than you. Therefore, follow me and I will direct you.'"

Surah: 7 Ayah: 22 & Ayah: 23

﴿ فَدَلَّىٰهُمَا بِغُرُورٍ ۚ فَلَمَّا ذَاقَا ٱلشَّجَرَةَ بَدَتْ لَهُمَا سَوْءَٰتُهُمَا وَطَفِقَا يَخْصِفَانِ عَلَيْهِمَا مِن وَرَقِ ٱلْجَنَّةِ ۖ وَنَادَىٰهُمَا رَبُّهُمَآ أَلَمْ أَنْهَكُمَا عَن تِلْكُمَا ٱلشَّجَرَةِ وَأَقُل لَّكُمَآ إِنَّ ٱلشَّيْطَٰنَ لَكُمَا عَدُوٌّ مُّبِينٌ ﴾

22. So he misled them with deception. Then when they tasted of the tree, that which was hidden from them of their shame (private parts) became manifest to them and they began to cover themselves with the leaves of Paradise (in order to cover their shame). And their Lord called out to them (saying): "Did I not forbid you that tree and tell you: Verily, Shaitân (Satan) is an open enemy unto you?"

﴿ قَالَا رَبَّنَا ظَلَمْنَآ أَنفُسَنَا وَإِن لَّمْ تَغْفِرْ لَنَا وَتَرْحَمْنَا لَنَكُونَنَّ مِنَ ٱلْخَٰسِرِينَ ﴾

23. They said: "Our Lord! We have wronged ourselves. If You forgive us not, and bestow not upon us Your Mercy, we shall certainly be of the losers."

Transliteration

22. Fadallahuma bighuroorin falamma thaqa alshshajarata badat lahuma sawatuhuma watafiqa yakhsifani AAalayhima min waraqi aljannati wanadahuma rabbuhuma alam anhakuma AAan tilkuma alshshajarati waaqul lakuma inna alshshaytana lakuma AAaduwwun mubeenun 23. Qala rabbana thalamna anfusana wa-in lam taghfir lana watarhamna lanakoonanna mina alkhasireena

Tafsir Ibn Kathir:

Ubayy bin Ka`b said, "Adam was a tall man, about the height of a palm tree, and he had thick hair on his head. When he committed the error that he committed, his private part appeared to him while before, he did not see it. So he started running in fright through Paradise, but a tree in Paradise took him by the head. He said to it, `Release me,' but it said, `No, I will not release you.' So his Lord called him, `O Adam! Do you run away from Me' He said, `O Lord! I felt ashamed before You.'" Ibn Jarir and Ibn Marduwyah collected this statement using several chains of narration from Al-Hasan from Ubayy bin Ka`b who narrated it from the Prophet . However, relating the Hadith to Ubayy is more correct. Ibn `Abbas commented on the Ayah,

(And they began to cover themselves with the leaves of Paradise.) "Using fig leaves." This statement has an authentic chain of narration leading to Ibn `Abbas. Mujahid said that they began to cover themselves with the leaves of Paradise, "Making them as a dress (or garment)." Commenting on Allah's statement,

(Stripping them of their raiment) (7:27) Wahb bin Munabbih said, "The private parts of Adam and Hawwa' had a light covering them which prevented them from seeing the private parts of each other. When they ate from the tree, their private parts appeared to them." Ibn Jarir reported this statement with an authentic chain of narration. Abdur-Razzaq reported from Qatadah, "Adam said, `O Lord! What if I repented and sought forgiveness' Allah said, `Then, I will admit you into Paradise.' As for Shaytan, he did not ask for forgiveness, but for respite. Each one of them was given what he asked for." Ad-Dahhak bin Muzahim commented,

("Our Lord! We have wronged ourselves. If You forgive us not, and bestow not upon us Your mercy, we shall certainly be of the losers.") "These are the words that Adam received from his Lord."

Surah: 7 Ayah: 24 & Ayah: 25

﴿ قَالَ ٱهْبِطُواْ بَعْضُكُمْ لِبَعْضٍ عَدُوٌّ ۖ وَلَكُمْ فِى ٱلْأَرْضِ مُسْتَقَرٌّ وَمَتَـٰعٌ إِلَىٰ حِينٍ ﴾

24. (Allâh) said: "Get down, one of you an enemy to the other (i.e. Adam, Hawwâ' (Eve), and Shaitân (Satan)) On earth will be a dwelling-place for you and an enjoyment for a time."

﴿ قَالَ فِيهَا تَحْيَوْنَ وَفِيهَا تَمُوتُونَ وَمِنْهَا تُخْرَجُونَ ﴾

25. He said: "Therein you shall live, and therein you shall die, and from it you shall be brought out (i.e. resurrected)."

Transliteration

24. Qala ihbitoo baAAdukum libaAAdin AAaduwwun walakum fee al-ardi mustaqarrun wamataAAun ila heenin   25. Qala feeha tahyawna wafeeha tamootoona waminha tukhrajoona

Tafsir Ibn Kathir:

Sending Them All Down to Earth

It was said that,

(Get down), was addressed to Adam, Hawwa', Iblis and the snake. Some scholars did not mention the snake, and Allah knows best. The enmity is primarily between Adam and Iblis, and Hawwa' follows Adam in this regard. Allah said in Surah Ta Ha,

("Get you down (from the Paradise to the earth), both of you, together...") (20:123). If the story about the snake is true, then it is a follower of Iblis. Some scholars mentioned the location on earth they were sent down, but these accounts are taken from the Israelite tales, and only Allah knows if they are true. If having known these areas was useful for the people in matters of religion or life, Allah would have mentioned them in His Book, and His Messenger would have mentioned them too. Allah's statement,

(On earth will be a dwelling place for you and an enjoyment for a time.) means, on earth you will have dwellings and known, designated, appointed terms that have been recorded by the Pen, counted by Predestination and written in the First Record.

(He (Allah) said: "Therein you shall live, and therein you shall die, and from it you shall be brought out (resurrected).") This Ayah is similar to Allah's other statement,

(Thereof (the earth) We created you, and into it We shall return you, and from it We shall bring you out once again.) (20:55). Allah states that He has made the earth a dwelling place for the Children of Adam, for the remainder of this earthly life. On it, they will live, die and be buried in their graves; and from it, they will be resurrected for the Day of Resurrection. On that Day, Allah will gather the first and last of creatures and reward or punish each according to his or her deeds.

Surah: 7 Ayah: 26

﴿ يَبَنِى ءَادَمَ قَدْ أَنزَلْنَا عَلَيْكُمْ لِبَاسًا يُوَارِى سَوْءَٰتِكُمْ وَرِيشًا ۖ وَلِبَاسُ ٱلتَّقْوَىٰ ذَٰلِكَ خَيْرٌ ۚ ذَٰلِكَ مِنْ ءَايَٰتِ ٱللَّهِ لَعَلَّهُمْ يَذَّكَّرُونَ ﴾

26. O Children of Adam! We have bestowed raiment upon you to cover yourselves (screen your private parts) and as an adornment; and the raiment of righteousness, that is better. Such are among the Ayât (proofs, evidences, verses, lessons, signs, revelations, etc.) of Allâh, that they may remember (i.e. leave falsehood and follow truth).

Transliteration

26. Ya banee adama qad anzalna AAalaykum libasan yuwaree saw-atikum wareeshan walibasu alttaqwa thalika khayrun thalika min ayati Allahi laAAallahum yaththakkaroona

Tafsir Ibn Kathir:

Bestowing Raiment and Adornment on Mankind

Allah reminds His servants that He has given them Libas and Rish. Libas refers to the clothes that are used to cover the private parts, while Rish refers to the outer adornments used for purposes of beautification. Therefore, the first type is essential while the second type is complimentary. Ibn Jarir said that Rish includes furniture and outer clothes. `Abdur-Rahman bin Zayd bin Aslam commented on the Ayah,

(and the Libas (raiment) of Taqwa...) "When one fears Allah, Allah covers his errors. Hence the `Libas of Taqwa' (that the Ayah mentions)."

Surah: 7 Ayah: 27

﴿ يَـٰبَنِىٓ ءَادَمَ لَا يَفْتِنَنَّكُمُ ٱلشَّيْطَـٰنُ كَمَآ أَخْرَجَ أَبَوَيْكُم مِّنَ ٱلْجَنَّةِ يَنزِعُ عَنْهُمَا لِبَاسَهُمَا لِيُرِيَهُمَا سَوْءَٰتِهِمَآ إِنَّهُۥ يَرَىٰكُمْ هُوَ وَقَبِيلُهُۥ مِنْ حَيْثُ لَا تَرَوْنَهُمْ إِنَّا جَعَلْنَا ٱلشَّيَـٰطِينَ أَوْلِيَآءَ لِلَّذِينَ لَا يُؤْمِنُونَ ۝ ﴾

27. O Children of Adam! Let not Shaitân (Satan) deceive you, as he got your parents (adam and Hawwâ' (Eve)) out of Paradise, stripping them of their raiments, to show them their private parts. Verily, he and Qabîluhu (his soldiers from the jinn or his tribe) see you from where you cannot see them. Verily, We made the Shayâtîn (devils) Auliyâ' (protectors and helpers) for those who believe not.

Transliteration

27. Ya banee adama la yaftinannakumu alshshaytanu kama akhraja abawaykum mina aljannati yanziAAu AAanhuma libasahuma liyuriyahuma saw-atihima innahu yarakum huwa waqabeeluhu min haythu la tarawnahum inna jaAAalna alshshayateena awliyaa lillatheena la yu/minoona

Tafsir Ibn Kathir:

Warning against the Lures of Shaytan

Allah warns the Children of Adam against Iblis and his followers, by explaining about his ancient enmity for the father of mankind, Adam peace be upon him. Iblis plotted to have Adam expelled from Paradise, which is the dwelling of comfort, to the dwelling of hardship and fatigue (this life) and caused him to have his private part uncovered, after it had been hidden from him. This, indeed, is indicative of deep hatred (from Shaytan towards Adam and mankind). Allah said in a similar Ayah,

(Will you then take him (Iblis) and his offspring as protectors and helpers rather than Me, while they are enemies to you What an evil is the exchange for the wrongdoers.) (18:50).

Surah: 7 Ayah: 28, Ayah: 29 & Ayah: 30

﴿ وَإِذَا فَعَلُوا۟ فَـٰحِشَةً قَالُوا۟ وَجَدْنَا عَلَيْهَآ ءَابَآءَنَا وَٱللَّهُ أَمَرَنَا بِهَا قُلْ إِنَّ ٱللَّهَ لَا يَأْمُرُ بِٱلْفَحْشَآءِ أَتَقُولُونَ عَلَى ٱللَّهِ مَا لَا تَعْلَمُونَ ۝ ﴾

28. And when they commit a Fâhisha (evil deed, going round the Ka'bah in naked state, and every kind of unlawful sexual intercourse), they say: "We found our fathers doing it, and Allâh has commanded us on it." Say: "Nay, Allâh never commands of Fâhisha. Do you say of Allâh what you know not?

$$\text{﴿ قُلْ أَمَرَ رَبِّى بِالْقِسْطِ وَأَقِيمُواْ وُجُوهَكُمْ عِندَ كُلِّ مَسْجِدٍ وَادْعُوهُ مُخْلِصِينَ لَهُ الدِّينَ كَمَا بَدَأَكُمْ تَعُودُونَ ۝ ﴾}$$

29. Say (O Muhammad (peace be upon him)) My Lord has commanded justice and (said) that you should face Him only (i.e. worship none but Allâh and face the Qiblah, i.e. the Ka'bah at Makkah during prayers) in every place of worship, in prayers (and not to face other false deities and idols), and invoke Him only making your religion sincere to Him (by not joining in worship any partner with Him and with the intention that you are doing your deeds for Allâh's sake only). As He brought you (into being) in the beginning, so shall you be brought into being (on the Day of Resurrection in two groups, one as a blessed one (believers), and the other as a wretched one (disbelievers))

$$\text{﴿ فَرِيقًا هَدَى وَفَرِيقًا حَقَّ عَلَيْهِمُ الضَّلَلَةُ إِنَّهُمُ اتَّخَذُواْ الشَّيَطِينَ أَوْلِيَآءَ مِن دُونِ اللَّهِ وَيَحْسَبُونَ أَنَّهُم مُّهْتَدُونَ ۝ ﴾}$$

30. A group He has guided, and a group deserved to be in error; (because) surely they took the Shayâtîn (devils) as Auliyâ' (protectors and helpers) instead of Allâh, and think that they are guided.

Transliteration

28. Wa-itha faAAaloo fahishatan qaloo wajadna AAalayha abaana waAllahu amarana biha qul inna Allaha la ya/muru bialfahsha-i ataqooloona AAala Allahi ma la taAAlamoona 29. Qul amara rabbee bialqisti waaqeemoo wujoohakum AAinda kulli masjidin waodAAoohu mukhliseena lahu alddeena kama badaakum taAAoodoona 30. Fareeqan hada wafareeqan haqqa AAalayhimu alddalalatu innahumu ittakhathoo alshshayateena awliyaa min dooni Allahi wayahsaboona annahum muhtadoona

Tafsir Ibn Kathir:

Disbelievers commit Sins and claim that Allah commanded Them to do so!

Mujahid said, "The idolators used to go around the House (Ka`bah) in Tawaf while naked, saying, `We perform Tawaf as our mothers gave birth to us.' The woman would cover her sexual organ with something saying, `Today, some or all of it will appear, but whatever appears from it, I do not allow it (it is not for adultery or for men to enjoy looking at!).'" Allah sent down the Ayah,

(And when they commit a Fahishah (sin), they say: "We found our fathers doing it, and Allah has commanded it for us.")(7:28) I say, the Arabs, with the exception of the Quraysh, used to perform Tawaf naked. They claimed they would not make Tawaf while wearing the clothes that they disobeyed Allah in. As for the Quraysh, known as Al-Hums, they used to perform Tawaf in their regular clothes. Whoever among the Arabs borrowed a garment from one of Al-Hums, he would wear it while in Tawaf. And whoever wore a new garment, would discard it and none would wear it after him on completion of Tawaf. Those who did not have a new garment, or were not given one by Al-Hums, then they would perform Tawaf while naked. Even women would go around in Tawaf while naked, and one of them would cover her sexual organ with something and proclaim, "Today, a part or all of it will appear, but whatever appears from it I do not allow it." Women used to perform Tawaf while naked usually at night. This was a practice that the idolators invented on their own, following only their forefathers in this regard. They falsely claimed that what their forefathers did was in fact following the order and legislation of Allah. Allah then refuted them, Allah said,

(And when they commit a Fahishah, they say: "We found our fathers doing it, and Allah has commanded it for us.")

Allah does not order Fahsha', but orders Justice and Sincerity

Allah replied to this false claim,

(Say), O Muhammad, to those who claimed this,

("Nay, Allah never commands Fahsha'...") meaning, the practice you indulge in is a despicable sin, and Allah does not command such a thing.

("Do you say about Allah what you know not") that is, do you attribute to Allah statements that you are not certain are true Allah said next,

(Say: "My Lord has commanded justice, (fairness and honesty)"),

("And that you should face Him only, in every Masjid, and invoke Him only making your religion sincere to Him...") This Ayah means, Allah commands you to be straightforward in worshipping Him, by following the Messengers who were supported with miracles and obeying what they conveyed from Allah and the Law that they brought. He also commands sincerity in worshipping Him, for He, Exalted He is, does not accept a good deed until it satisfies these two conditions: being correct and in conformity with His Law, and being free of Shirk.

The Meaning of being brought into Being in the Beginning and brought back again

Allah's saying

(As He brought you in the beginning, so shall you be brought into being again) (7:29). Until;

(error.) There is some difference over the meaning of:

(As He brought you in the beginning, so shall you be brought into being again.) Ibn Abi Najih said that Mujahid said that it means, "He will bring you back to life after you die." Al-Hasan Al-Basri commented, "As He made you begin in this life, He will bring you back to life on the Day of Resurrection." Qatadah commented on:

(As He brought you in the beginning, so shall you be brought into being again.) "He started their creation after they were nothing, and they perished later on, and He shall bring them back again." `Abdur-Rahman bin Zayd bin Aslam said, "As He created you in the beginning, He will bring you back in the end." This last explanation was preferred by Abu Ja`far Ibn Jarir and he supported it with what he reported from Ibn `Abbas, "The Messenger of Allah stood up and gave us a speech, saying,

«يَا أَيُّهَا النَّاسُ إِنَّكُمْ تُحْشَرُونَ إِلَى اللهِ حُفَاةً عُرَاةً غُرْلًا

(كَمَا بَدَأْنَا أَوَّلَ خَلْقٍ نُعِيدُهُ وَعْداً عَلَيْنَا إِنَّا كُنَّا فَعِلِينَ)»

(O people! You will be gathered to Allah while barefooted, naked and uncircumcised, (As We began the first creation, We shall repeat it. (It is) a promise binding upon Us. Truly, We shall do it)).(21:104) This Hadith was collected in the Two Sahihs. `Ali bin Abi Talhah reported that Ibn `Abbas commented on the Ayah,

(As He brought you in the beginning, so shall you be brought into being again. A group He has guided, and a group deserved to be in error;) "Allah, the Exalted, began the creation of the Sons of Adam, some believers and some disbelievers, just as He said,

(He it is Who created you, then some of you are disbelievers and some of you are believers) (64:2). He will then return them on the Day of Resurrection as He started them, some believers and some disbelievers. I say, what supports this meaning, is the Hadith from Ibn Mas`ud that Al-Bukhari recorded, (that the Prophet said:)

«فَوَالَّذِي لَا إِلَهَ غَيْرُهُ إِنَّ أَحَدَكُمْ لَيَعْمَلُ بِعَمَلِ أَهْلِ الْجَنَّةِ حَتَّى مَا يَكُونُ بَيْنَهُ وَبَيْنَهَا إِلَّا بَاعٌ أَوْ ذِرَاعٌ، فَيَسْبِقُ عَلَيْهِ الْكِتَابُ فَيَعْمَلُ بِعَمَلِ أَهْلِ النَّارِ فَيَدْخُلُهَا، وَإِنَّ أَحَدَكُمْ لَيَعْمَلُ بِعَمَلِ أَهْلِ النَّارِ حَتَّى مَا يَكُونُ بَيْنَهُ وَبَيْنَهَا إِلَّا بَاعٌ أَوْ ذِرَاعٌ فَيَسْبِقُ عَلَيْهِ الْكِتَابُ، فَيَعْمَلُ بِعَمَلِ أَهْلِ الْجَنَّةِ فَيَدْخُلُ الْجَنَّةَ»

(By He, other than Whom there is no god, one of you might perform the deeds of the people of Paradise until only the length of an arm or a forearm would separate him from it. However, that which was written in the Book takes precedence, and he commits the work of the people of the Fire and thus enters it. And one of you might perform the deeds of the people of the Fire until only the length of an arm or a forearm separates between him and the Fire. However, that which was written in the Book takes precedence, and he performs the work of the people of Paradise and thus enters Paradise.) We should combine this meaning -- if it is held to be the correct meaning for the Ayah -- with Allah's statement:

(So set you your face towards the religion, Hanifan. Allah's Fitrah with which He has created mankind) (30:30), and what is recorded in the Two Sahihs from Abu Hurayrah who said that the Messenger of Allah said:

»كُلُّ مَوْلُودٍ يُولَدُ عَلَى الْفِطْرَةِ، فَأَبَوَاهُ يُهَوِّدَانِهِ وَيُنَصِّرَانِهِ وَيُمَجِّسَانِهِ«

(Every child is born upon the Fitrah, it is only his parents who turn him into a Jew, a Christian or a Zoroastrian.) Muslim recorded that `Iyad bin Himar said that the Messenger of Allah said,

»يَقُولُ اللهُ تَعَالَى: إِنِّي خَلَقْتُ عِبَادِي حُنَفَاءَ، فَجَاءَتْهُمُ الشَّيَاطِينُ فَاجْتَالَتْهُمْ عَنْ دِينِهِم«

(Allah said, `I created My servants Hunafa' (monotheists), but the devils came to them and deviated them from their religion.) The collective meaning here is, Allah created His creatures so that some of them later turn believers and some turn disbelievers. Allah has originally created all of His servants able to recognize Him, to single Him out in worship, and know that there is no deity worthy of worship except Him. He also took their covenant to fulfill the implications of this knowledge, which He placed in their consciousness and souls. He has decided that some of them will be miserable and some will be happy,

(He it is Who created you, then some of you are disbelievers and some of you are believers) (64:2). Also, a Hadith states,

»كُلُّ النَّاسِ يَغْدُو فَبَائِعٌ نَفْسَهُ فَمُعْتِقُهَا أَوْ مُوبِقُهَا«

(All people go out in the morning and sell themselves, and some of them free themselves while some others destroy themselves.) Allah's decree will certainly come to pass in His creation. Verily, He it is

(Who has measured (everything); and then guided) (87:3), and,

(He Who gave to each thing its form and nature, then guided it aright) (20:50). And in the Two Sahihs:

»فَأَمَّا مَنْ كَانَ مِنْكُمْ مِنْ أَهْلِ السَّعَادَةِ فَسَيُيَسَّرُ لِعَمَلِ أَهْلِ السَّعَادَةِ، وَأَمَّا مَنْ كَانَ مِنْ أَهْلِ الشَّقَاوَةِ فَسَيُيَسَّرُ لِعَمَلِ أَهْلِ الشَّقَاوَةِ«

(As for those among you who are among the people of happiness, they will be facilitated to perform the deeds of the people of happiness. As for those who are among the miserable, they will be facilitated to commit the deeds of the miserable). This is why Allah said here,

(A group He has guided, and a group deserved to be in error;) Allah then explained why,

(because) surely, they took the Shayatin as supporters instead of Allah). Ibn Jarir said, "This is one of the clearest arguments proving the mistake of those who claim that Allah does not punish anyone for disobedient acts he commits of deviations he believes in until after knowledge of what is correct reaches him, then he were to obstinately avoid it anyway. If this were true, then there would be no difference between the deviations of the misguided group - their belief that they are guided - and the group that is in fact guided. Yet Allah has differentiated between the two in this noble Ayah, doing so in both name and judgement."

Surah: 7 Ayah: 31

﴿۞ يَـٰبَنِىٓ ءَادَمَ خُذُواْ زِينَتَكُمْ عِندَ كُلِّ مَسْجِدٍ وَكُلُواْ وَٱشْرَبُواْ وَلَا تُسْرِفُوٓاْ إِنَّهُۥ لَا يُحِبُّ ٱلْمُسْرِفِينَ ۝﴾

31. O Children of Adam! Take your adornment (by wearing your clean clothes), while praying and going round (the Tawâf of) the Ka'bah, and eat and drink but waste not by extravagance, certainly He (Allâh) likes not Al-Musrifûn (those who waste by extravagance).

Transliteration

31. Ya banee adama khuthoo zeenatakum AAinda kulli masjidin wakuloo waishraboo wala tusrifoo innahu la yuhibbu almusrifeena

Tafsir Ibn Kathir:

Allah commands taking Adornment when going to the Masjid

This honorable Ayah refutes the idolators' practice of performing Tawaf around the Sacred House while naked. Muslim, An-Nasa'i and Ibn Jarir, (the following wording is that of Ibn Jarir) recorded that Shu`bah said that Salamah bin Kuhayl said that Muslim Al-Batin said that Sa`id bin Jubayr said that Ibn `Abbas said, "The idolators used to go around the House while naked, both men and women, men in the day and women by night. The woman would say, "Today, a part or all of it will be unveiled, but whatever is exposed of it, I do not allow." Allah said in reply,

(Take your adornment to every Masjid,) Al-`Awfi said that Ibn `Abbas commented on:

(Take your adornment to every Masjid) o"There were people who used to perform Tawaf around the House while naked, and Allah ordered them to take adornment, meaning, wear clean, proper clothes that cover the private parts. people were commanded to wear their best clothes when performing every prayer." Mujahid, `Ata', Ibrahim An-Nakha`i, Sa`id bin Jubayr, Qatadah, As-Suddi, Ad-Dahhak and

Malik narrated a similar saying from Az-Zuhri, and from several of the Salaf. They said that this Ayah was revealed about the idolators who used to perform Tawaf around the House while naked. This Ayah (7:31), as well as the Sunnah, encourage wearing the best clothes when praying, especially for Friday and `Id prayers. It is also recommended (for men) to wear perfume for prayer, because it is adornment, and to use Siwak for it is part of what completes adornment. The best color for clothes is white, for Imam Ahmad narrated that Ibn `Abbas said that the Messenger of Allah said,

«الْبَسُوا مِنْ ثِيَابِكُمُ الْبَيَاضَ فَإِنَّهَا مِنْ خَيْرِ ثِيَابِكُمْ، وَكَفِّنُوا فِيهَا مَوْتَاكُمْ وَإِنَّ خَيْرَ أَكْحَالِكُمُ الْإِثْمُدُ فَإِنَّهُ يَجْلُو الْبَصَرَ وَيُنْبِتُ الشَّعَرَ»

(Wear white clothes, for it is among your best clothes, and also wrap your dead with it. And Ithmid (antimony) is among the best of your Kuhl, for it clears the sight and helps the hair grow.) This Hadith has a sound chain of narration, consisting of narrators who conform to the conditions and guidelines of Imam Muslim. Abu Dawud, At-Tirmidhi and Ibn Majah also recorded it, and At-Tirmidhi said, "Hasan Sahih."

Prohibiting Extravagance

Allah said,

(And eat and drink..). Al-Bukhari said that Ibn `Abbas said, "Eat what you wish and wear what you wish, as long as you avoid two things: extravagance and arrogance." Ibn Jarir said that Muhammad bin `Abdul-A`la narrated to us that Muhammad bin Thawr narrated to us from Ma`mar from Ibn Tawus from his father who said that Ibn `Abbas said, "Allah has allowed eating and drinking, as long as it does not contain extravagance or arrogance." This chain is Sahih. Imam Ahmad recorded that Al-Miqdam bin Ma`dikarib Al-Kindi said that he heard the Messenger of Allah saying,

«مَا مَلَأَ ابْنُ آدَمَ وِعَاءً شَرًّا مِنْ بَطْنِهِ بِحَسْبِ ابْنِ آدَمَ أَكَلَاتٌ يُقِمْنَ صُلْبَهُ فَإِنْ كَانَ فَاعِلًا لَا مَحَالَةَ فَثُلُثٌ طَعَامٌ وَثُلُثٌ شَرَابٌ وَثُلُثٌ لِنَفَسِهِ»

(The Son of Adam will not fill a pot worse for himself than his stomach. It is enough for the Son of Adam to eat a few bites that strengthens his spine. If he likes to have more, then let him fill a third with food, a third with drink and leave a third for his breathing.) An-Nasa'i and At-Tirmidhi collected this Hadith, At-Tirmidhi said, "Hasan" or "Hasan Sahih" according to another manuscript. `Ata' Al-Khurasani said that Ibn `Abbas commented on the Ayah,

(And eat and drink but waste not by extravagance, certainly He (Allah) likes not the wasteful.) "With food and drink." Ibn Jarir commented on Allah's statement,

(Certainly He (Allah) likes not the wasteful.) "Allah the Exalted says that He does not like those who trespass the limits on an allowed matter or a prohibited matter, those who go to the extreme over what He has allowed, allow what He has prohibited, or prohibit what He has allowed. But, He likes that what He has allowed be considered as such (without extravagance) and what He has prohibited be considered as such. This is the justice that He has commanded."

Surah: 7 Ayah: 32

﴿ قُلْ مَنْ حَرَّمَ زِينَةَ ٱللَّهِ ٱلَّتِىٓ أَخْرَجَ لِعِبَادِهِۦ وَٱلطَّيِّبَـٰتِ مِنَ ٱلرِّزْقِ قُلْ هِىَ لِلَّذِينَ ءَامَنُوا۟ فِى ٱلْحَيَوٰةِ ٱلدُّنْيَا خَالِصَةً يَوْمَ ٱلْقِيَـٰمَةِ كَذَٰلِكَ نُفَصِّلُ ٱلْـَٔايَـٰتِ لِقَوْمٍ يَعْلَمُونَ ﴾

32. Say (O Muhammad (peace be upon him)) "Who has forbidden the adoration with clothes given by Allâh, which He has produced for His slaves, and At-Taiyyibât (all kinds of Halâl (lawful) things) of food?" Say: "They are, in the life of this world, for those who believe, (and) exclusively for them (believers) on the Day of Resurrection (the disbelievers will not share them)." Thus We explain the Ayât (Islâmic laws) in detail for people who have knowledge.

Transliteration

32. Qul man harrama zeenata Allahi allatee akhraja liAAibadihi waalttayyibati mina alrrizqi qul hiya lillatheena amanoo fee alhayati alddunya khalisatan yawma alqiyamati kathalika nufassilu al-ayati liqawmin yaAAlamoona

Tafsir Ibn Kathir:

Allah refutes those who prohibit any type of food, drink or clothes according to their own understanding, without relying on what Allah has legislated,

(Say) O Muhammad, to the idolators who prohibit some things out of false opinion and fabrication,

(Who has forbidden the adornment with clothes given by Allah, which He has produced for His servants) meaning, these things were created for those who believe in Allah and worship Him in this life, even though the disbelievers share in these bounties in this life. In the Hereafter, the believers will have all this to themselves and none of the disbelievers will have a share in it, for Paradise is prohibited for the disbelievers.

Surah: 7 Ayah: 33

﴿ قُلْ إِنَّمَا حَرَّمَ رَبِّىَ ٱلْفَوَٰحِشَ مَا ظَهَرَ مِنْهَا وَمَا بَطَنَ وَٱلْإِثْمَ وَٱلْبَغْىَ بِغَيْرِ ٱلْحَقِّ وَأَن تُشْرِكُوا۟ بِٱللَّهِ مَا لَمْ يُنَزِّلْ بِهِۦ سُلْطَٰنًا وَأَن تَقُولُوا۟ عَلَى ٱللَّهِ مَا لَا تَعْلَمُونَ ۝ ﴾

33. Say (O Muhammad (peace be upon him)) "(But) the things that my Lord has indeed forbidden are Al-Fawâhish (great evil sins, every kind of unlawful sexual intercourse) whether committed openly or secretly, sins (of all kinds), unrighteous oppression, joining partners (in worship) with Allâh for which He has given no authority, and saying things about Allâh of which you have no knowledge."

Transliteration

33. Qul innama harrama rabbiya alfawahisha ma thahara minha wama batana waal-ithma waalbaghya bighayri alhaqqi waan tushrikoo biAllahi ma lam yunazzil bihi sultanan waan taqooloo AAala Allahi ma la taAAlamoona

Tafsir Ibn Kathir:

Fahishah, Sin, Transgression, Shirk and Lying about Allah are prohibited

Imam Ahmad recorded that `Abdullah said that the Messenger of Allah said,

«لَا أَحَدَ أَغْيَرُ مِنَ اللهِ فَلِذَلِكَ حَرَّمَ الْفَوَاحِشَ مَا ظَهَرَ مِنْهَا وَمَا بَطَنَ، وَلَا أَحَدَ أَحَبُّ إِلَيْهِ الْمَدْحُ مِنَ اللهِ»

(None is more jealous than Allah, and this is why He prohibited Fawahish, committed openly or in secret. And none likes praise more than Allah). This was also recorded in the Two Sahihs. In the explanation of Surat Al-An`am, we explained the Fahishah that is committed openly and in secret. Allah said next,

(and Ithm, and transgression without right,) (7:33). As-Suddi commented, "Al-Ithm means, `disobedience'. As for unrighteous oppression, it occurs when you transgress against people without justification." Mujahid said, "Ithm includes all types of disobedience. Allah said that the oppressor commits oppression against himself." Therefore, the meaning of, Ithm is the sin that one commits against himself, while `oppression' pertains to transgression against other people, and Allah prohibited both. Allah's statement,

(and joining partners with Allah for which He has given no authority,) prohibits calling partners with Allah in worship.

(and saying things about Allah of which you have no knowledge.) such as lies and inventions, like claiming that Allah has a son, and other evil creeds that you -- O idolators -- have no knowledge of. This is similar to His saying:

(So shun the abomination (worshipping) of the idols) (22:30).

Surah: 7 Ayah: 34, Ayah: 35 & Ayah: 36

﴿ وَلِكُلِّ أُمَّةٍ أَجَلٌ فَإِذَا جَاءَ أَجَلُهُمْ لَا يَسْتَأْخِرُونَ سَاعَةً وَلَا يَسْتَقْدِمُونَ ﴾

34. And every nation has its appointed term; when their term comes, neither can they delay it nor can they advance it an hour (or a moment).

﴿ يَـٰبَنِى ءَادَمَ إِمَّا يَأْتِيَنَّكُمْ رُسُلٌ مِّنكُمْ يَقُصُّونَ عَلَيْكُمْ ءَايَـٰتِى فَمَنِ ٱتَّقَىٰ وَأَصْلَحَ فَلَا خَوْفٌ عَلَيْهِمْ وَلَا هُمْ يَحْزَنُونَ ﴾

35. O Children of Adam! If there come to you Messengers from amongst you, reciting to you, My Verses, then whosoever becomes pious and righteous, on them shall be no fear, nor shall they grieve.

﴿ وَٱلَّذِينَ كَذَّبُوا بِـَٔايَـٰتِنَا وَٱسْتَكْبَرُوا عَنْهَا أُوْلَـٰٓئِكَ أَصْحَـٰبُ ٱلنَّارِ هُمْ فِيهَا خَـٰلِدُونَ ﴾

36. But those who reject Our Ayât (proofs, evidences, verses, lessons, signs, revelations) and treat them with arrogance, they are the dwellers of the (Hell) Fire, they will abide therein forever.

Transliteration

34. Walikulli ommatin ajalun fa-itha jaa ajaluhum la yasta/khiroona saAAatan wala yastaqdimoona   35. Ya banee adama imma ya/tiyannakum rusulun minkum yaqussoona AAalaykum ayatee famani ittaqa waaslaha fala khawfun AAalayhim wala hum yahzanoona 36. Waallatheena kaththaboo bi-ayatina waistakbaroo AAanha ola-ika as-habu alnnari hum feeha khalidoona

Tafsir Ibn Kathir:

Allah said,

(And every Ummah has), meaning, each generation and nation,

(its appointed term; when their term comes) which they were destined for,

(neither can they delay it nor can they advance it an hour (or a moment)). Allah then warned the Children of Adam that He sent to them Messengers who conveyed to them His Ayat. Allah also conveyed good news, as well as warning,

(then whosoever has Taqwa and becomes righteous) by abandoning the prohibitions and performing acts of obedience,

Chapter 7: Al-Araf (The Heights), Verses 001-087   *111*

(on them shall be no fear nor shall they grieve. But those who reject Our Ayat and treat them with arrogance,) meaning, their hearts denied the Ayat and they were too arrogant to abide by them,

(they are the dwellers of the Fire, they will abide therein forever.) without end to their dwelling in it.

Surah: 7 Ayah: 37

﴿ فَمَنْ أَظْلَمُ مِمَّنِ افْتَرَىٰ عَلَى ٱللَّهِ كَذِبًا أَوْ كَذَّبَ بِـَٔايَـٰتِهِۦٓ ۚ أُو۟لَـٰٓئِكَ يَنَالُهُمْ نَصِيبُهُم مِّنَ ٱلْكِتَـٰبِ ۖ حَتَّىٰٓ إِذَا جَآءَتْهُمْ رُسُلُنَا يَتَوَفَّوْنَهُمْ قَالُوٓا۟ أَيْنَ مَا كُنتُمْ تَدْعُونَ مِن دُونِ ٱللَّهِ ۖ قَالُوا۟ ضَلُّوا۟ عَنَّا وَشَهِدُوا۟ عَلَىٰٓ أَنفُسِهِمْ أَنَّهُمْ كَانُوا۟ كَـٰفِرِينَ ﴿٣٧﴾ ﴾

37. Who is more unjust than one who invents a lie against Allâh or rejects His Ayât (proofs, evidences, verses, lessons, signs, revelations)? For such their appointed portion (good things of this worldly life and their period of stay therein) will reach them from the Book (of Decrees) until, when Our Messengers (the angel of death and his assistants) come to them to take their souls, they (the angels) will say: "Where are those whom you used to invoke and worship besides Allâh," they will reply, "They have vanished and deserted us." And they will bear witness against themselves, that they were disbelievers.

Transliteration

37. Faman athlamu mimmani iftara AAala Allahi kathiban aw kaththaba bi-ayatihi ola-ika yanaluhum naseebuhum mina alkitabi hatta itha jaat-hum rusuluna yatawaffawnahum qaloo ayna ma kuntum tadAAoona min dooni Allahi qaloo dalloo AAanna washahidoo AAala anfusihim annahum kanoo kafireena

Tafsir Ibn Kathir:

Idolators enjoy Their destined Share in This Life, but will lose Their Supporters upon Death

Allah said,

(Who is more unjust than one who invents a lie against Allah or rejects His Ayat) meaning, none is more unjust than whoever invents a lie about Allah or rejects the Ayat that He has revealed. Muhammad bin Ka`b Al-Qurazi said that,

(For such their appointed portion will reach them from the Book) refers to each person's deeds, alloted provisions and age. Similar was said by Ar-Rabi` bin Anas and `Abdur-Rahman bin Zayd bin Aslam. Allah said in similar statements,

(Verily, those who invent a lie against Allah, will never be successful. (A brief) enjoyment in this world! And then unto Us will be their return, then We shall make them taste the severest torment because they used to disbelieve.) (10:69-70) and,

(And whoever disbelieves, let not his disbelief grieve you. To Us is their return, and We shall inform them what they have done. Verily, Allah is the All-Knower of what is in the breasts (of men). We let them enjoy for a little while.) (31:23-24). Allah said next,

(until when Our messengers come to them to take their souls.) Allah states that when death comes to the idolators and the angels come to capture their souls to take them to Hellfire, the angels horrify them, saying, "Where are the so-called partners (of Allah) whom you used to call in the life of this world, invoking and worshipping them instead of Allah Call them so that they save you from what you are suffering." However, the idolators will reply,

("They have vanished and deserted us") meaning, we have lost them and thus, we do not hope in their benefit or aid,

(And they will bear witness against themselves) they will admit and proclaim against themselves,

(that they were disbelievers.)

Surah: 7 Ayah: 38 & Ayah: 39

﴿ قَالَ ٱدْخُلُواْ فِىٓ أُمَمٍ قَدْ خَلَتْ مِن قَبْلِكُم مِّنَ ٱلْجِنِّ وَٱلْإِنسِ فِى ٱلنَّارِ كُلَّمَا دَخَلَتْ أُمَّةٌ لَّعَنَتْ أُخْتَهَا حَتَّىٰٓ إِذَا ٱدَّارَكُواْ فِيهَا جَمِيعًا قَالَتْ أُخْرَىٰهُمْ لِأُولَىٰهُمْ رَبَّنَا هَـٰٓؤُلَآءِ أَضَلُّونَا فَـَٔاتِهِمْ عَذَابًا ضِعْفًا مِّنَ ٱلنَّارِ قَالَ لِكُلٍّ ضِعْفٌ وَلَـٰكِن لَّا تَعْلَمُونَ ۝ ﴾

38. (Allâh) will say: "Enter you in the company of nations who passed away before you, of men and jinn, into the Fire." Every time a new nation enters, it curses its sister nation (that went before), until they will be gathered all together in the Fire. The last of them will say to the first of them: "Our Lord! These misled us, so give them a double torment of the Fire." He will say: "For each one there is double (torment), but you know not."

﴿ وَقَالَتْ أُولَىٰهُمْ لِأُخْرَىٰهُمْ فَمَا كَانَ لَكُمْ عَلَيْنَا مِن فَضْلٍ فَذُوقُواْ ٱلْعَذَابَ بِمَا كُنتُمْ تَكْسِبُونَ ۝ ﴾

39. The first of them will say to the last of them: "You were not better than us, so taste the torment for what you used to earn."

Transliteration

38. Qala odkhuloo fee omamin qad khalat min qablikum mina aljinni waal-insi fee alnnari kullama dakhalat ommatun laAAanat okhtaha hatta itha iddarakoo feeha jameeAAan qalat okhrahum li-oolahum rabbana haola-i adalloona faatihim AAathaban

diAAfan mina alnnari qala likullin diAAfun walakin la taAAlamoona 39. Waqalat oolahum li-okhrahum fama kana lakum AAalayna min fadlin fathooqoo alAAathaba bima kuntum taksiboona

Tafsir Ibn Kathir:

People of the Fire will dispute and curse Each Other Allah mentioned what He will say to those who associate others with Him, invent lies about Him, and reject His Ayat,

(Enter you in the company of nations), who are your likes and similar to you in conduct,

(Who passed away before you) from the earlier disbelieving nations,

(Of men and Jinn, into the Fire.) Allah said next,

(Every time a new nation enters, it curses its sister nation (that went before)) Al-Khalil (Prophet Ibrahim), peace be upon him, said,

("But on the Day of Resurrection, you shall deny each other) (29:25). Also, Allah said,

(When those who were followed declare themselves innocent of those who followed (them), and they see the torment, then all their relations will be cut off from them. And those who followed will say: "If only we had one more chance to return (to the worldly life), we would declare ourselves as innocent from them as they have declared themselves as innocent from us." Thus Allah will show them their deeds as regrets for them. And they will never get out of the Fire) (2:166-167). Allah's statement,

(until they are all together in the Fire) means, they are all gathered in the Fire,

(The last of them will say to the first of them) that is, the nation of followers that enter last will say this to the first nations to enter. This is because the earlier nations were worse criminals than those who followed them, and this is why they entered the Fire first. For this reason, their followers will complain against them to Allah, because they were the ones who misguided them from the correct path, saying,

("Our Lord! These misled us, so give them a double torment of the Fire.") multiply their share of the torment. Allah said in another instance,

(On the Day when their faces will be turned over in the Fire, they will say: "Oh! Would that we had obeyed Allah and obeyed the Messenger." And they will say: "Our Lord! Verily, we obeyed our chiefs and our great ones, and they misled us from the (right) way. Our Lord! Give them a double torment.") (33:66-68). Allah said in reply,

(He will say: "For each one there is double (torment)..."), We did what you asked, and recompensed each according to their deeds.' Allah said in another Ayah,

(Those who disbelieved and hinder (men) from the path of Allah, for them We will add torment)(16:88). Furthermore, Allah said,

(And verily, they shall bear their own loads, and other loads besides their own) (29:13) and,

(And also (some thing) of the burdens of those whom they misled without knowledge) (16:25).

(The first of them will say to the last of them) meaning, the followed will say to the followers,

("You were not better than us. ..") meaning, you were led astray as we were led astray, according to As-Suddi.

("So taste the torment for what you used to earn.") Allah again described the condition of the idolators during the gathering (of Resurrection), when He said;

(And those who were arrogant will say to those who were deemed weak: "Did we keep you back from guidance after it come to you Nay, but you were criminals." Those who were deemed weak will say to those who were arrogant: "Nay, but it was your plotting by night and day, when you ordered us to disbelieve in Allah and set up rivals to Him!" And each of them (parties) will conceal their own regrets, when they behold the torment. And We shall put iron collars round the necks of those who disbelieved. Are they requited aught except what they used to do) (34:32-33)

Surah: 7 Ayah: 40 & Ayah: 41

﴿ إِنَّ ٱلَّذِينَ كَذَّبُوا۟ بِـَٔايَـٰتِنَا وَٱسْتَكْبَرُوا۟ عَنْهَا لَا تُفَتَّحُ لَهُمْ أَبْوَٰبُ ٱلسَّمَآءِ وَلَا يَدْخُلُونَ ٱلْجَنَّةَ حَتَّىٰ يَلِجَ ٱلْجَمَلُ فِى سَمِّ ٱلْخِيَاطِ ۚ وَكَذَٰلِكَ نَجْزِى ٱلْمُجْرِمِينَ ﴾

40. Verily, those who belie Our Ayât (proofs, evidences, verses, lessons, signs, revelations) and treat them with arrogance, for them the gates of heaven will not be opened, and they will not enter Paradise until the camel goes through the eye of the needle (which is impossible). Thus do We recompense the Mujrimûn (criminals, polytheists, sinners).

﴿ لَهُم مِّن جَهَنَّمَ مِهَادٌ وَمِن فَوْقِهِمْ غَوَاشٍ ۚ وَكَذَٰلِكَ نَجْزِى ٱلظَّـٰلِمِينَ ﴾

41. Theirs will be a bed of Hell (Fire), and over them coverings (of Hell-fire). Thus do We recompense the Zâlimûn (polytheists and wrong-doers).

Transliteration

40. Inna allatheena kaththaboo bi-ayatina waistakbaroo AAanha la tufattahu lahum abwabu alssama-i wala yadkhuloona aljannata hatta yalija aljamalu fee sammi alkhiyati wakathalika najzee almujrimeena 41. Lahum min jahannama mihadun wamin fawqihim ghawashin wakathalika najzee alththalimeena

Tafsir Ibn Kathir:

Doors of Heaven shall not open for Those Who deny Allah's Ayat, and They shall never enter Paradise

Allah said,

(for them the gates of the heavens will not be opened,) meaning, their good deeds and supplication will not ascend through it, according to Mujahid, Sa`id bin Jubayr and Ibn `Abbas, as Al-`Awfi and `Ali bin Abi Talhah reported from him. Ath-Thawri narrated that, Layth said that `Ata' narrated this from Ibn `Abbas. It was also said that the meaning here is that the doors of the heavens will not be opened for the disbelievers' souls, according to Ad-Dahhak who reported this from Ibn `Abbas. As-Suddi and several others mentioned this meaning. What further supports this meaning, is the report from Ibn Jarir that Al-Bara' said that the Messenger of Allah mentioned capturing the soul of the `Fajir' (wicked sinner or disbeliever), and that his or her soul will be ascended to heaven. The Prophet said,

»فَيَصْعَدُونَ بِهَا، فَلَا تَمُرُّ عَلَى مَلَإٍ مِنَ الْمَلَائِكَةِ إِلَّا قَالُوا مَا هَذِهِ الرُّوحُ الْخَبِيثَةُ؟ فَيَقُولُونَ: فُلَانٌ بِأَقْبَحِ أَسْمَائِهِ الَّتِي كَانَ يُدْعَى بِهَا فِي الدُّنْيَا، حَتَّى يَنْتَهُوا بِهَا إِلَى السَّمَاءِ فَيَسْتَفْتِحُونَ بَابَهَا لَهُ فَلَا يُفْتَحُ لَهُ«

(So they (angels) ascend it and it will not pass by a gathering of the angels, but they will ask, `who's wicked soul is this' They will reply, `The soul of so-and-so,' calling him by the worst names he was called in this life. When they reach the (lower) heaven, they will ask that its door be opened for the soul, but it will not be opened for it.) The Prophet then recited,

(لاَ تُفَتَّحُ لَهُمْ أَبْوَبُ السَّمَآءِ)

(For them the gates of heaven will not be opened). This is a part of a long Hadith which was also recorded by Abu Dawud, An-Nasa'i and Ibn Majah. Ibn Jurayj commented on the Ayah,

(for them the gates of heaven will not be opened,) "(The gates of heaven) will not be opened for their deeds or souls." This explanation combines the two meanings we gave above, and Allah knows best. Allah's statement,

(and they will not enter Paradise until the Jamal goes through the eye of the needle.) refers to the male camel. Ibn Mas`ud said it is a male camel from the she camel. In another narration it refers to the spouse of the she camel. Mujahid and `Ikrimah said that Ibn `Abbas used to recite this Ayah this way, "Until the Jummal goes through the eye of the needle", whereas `Jummal' is a thick rope. Allah's statement,

(Theirs will be Mihad from the Fire) means, beds, while;

(and over them Ghawash), means, coverings, according to Muhammad bin Ka`b Al-Qurazi. Similar was said by Ad-Dahhak bin Muzahim and As-Suddi. Allah said next,

(Thus do We recompense the wrongdoers.)

Surah: 7 Ayah: 42 & Ayah: 43

﴿ وَٱلَّذِينَ ءَامَنُواْ وَعَمِلُواْ ٱلصَّٰلِحَٰتِ لَا نُكَلِّفُ نَفْسًا إِلَّا وُسْعَهَآ أُوْلَٰٓئِكَ أَصْحَٰبُ ٱلْجَنَّةِ هُمْ فِيهَا خَٰلِدُونَ ﴾

42. But those who believed (in the Oneness of Allâh - Islâmic Monotheism), and worked righteousness - We tax not any person beyond his scope - such are the dwellers of Paradise. They will abide therein.

﴿ وَنَزَعْنَا مَا فِى صُدُورِهِم مِّنْ غِلٍّ تَجْرِى مِن تَحْتِهِمُ ٱلْأَنْهَٰرُ وَقَالُواْ ٱلْحَمْدُ لِلَّهِ ٱلَّذِى هَدَىٰنَا لِهَٰذَا وَمَا كُنَّا لِنَهْتَدِىَ لَوْلَآ أَنْ هَدَىٰنَا ٱللَّهُ لَقَدْ جَآءَتْ رُسُلُ رَبِّنَا بِٱلْحَقِّ وَنُودُوٓاْ أَن تِلْكُمُ ٱلْجَنَّةُ أُورِثْتُمُوهَا بِمَا كُنتُمْ تَعْمَلُونَ ﴾

43. And We shall remove from their breasts any (mutual) hatred or sense of injury (which they had, if at all, in the life of this world); rivers flowing under them, and they will say: "All the praises and thanks be to Allâh, Who has guided us to this, and never could we have found guidance, were it not that Allâh had guided us! Indeed, the Messengers of our Lord did come with the truth." And it will be cried out to them: "This is the Paradise which you have inherited for what you used to do."

Transliteration

42. Waallatheena amanoo waAAamiloo alssalihati la nukallifu nafsan illa wusAAaha ola-ika as-habu aljannati hum feeha khalidoona 43. WanazaAAna ma fee sudoorihim min ghillin tajree min tahtihimu al-anharu waqaloo alhamdu lillahi allathee hadana lihatha wama kunna linahtadiya lawla an hadana Allahu laqad jaat rusulu rabbina bialhaqqi wanoodoo an tilkumu aljannatu oorithtumooha bima kuntum taAAmaloona

Tafsir Ibn Kathir:

Destination of Righteous Believers

After Allah mentioned the condition of the miserable ones, He then mentioned the condition of the happy ones, saying,

(But those who believed, and worked righteousness) Their hearts have believed and they performed good deeds with their limbs and senses, as compared to those who disbelieved in the Ayat of Allah and were arrogant with them. Allah also said that embracing faith and implementing it are easy, when He said,

Chapter 7: Al-Araf (The Heights), Verses 001-087

(But those who believed, and worked righteousness -- We burden not any person beyond his scope -- such are the dwellers of Paradise. They will abide therein. And We shall remove from their breasts any Ghill;) meaning, envy and hatred. Al-Bukhari recorded that Abu Sa`id Al-Khudri said that the Messenger of Allah said,

«إِذَا خَلَصَ الْمُؤْمِنُونَ مِنَ النَّارِ حُبِسُوا عَلَى قَنْطَرَةٍ بَيْنَ الْجَنَّةِ وَالنَّارِ فَاقْتُصَّ لَهُمْ مَظَالِمُ كَانَتْ بَيْنَهُمْ فِي الدُّنْيَا حَتَّى إِذَا هُذِّبُوا وَنُقُّوا أُذِنَ لَهُمْ فِي دُخُولِ الْجَنَّةِ فَوَالَّذِي نَفْسِي بِيَدِهِ إِنَّ أَحَدَهُمْ بِمَنْزِلِهِ فِي الْجَنَّةِ أَدَلُّ مِنْهُ بِمَسْكَنِهِ كَانَ فِي الدُّنْيَا»

(After the believers are saved from entering the Fire, they will be kept in wait by a bridge between Paradise and Hellfire. Then, transgression that occurred between them in the life of this world will be judged. Until, when they are purified and cleansed, they will be given permission to enter Paradise. By He in Whose Hand is my soul! One of them will be able to find his dwelling in Paradise more so than he did in the life of this world.) As-Suddi said about Allah's statement,

(And We shall remove from their breasts any Ghill; rivers flowing under them,) "When the people of Paradise are taken to it, they will find a tree close to its door, and two springs from under the trunk of that tree. They will drink from one of them, and all hatred will be removed from their hearts, for it is the cleansing drink. They will take a bath in the other, and the brightness of delight will radiate from their faces. Ever after, they will never have messy hair or become dirty." An-Nasa'i and Ibn Marduwyah (this being his wording) recorded that Abu Hurayrah said that the Messenger of Allah said,

«كُلُّ أَهْلِ الْجَنَّةِ يَرَى مَقْعَدَهُ مِنَ النَّارِ، فَيَقُولُ: لَوْلَا أَنَّ اللهَ هَدَانِي، فَيَكُونُ لَهُ شُكْرًا، وَكُلُّ أَهْلِ النَّارِ يَرَى مَقْعَدَهُ مِنَ الْجَنَّةِ فَيَقُولُ: لَوْ أَنَّ اللهَ هَدَانِي، فَيَكُونُ لَهُ حَسْرَةً»

(Each of the people of Paradise will see his seat in the Fire and he will say, `Had not Allah guided me! And this will cause him to be grateful. Each of the people of the Fire will see his seat in Paradise, and he will say, `Might that Allah had guided me!' So it will be a cause of anguish for him.) This is why when the believers are awarded seats in Paradise that belonged to the people of the Fire, they will be told, "This is the Paradise that you inherited because of what you used to do. " This means, because of your good deeds, you earned Allah's mercy and thus entered Paradise and took your designated dwellings in it, comparable to your deeds. This is the proper meaning here, for it is recorded in the Two Sahihs that the Prophet said,

»وَاعْلَمُوا أَنَّ أَحَدَكُمْ لَنْ يُدْخِلَهُ عَمَلُهُ الجَنَّةَ«

(And know that the good deeds of one of you will not admit him into Paradise.) They said, "Not even you, O Allah's Messenger" He said,

»وَلَا أَنَا إِلَّا أَنْ يَتَغَمَّدَنِي اللهُ بِرَحْمَةٍ مِنْهُ وَفَضْلٍ«

(Not even I, unless Allah grants it to me out of His mercy and favor.)

Surah: 7 Ayah: 44 & Ayah: 45

﴿ وَنَادَىٰ أَصْحَٰبُ ٱلْجَنَّةِ أَصْحَٰبَ ٱلنَّارِ أَن قَدْ وَجَدْنَا مَا وَعَدَنَا رَبُّنَا حَقًّا فَهَلْ وَجَدتُّم مَّا وَعَدَ رَبُّكُمْ حَقًّا ۖ قَالُوا۟ نَعَمْ ۚ فَأَذَّنَ مُؤَذِّنٌۢ بَيْنَهُمْ أَن لَّعْنَةُ ٱللَّهِ عَلَى ٱلظَّٰلِمِينَ ﴿٤٤﴾

44. And the dwellers of Paradise will call out to the dwellers of the Fire (saying): "We have indeed found true what our Lord had promised us; have you also found true, what your Lord promised (warnings)?" They shall say: "Yes." Then a crier will proclaim between them: "The Curse of Allâh is on the Zâlimûn (polytheists and wrong-doers)."

﴿ ٱلَّذِينَ يَصُدُّونَ عَن سَبِيلِ ٱللَّهِ وَيَبْغُونَهَا عِوَجًا وَهُم بِٱلْءَاخِرَةِ كَٰفِرُونَ ﴿٤٥﴾

45. Those who hindered (men) from the Path of Allâh, and would seek to make it crooked, and they were disbelievers in the Hereafter.

Transliteration

44. Wanada as-habu aljannati as-haba alnnari an qad wajadna ma waAAadana rabbuna haqqan fahal wajadtum ma waAAada rabbukum haqqan qaloo naAAam faaththana mu-aththinun baynahum an laAAnatu Allahi AAala alththalimeena 45. Allatheena yasuddoona AAan sabeeli Allahi wayabghoonaha AAiwajan wahum bial-akhirati kafiroona

Tafsir Ibn Kathir:

People of Hellfire will feel Anguish upon Anguish

Allah mentioned how the people of the Fire will be addressed, chastised and admonished when they take their places in the Fire,

Chapter 7: Al-A`raf (The Heights), Verses 001-087

("We (dwellers of Paradise) have indeed found true what our Lord had promised us; have you (dwellers of Hell) also found true what your Lord promised (warned)" They shall say: "Yes.") In Surat As-Saffat, Allah mentioned the one who had a disbelieving companion,

(So he looked down and saw him in the midst of the Fire. He said: "By Allah! You have nearly ruined me. Had it not been for the grace of my Lord, I would certainly have been among those brought forth (to Hell)." (The dwellers of Paradise will say!) "Are we then not to die (any more) Except our first death, and we shall not be punished") (37:55-59). Allah will punish the disbeliever for the claims he used to utter in this life. The angels will also admonish the disbelievers, saying,

(This is the Fire which you used to belie. Is this magic or do you not see Taste you therein its heat and whether you are patient of it or impatient of it, it is all the same. You are only being requited for what you used to do) (52:14-16). The Messenger of Allah admonished the inhabitants of the well at Badr:

«يَا أَبَا جَهْلِ بْنَ هِشَامٍ وَيَا عُتْبَةَ بْنَ رَبِيعَةَ وَيَا شَيْبَةَ بْنَ رَبِيعَةَ وَسَمَّى رُؤُوسَهُمْ هَلْ وَجَدْتُمْ مَا وَعَدَ رَبُّكُمْ حَقًّا فَإِنِّي وَجَدْتُ مَا وَعَدَنِي رَبِّي حَقًّا»

(O Abu Jahl bin Hisham! O `Utbah bin Rabi`ah! O Shaybah bin Rabi`ah (and he called their leaders by name)! Have you found what your Lord promised to be true (the Fire) I certainly found what my Lord has promised me to be true (victory).) `Umar said, "O Allah's Messenger! Do you address a people who have become rotten carrion" He said,

«وَالَّذِي نَفْسِي بِيَدِهِ مَا أَنْتُمْ بِأَسْمَعَ لِمَا أَقُولُ مِنْهُمْ وَلَكِنْ لَا يَسْتَطِيعُونَ أَنْ يُجِيبُوا»

(By He in Whose Hand is my soul! You do not hear what I am saying better than they do, but they cannot reply.) Allah's statement, (Then a crier will proclaim between them) will herald and announce, (The curse of Allah is on the wrongdoers) meaning, the curse will reside with the wrongdoers. Allah then described them by saying,

(Those who hindered (men) from the path of Allah, and would seek to make it crooked) meaning, they hindered the people from following Allah's path, His Law, and what the Prophets brought. They sought to make Allah's path appear crooked and winding, so that no one would follow it. Allah said,

(and they were disbelievers in the Hereafter) They disbelieved in the Meeting with Allah in the Hereafter, They used to deny this will ever occur, not accepting it nor believing in it. This is why they used to discount the seriousness of the evil deeds and statements that they committed, because they did not fear any reckoning or punishment. Therefore, they were and are indeed the worst people in statement and action.

Surah: 7 Ayah: 46 & Ayah: 47

﴿ وَبَيْنَهُمَا حِجَابٌ وَعَلَى ٱلْأَعْرَافِ رِجَالٌ يَعْرِفُونَ كُلاًّ بِسِيمَـٰهُمْ وَنَادَوْاْ أَصْحَـٰبَ ٱلْجَنَّةِ أَن سَلَـٰمٌ عَلَيْكُمْ لَمْ يَدْخُلُوهَا وَهُمْ يَطْمَعُونَ ۝ ﴾

46. And between them will be a barrier screen and on Al-A'râf (a wall with elevated places) will be men (whose good and evil deeds would be equal in scale), who would recognize all (of the Paradise and Hell people), by their marks (the dwellers of Paradise by their white faces and the dwellers of Hell by their black faces), they will call out to the dwellers of Paradise, "Salâmun 'Alaikûm" (peace be on you), and at that time they (men on Al-A'râf) will not yet have entered it (Paradise), but they will hope to enter (it) with certainty.

﴿ ۞ وَإِذَا صُرِفَتْ أَبْصَـٰرُهُمْ تِلْقَآءَ أَصْحَـٰبِ ٱلنَّارِ قَالُواْ رَبَّنَا لَا تَجْعَلْنَا مَعَ ٱلْقَوْمِ ٱلظَّـٰلِمِينَ ۝ ﴾

47. And when their eyes will be turned towards the dwellers of the Fire, they will say: "Our Lord! Place us not with the people who are Zâlimûn (polytheists and wrong-doers)."

Transliteration

46. Wabaynahuma hijabun waAAala al-aAArafi rijalun yaAArifoona kullan biseemahum wanadaw as-haba aljannati an salamun AAalaykum lam yadkhulooha wahum yatmaAAoona 47. Wa-itha surifat absaruhum tilqaa as-habi alnnari qaloo rabbana la tajAAalna maAAa alqawmi alththalimeena

Tafsir Ibn Kathir:

The People of Al-A`raf

After Allah mentioned that the people of Paradise will address the people of the Fire, He stated that there is a barrier between Paradise and the Fire, which prevents the people of the Fire from reaching Paradise. Ibn Jarir said, "It is the wall that Allah described,

(So a wall will be put up between them, with a gate therein. Inside it will be mercy, and outside it will be torment.) (57:13) It is also about Al-A`raf that Allah said,

(and on Al-A`raf will be men)." Ibn Jarir recorded that As-Suddi said about Allah's statement,

(And between them will be a screen) "It is the wall, it is Al-A`raf." Mujahid said, "Al-A`raf is a barrier between Paradise and the Fire, a wall that has a gate." Ibn Jarir said, "Al-A`raf is plural for `Urf, where every elevated piece of land is known as `Urf to the Arabs." As-Suddi said, "Al-A`raf is so named because its residents recognize (Ya`rifun) the people. Al-A`raf's residents are those whose good and bad deeds are equal, as Hudhayfah, Ibn `Abbas, Ibn Mas`ud and several of the Salaf and later generations said." Ibn Jarir recorded that Hudhayfah was asked about the people of Al-A`raf and he said, "A people whose good and bad deeds are equal. Their evil deeds prevented them from qualifying to enter Paradise, and their good deeds qualified them to avoid the Fire. Therefore, they are stopped there on the wall until Allah judges them." Ma`mar said that Al-Hasan recited this Ayah,

(and at that time they will not yet have entered it (Paradise), but they will hope to enter (it).) Then he said, "By Allah! Allah did not put this hope in their hearts, except for an honor that He intends to bestow on them." Qatadah said; "Those who hope are those among you whom Allah informed of their places." Allah said next,

(And when their eyes will be turned towards the dwellers of the Fire, they will say: "Our Lord! Place us not with the people who are wrongdoers.") Ad-Dahhak reported that Ibn `Abbas said, "When the people of Al-A`raf look at the people of the Fire and recognize them, they will supplicate, `O Lord! Do not place us with the people who are wrongdoers.'"

Surah: 7 Ayah: 48 & Ayah: 49

﴿ وَنَادَىٰ أَصْحَـٰبُ ٱلْأَعْرَافِ رِجَالًا يَعْرِفُونَهُم بِسِيمَـٰهُمْ قَالُوا۟ مَآ أَغْنَىٰ عَنكُمْ جَمْعُكُمْ وَمَا كُنتُمْ تَسْتَكْبِرُونَ ﴿٤٨﴾ ﴾

48. And the men on Al-A'râf (the wall) will call unto the men whom they would recognize by their marks, saying: "Of what benefit to you were your great numbers (and hoards of wealth), and your arrogance against Faith?"

﴿ أَهَـٰٓؤُلَآءِ ٱلَّذِينَ أَقْسَمْتُمْ لَا يَنَالُهُمُ ٱللَّهُ بِرَحْمَةٍ ٱدْخُلُوا۟ ٱلْجَنَّةَ لَا خَوْفٌ عَلَيْكُمْ وَلَآ أَنتُمْ تَحْزَنُونَ ﴿٤٩﴾ ﴾

49. Are they those, of whom you swore that Allâh would never show them mercy. (Behold! It has been said to them): "Enter Paradise, no fear shall be on you, nor shall you grieve."

Transliteration

48. Wanada as-habu al-aAArafi rijalan yaAArifoonahum biseemahum qaloo ma aghna AAankum jamAAukum wama kuntum tastakbiroona 49. Ahaola-i allatheena aqsamtum la yanaluhumu Allahu birahmatin odkhuloo aljannata la khawfun AAalaykum wala antum tahzanoona

Tafsir Ibn Kathir:

Allah states that the people of Al-A`raf will admonish some of the chiefs of the idolators whom they recognize by their marks in the Fire, saying,

("Of what benefit to you was your gathering...") meaning, your great numbers,

("...and your arrogance") This Ayah means, your great numbers and wealth did not save you from Allah's torment. Rather, you are dwelling in His torment and punishment. `Ali bin Abi Talhah reported from Ibn `Abbas,

(Are they those, of whom you swore that Allah would never show them mercy) refers to the people of Al-A`raf who will be told when Allah decrees:

((Behold! It has been said to them): "Enter Paradise, no fear shall be on you, nor shall you grieve.")

Surah: 7 Ayah: 50 & Ayah: 51

﴿ وَنَادَىٰ أَصْحَٰبُ ٱلنَّارِ أَصْحَٰبَ ٱلْجَنَّةِ أَنْ أَفِيضُوا۟ عَلَيْنَا مِنَ ٱلْمَآءِ أَوْ مِمَّا رَزَقَكُمُ ٱللَّهُ قَالُوٓا۟ إِنَّ ٱللَّهَ حَرَّمَهُمَا عَلَى ٱلْكَٰفِرِينَ ﴾

50. And the dwellers of the Fire will call to the dwellers of Paradise: "Pour on us some water or anything that Allâh has provided you with." They will say: "Both (water and provision) Allâh has forbidden to the disbelievers."

﴿ ٱلَّذِينَ ٱتَّخَذُوا۟ دِينَهُمْ لَهْوًا وَلَعِبًا وَغَرَّتْهُمُ ٱلْحَيَوٰةُ ٱلدُّنْيَا ۚ فَٱلْيَوْمَ نَنسَىٰهُمْ كَمَا نَسُوا۟ لِقَآءَ يَوْمِهِمْ هَٰذَا وَمَا كَانُوا۟ بِـَٔايَٰتِنَا يَجْحَدُونَ ﴾

51. "Who took their religion as an amusement and play, and the life of the world deceived them." So this Day We shall forget them as they forgot their meeting of this Day, and as they used to reject Our Ayât (proofs, evidences, verses, lessons, signs, revelations).

Transliteration

50. Wanada as-habu alnari as-haba aljannati an afeedoo AAalayna mina alma-i aw mimma razaqakumu Allahu qaloo inna Allaha harramahuma AAala alkafireena 51. Allatheena ittakhathoo deenahum lahwan walaAAiban wagharrat-humu alhayatu alddunya faalyawma nansahum kama nasoo liqaa yawmihim hatha wama kanoo bi-ayatina yajhadoona

Tafsir Ibn Kathir:

The Favors of paradise are Prohibited for the People of the Fire

Allah emphasizes the disgrace of the people of the Fire. They will ask the people of Paradise for some of their drink and food, but they will not be given any of that. As-Suddi said,

(And the dwellers of the Fire will call to the dwellers of Paradise: "Pour on us some water or anything that Allah has provided you with.") "That is food". Ath-Thawri said that `Uthman Ath-Thaqafi said that Sa`id bin Jubayr commented on this Ayah, "One of them will call his father or brother, 'I have been burned, so pour some water on me.' The believers will be asked to reply, and they will reply,

("Both Allah has forbidden to the disbelievers.")" `Abdur-Rahman bin Zayd bin Aslam said that,

("Both Allah has forbidden to the disbelievers.") "Refers to the food and drink of Paradise." Allah describes the disbelievers by what they used to do in this life, taking the religion as amusement and play, and being deceived by this life and its adornment, rather than working for the Hereafter as Allah commanded,

(So this Day We shall forget them as they forgot their meeting of this Day) meaning, Allah will treat them as if He has forgotten them. Certainly, nothing escapes Allah's perfect watch and He never forgets anything. Allah said in another Ayah,

(In a Record. My Lord neither errs nor forgets) (20:52) Allah said -- that He will forget them on that Day -- as just recompense for them, because,

(They have forgotten Allah, so He has forgotten them) (9:67)

(Like this: Our Ayat came unto you, but you disregarded them, and so this Day, you will be neglected) (20:126) and,

(And it will be said: "This Day We will forget you as you forgot the meeting of this Day of yours.") (45:34) Al-`Awfi reported that Ibn `Abbas commented on,

(So this Day We shall forget them as they forgot their meeting of this Day) "Allah will forget the good about them, but not their evil." And `Ali bin Abi Talhah reported that Ibn `Abbas said, "We shall forsake them as they have forsaken the meeting of this Day of theirs." Mujahid said, "We shall leave them in the Fire." As-Suddi said, "We shall leave them from any mercy, just as they left any action on behalf of the meeting on this Day of theirs." It is recorded in the Sahih that Allah will say to the servant on the Day of Resurrection:

«أَلَمْ أُزَوِّجْكَ؟ أَلَمْ أُكْرِمْكَ؟ أَلَمْ أُسَخِّرْ لَكَ الْخَيْلَ وَالْإِبِلَ وَأَذَرْكَ تَرْأَسُ وَتَرْبَعُ؟ فَيَقُولُ: بَلَى، فَيَقُولُ: أَظَنَنْتَ أَنَّكَ مُلَاقِيَّ؟ فَيَقُولُ: لَا، فَيَقُولُ اللهُ تَعَالَى: فَالْيَوْمَ أَنْسَاكَ كَمَا نَسِيتَنِي»

("Have I not gotten you married Have I not honored you Have I not made horses and camels subservient for you and allowed you to become a leader and a master" He will say, "Yes." Allah will say, "Did you think that you will meet Me" He will say, "No." Allah the Exalted will say, `Then this Day, I will forget you as you have forgotten Me.")

Surah: 7 Ayah: 52 & Ayah: 53

﴿ وَلَقَدْ جِئْنَـٰهُم بِكِتَـٰبٍ فَصَّلْنَـٰهُ عَلَىٰ عِلْمٍ هُدًى وَرَحْمَةً لِّقَوْمٍ يُؤْمِنُونَ ۝ ﴾

52. Certainly, We have brought them a Book (the Qur'ân) which We have explained in detail with knowledge, - a guidance and a mercy to a people who believe.

﴿ هَلْ يَنظُرُونَ إِلَّا تَأْوِيلَهُ ۚ يَوْمَ يَأْتِى تَأْوِيلُهُ يَقُولُ ٱلَّذِينَ نَسُوهُ مِن قَبْلُ قَدْ جَآءَتْ رُسُلُ رَبِّنَا بِٱلْحَقِّ فَهَل لَّنَا مِن شُفَعَآءَ فَيَشْفَعُوا لَنَآ أَوْ نُرَدُّ فَنَعْمَلَ غَيْرَ ٱلَّذِى كُنَّا نَعْمَلُ ۚ قَدْ خَسِرُوٓا أَنفُسَهُمْ وَضَلَّ عَنْهُم مَّا كَانُوا۟ يَفْتَرُونَ ۝ ﴾

53. Await they just for the final fulfillment of the event? On the Day the event is finally fulfilled (i.e. the Day of Resurrection), those who neglected it before will say: "Verily, the Messengers of our Lord did come with the truth, now are there any intercessors for us that they might intercede on our behalf? Or could we be sent back (to the first life of the world) so that we might do (good) deeds other than those (evil) deeds which we used to do?" Verily, they have lost their own selves (i.e. destroyed themselves) and that which they used to fabricate (invoking and worshipping others besides Allâh) has gone away from them.

Transliteration

52. Walaqad ji/nahum bikitabin fassalnahu AAala AAilmin hudan warahmatan liqawmin yu/minoona 53. Hal yanthuroona illa ta/weelahu yawma ya/tee ta/weeluhu yaqoolu allatheena nasoohu min qablu qad jaat rusulu rabbina bialhaqqi fahal lana min shufaAAaa fayashfaAAoo lana aw nuraddu fanaAAmala ghayra allathee kunna naAAmalu qad khasiroo anfusahum wadalla AAanhum ma kanoo yaftaroona

Tafsir Ibn Kathir:

The Idolators have no Excuse

Allah states that He has left no excuse for the idolators, for He has sent to them the Book that the Messenger came with, and which is explained in detail,

((This is) a Book, the Ayat whereof are perfected (in every sphere of knowledge), and then explained in detail) (11:1) Allah said next,

(We have explained in detail with knowledge) meaning, `We have perfect knowledge of what We explained in it'. Allah said in another Ayah,

(He has sent it down with His Knowledge,) (4:166) The meaning here is that after Allah mentioned the loss the idolators end up with in the Hereafter, He stated that He has indeed sent Prophets and revealed Books in this life, thus leaving no excuse for them. Allah also said;

(And We never punish until We have sent a Messenger (to give warning).) (17:15) This is why Allah said here,

(Await they just for the final fulfillment of the event) in reference to what they were promised of torment, punishment, the Fire; or Paradise, according to Mujahid and several others.

(On the Day the event is finally fulfilled,) on the Day of Resurrection, according to Ibn `Abbas,

(those who neglected it before will say) those who ignored it in this life and neglected abiding by its implications will say,

("Verily, the Messengers of our Lord did come with the truth, now are there any intercessors for us that they might intercede on our behalf") so that we are saved from what we ended up in.

("Or could we be sent back"), to the first life,

("So that we might do (good) deeds other than those (evil) deeds which we used to do"). This part of the Ayah is similar to Allah's statement,

(If you could but see when they will be held over the (Hell) Fire! They will say: "Would that we were but sent back! Then we would not deny the Ayat of our Lord, and we would be of the believers!" Nay, it has become manifest to them what they had been concealing before. But if they were returned (to the world), they would certainly revert to that which they were forbidden. And indeed they are liars) (6:27-28) Allah said here,

(Verily, they have lost themselves and that which they used to fabricate has gone away from them.) meaning, they destroyed themselves by entering the Fire for eternity,

(And that which they used to fabricate has gone away from them.) What they used to worship instead of Allah abandoned them and will not intercede on their behalf, aid them or save them from their fate.

Surah: 7 Ayah: 54

﴿ إِنَّ رَبَّكُمُ ٱللَّهُ ٱلَّذِى خَلَقَ ٱلسَّمَٰوَٰتِ وَٱلْأَرْضَ فِى سِتَّةِ أَيَّامٍ ثُمَّ ٱسْتَوَىٰ عَلَى ٱلْعَرْشِ يُغْشِى ٱلَّيْلَ ٱلنَّهَارَ يَطْلُبُهُۥ حَثِيثًا وَٱلشَّمْسَ وَٱلْقَمَرَ وَٱلنُّجُومَ مُسَخَّرَٰتٍۭ بِأَمْرِهِۦٓ ۗ أَلَا لَهُ ٱلْخَلْقُ وَٱلْأَمْرُ ۗ تَبَارَكَ ٱللَّهُ رَبُّ ٱلْعَٰلَمِينَ ﴾

54. Indeed your Lord is Allâh, Who created the heavens and the earth in Six Days, and then He rose over (Istawâ) the Throne (really in a manner that suits His Majesty). He brings the night as a cover over the day, seeking it rapidly, and (He created) the sun, the moon, the stars subjected to His Command. Surely, His is

the Creation and Commandment. Blessed be Allâh, the Lord of the 'Alamîn (mankind, jinn and all that exists)!

Transliteration

54. Inna rabbakumu Allahu allathee khalaqa alssamawati waal-arda fee sittati ayyamin thumma istawa AAala alAAarshi yughshee allayla alnnahara yatlubuhu hatheethan waalshshamsa waalqamara waalnnujooma musakhkharatin bi-amrihi ala lahu alkhalqu waal-amru tabaraka Allahu rabbu alAAalameena

Tafsir Ibn Kathir:

The Universe was created in Six Days

Allah states that He created the universe, the heavens and earth and all that is in, on and between them in six days, as He has stated in several Ayat in the Qur'an. These six days are: Sunday, Monday, Tuesday, Wednesday, Thursday and Friday. On Friday, the entire creation was assembled and on that day, Adam was created. There is a difference of opinion whether these days were the same as our standard days as suddenly comes to the mind, or each day constitutes one thousand years, as reported from Mujahid, Imam Ahmad bin Hanbal, and from Ibn `Abbas according to Ad-Dahhak's narration from him. As for Saturday, no creation took place in it since it is the seventh day of (of the week). The word `As-Sabt' means stoppage, or break. Imam Ahmad recorded Abu Hurayrah saying: `Allah's Messenger told me:

»خَلَقَ اللهُ، (عَزَّ وَجَلَّ)، التُّرْبَةَ يَوْمَ السَّبْتِ، وَخَلَقَ فِيهَا الْجِبَالَ يَوْمَ الْأَحَدِ، وَخَلَقَ الشَّجَرَ يَوْمَ الْاثْنَيْنِ، وَخَلَقَ الْمَكْرُوهَ يَوْمَ الثُّلَاثَاءِ، وَخَلَقَ النُّورَ يَوْمَ الْأَرْبِعَاءِ، وَبَثَّ فِيهَا الدَّوَابَّ يَوْمَ الْخَمِيسِ، وَخَلَقَ آدَمَ، عَلَيْهِ السَّلَامُ، بَعْدَ الْعَصْرِ مِنْ يَوْمِ الْجُمُعَةِ، فِي آخِرِ الْخَلْقِ، فِي آخِرِ سَاعَةٍ مِنْ سَاعَاتِ الْجُمُعَةِ، فِيمَا بَيْنَ الْعَصْرِ إِلَى اللَّيْلِ«

(Allah created the dust on Saturday, and He created the mountains on Sunday, and He created the trees on Monday, and He created the unpleasant things on Tuesday and He created the light on Wednesday and He spread the creatures throughout it on Thursday and He created Adam after `Asr on Friday. He was the last created during the last hour of Friday, between `Asr and the night.)

Meaning of Istawa

As for Allah's statement,

(and then He rose over (Istawa) the Throne) the people had several conflicting opinions over its meaning. However, we follow the way that our righteous predecessors took in this regard, such as Malik, Al-Awza`i, Ath-Thawri, Al-Layth bin Sa`d, Ash-Shafi`i, Ahmad, Ishaq bin Rahwayh and the rest of the scholars of Islam, in past and present times. Surely, we accept the apparent meaning of, Al-Istawa, without discussing its true essence, equating it (with the attributes of the creation), or altering or denying it (in any way or form). We also believe that the meaning that comes to those who equate Allah with the creation is to be rejected, for nothing is similar to Allah,

(There is nothing like Him, and He is the All-Hearer, the All-Seer.) (42:11) Indeed, we assert and affirm what the Imams said, such as Nu`aym bin Hammad Al-Khuza'i, the teacher of Imam Al-Bukhari, who said, "Whoever likens Allah with His creation, will have committed Kufr. Whoever denies what Allah has described Himself with, will have committed Kufr. Certainly, there is no resemblance (of Allah with the creation) in what Allah and His Messenger have described Him with. Whoever attests to Allah's attributes that the plain Ayat and authentic Hadiths have mentioned, in the manner that suits Allah's majesty, all the while rejecting all shortcomings from Him, will have taken the path of guidance."

The Day and the Night are among the Signs of Allah

Allah said,

(He brings the night as a cover over the day, seeking it rapidly,) meaning, the darkness goes away with the light, and the light goes away with the darkness. Each of them seeks the other rapidly, and does not come late, for when this vanishes, the other comes, and vice versa. Allah also said;

(And a sign for them is the night. We withdraw therefrom the day, and behold, they are in darkness. And the sun runs on its fixed course for a term (appointed). That is the decree of the All-Mighty, the All-Knowing. And the moon, We have measured for it mansions (to traverse) till it returns like the old dried curved date stalk. It is not for the sun to overtake the moon, nor does the night outstrip the day. They all float, each in an orbit.) (36:37-40) Allah's statement,

(Nor does the night outstrip the day) (36:40) means, the night follows the day in succession and does not come later or earlier than it should be. This is why Allah said here,

(seeking it rapidly, and (He created) the sun, the moon, the stars subjected to His command.) meaning, all are under His command, will and dominion. Allah alerted us afterwards,

(Surely, His is the creation and commandment) the dominion and the decision. Allah said next,

(Blessed is Allah, the Lord of all that exists!) which is similar to the Ayah,

(Blessed be He Who has placed in the heaven big stars) (25:61) Abu Ad-Darda' said a supplication, that was also attributed to the Prophet,

«اللَّهُمَّ لَكَ الْمُلْكُ كُلُّهُ وَلَكَ الْحَمْدُ كُلُّهُ وَإِلَيْكَ يُرْجَعُ الْأَمْرُ كُلُّهُ، أَسْأَلُكَ مِنَ الْخَيْرِ كُلِّهِ وَأَعُوذُ بِكَ مِنَ الشَّرِّ كُلِّهِ»

(O Allah! Yours is all the kingdom, all the praise, and Yours is the ownership of all affairs. I ask You for all types of good and seek refuge with You from all types of evil.)

Surah: 7 Ayah: 55 & Ayah: 56

﴿ ادْعُوا رَبَّكُمْ تَضَرُّعًا وَخُفْيَةً إِنَّهُ لَا يُحِبُّ الْمُعْتَدِينَ ۝ ﴾

55. Invoke your Lord with humility and in secret. He likes not the aggressors.

﴿ وَلَا تُفْسِدُوا فِي الْأَرْضِ بَعْدَ إِصْلَاحِهَا وَادْعُوهُ خَوْفًا وَطَمَعًا إِنَّ رَحْمَتَ اللَّهِ قَرِيبٌ مِنَ الْمُحْسِنِينَ ۝ ﴾

56. And do not do mischief on the earth, after it has been set in order, and invoke Him with fear and hope. Surely, Allâh's Mercy is (ever) near unto the good-doers.

Transliteration

55. OdAAoo rabbakum tadarruAAan wakhufyatan innahu la yuhibbu almuAAtadeena
56. Wala tufsidoo fee al-ardi baAAda islahiha waodAAoohu khawfan watamaAAan inna rahmata Allahi qareebun mina almuhsineena

Tafsir Ibn Kathir:

Encouraging supplicating to Allah

Allah commands His servants to supplicate to Him, for this will ensure their welfare in this life and the Hereafter. Allah said,

(Invoke your Lord Tadarru`an and Khufyah) meaning, in humbleness and humility. Allah said in a similar Ayah,

(And remember your Lord within yourself) (7:205) It is recorded in the Two Sahihs that Abu Musa Al-Ash`ari said, "The people raised their voices with supplications but the Messenger of Allah said,

«أَيُّهَا النَّاسُ ارْبَعُوا عَلَى أَنْفُسِكُمْ فَإِنَّكُمْ لَا تَدْعُونَ أَصَمَّ وَلَا غَائِبًا إِنَّ الَّذِي تَدْعُونَ سَمِيعٌ قَرِيب»

(O people! Take it easy on yourselves. Verily, you are not calling one who is deaf or absent, rather, the One you are calling is All-Hearer, Near (to His servants by His knowledge).) Ibn Jarir said that,

(Tadarru`an), means obeying Him in humility and humbleness,

(and Khufyah), with the humbleness in your hearts and certainty of His Oneness and Lordship not supplicating loudly to show off.

Forbidding Aggression in Supplications

It was reported that `Ata' Al-Khurasani narrated from Ibn `Abbas, who said about Allah's statement,

(He likes not the aggressors) "In the Du`a' and otherwise." Abu Mijlaz commented on,

(He likes not the aggressors), "Such (aggression) as asking to reach the grade of the Prophets." Imam Ahmad narrated that Abu Ni`amah said that `Abdullah bin Mughaffal heard his son supplicating, "O Allah! I ask you for the white castle on the right side of Paradise, if I enter it." So `Abdullah said, "O my son! Ask Allah for Paradise and seek refuge with Him from the Fire, for I heard the Messenger of Allah saying,

«يَكُونُ قَوْمٌ يَعْتَدُونَ فِي الدُّعَاءِ وَالطَّهُورِ»

(There will come some people who transgress in supplication and purification)" Ibn Majah and Abu Dawud recorded this Hadith with a good chain that there is no harm in, and Allah knows best.

The Prohibition of causing Mischief in the Land

Allah said next, (And do not do mischief on the earth, after it has been set in order) (5:56). Allah prohibits causing mischief on the earth, especially after it has been set in order. When the affairs are in order and then mischief occurs, it will cause maximum harm to the people; thus Allah forbids causing mischief and ordained worshipping Him, supplicating to Him, begging Him and being humble to Him. Allah said,

(and invoke Him with fear and hope) fearing what He has of severe torment and hoping in what He has of tremendous reward. Allah then said,

(Surely, Allah's mercy is (ever) near unto the good-doers) meaning, His mercy is for the good-doers who obey His commands and avoid what He prohibited. Allah said in another Ayah,

(And My mercy envelopes all things. That (mercy) I shall ordain for those who who have Taqwa.) (7:156). Matar Al-Warraq said, "Earn Allah's promise by obeying Him, for He ordained that His mercy is near to the good-doers. " Ibn Abi Hatim collected this statement.

Surah: 7 Ayah: 57 & Ayah: 58

﴿ وَهُوَ ٱلَّذِى يُرْسِلُ ٱلرِّيَـٰحَ بُشْرًۢا بَيْنَ يَدَىْ رَحْمَتِهِۦ ۖ حَتَّىٰٓ إِذَآ أَقَلَّتْ سَحَابًا ثِقَالًا سُقْنَـٰهُ لِبَلَدٍ مَّيِّتٍ فَأَنزَلْنَا بِهِ ٱلْمَآءَ فَأَخْرَجْنَا بِهِۦ مِن كُلِّ ٱلثَّمَرَٰتِ ۚ كَذَٰلِكَ نُخْرِجُ ٱلْمَوْتَىٰ لَعَلَّكُمْ تَذَكَّرُونَ ۝ ﴾

57. And it is He Who sends the winds as heralds of glad tidings, going before His Mercy (rain). Till when they have carried a heavy-laden cloud, We drive it to a land that is dead, then We cause water (rain) to descend thereon. Then We produce every kind of fruit therewith. Similarly, We shall raise up the dead, so that you may remember or take heed.

﴿ وَٱلْبَلَدُ ٱلطَّيِّبُ يَخْرُجُ نَبَاتُهُۥ بِإِذْنِ رَبِّهِۦ ۖ وَٱلَّذِى خَبُثَ لَا يَخْرُجُ إِلَّا نَكِدًا ۚ كَذَٰلِكَ نُصَرِّفُ ٱلْـَٔايَـٰتِ لِقَوْمٍ يَشْكُرُونَ ۝ ﴾

58. The vegetation of a good land comes forth (easily) by the Permission of its Lord; and that which is bad, brings forth nothing but a little with difficulty. Thus do We explain variously the Ayât (proofs, evidences, verses, lessons, signs, revelations, etc.) for a people who give thanks.

Transliteration

57. Wahuwa allathee yursilu alrriyaha bushran bayna yaday rahmatihi hatta itha aqallat sahaban thiqalan suqnahu libaladin mayyitin faanzalna bihi almaa faakhrajna bihi min kulli aththamarati kathalika nukhriju almawta laAAallakum tathakkaroona
58. Waalbaladu alttayyibu yakhruju nabatuhu bi-ithni rabbihi waallathee khabutha la yakhruju illa nakidan kathalika nusarrifu al-ayati liqawmin yashkuroona

Tafsir Ibn Kathir:

Among Allah's Signs, He sends down the Rain and brings forth the Produce

After Allah stated that He created the heavens and earth and that He is the Owner and Possessor of the affairs Who makes things subservient (for mankind), He ordained that He be invoked in Du`a', for He is able to do all things. Allah also stated that He is the Sustainer and He resurrects the dead on the Day of Resurrection. Here, Allah said that He sends the wind that spreads the clouds that are laden with rain. Allah said in another Ayah,

(And among His signs is this, that He sends the winds with glad tidings) (30:46). Allah's statement,

(going before His mercy) means, before the rain. Allah also said;

(And He it is Who sends down the rain after they have despaired, and spreads His mercy. And He is Al-Wali (the Guardian), Al-Hamid (the praiseworthy) (42:28) and,

(Look then at the results of Allah's mercy, how He revives the earth after its death. Verily, that (is the one Who) shall indeed raise the dead, and He is able to do all things) (30:50). Allah said next,

(Till when they have carried a heavy-laden cloud) when the wind carries clouds that are heavy with rain, and this is why these clouds are heavy, close to the earth, and their color is dark. Allah's statement,

(We drive it to a land that is dead) that is, a dry land that does not have any vegetation. This Ayah is similar to another Ayah,

(And a sign for them is the dead land. We give it life) (36:33). This is why Allah said here,

(Then We produce every kind of fruit therewith. Similarly, We shall raise up the dead.) meaning, just as We bring life to dead land, We shall raise up the dead on the Day of Resurrection, after they have disintegrated. Allah will send down rain from the sky and the rain will pour on the earth for forty days. The corpses will then be brought up in their graves, just as the seeds become grow in the ground (on receiving rain). Allah often mentions this similarity in the Qur'an when He gives the example of what will happen on the Day of Resurrection, and bringing life to dead land,

(so that you may remember or take heed.) Allah's statement,

(The vegetation of a good land comes forth (easily) by the permission of its Lord;) meaning, the good land produces its vegetation rapidly and proficiently. Allah said in another Ayah (about Maryam, mother of `Isa, peace be upon him);

(He made her grow in a good manner.) (3:37) The Ayah continues,

(and that which is bad, brings forth nothing but with difficulty.) Mujahid, and others such as As-Sibakh, etc. also said this. Al-Bukhari recorded that Abu Musa said that the Messenger of Allah said,

«مَثَلُ مَا بَعَثَنِي اللهُ بِهِ مِنَ الْعِلْمِ وَالْهُدَى كَمَثَلِ الْغَيْثِ الْكَثِيرِ أَصَابَ أَرْضًا فَكَانَتْ مِنْهَا نَقِيَّةٌ قَبِلَتِ الْمَاءَ فَأَنْبَتَتِ الْكَلَأَ وَالْعُشْبَ الْكَثِيرَ وَكَانَتْ مِنْهَا أَجَادِبُ أَمْسَكَتِ الْمَاءَ فَنَفَعَ اللهُ بِهَا النَّاسَ فَشَرِبُوا وَسَقَوْا وَزَرَعُوا وَأَصَابَ مِنْهَا طَائِفَةً أُخْرَى إِنَّمَا هِيَ قِيعَانٌ لَا تُمْسِكُ مَاءً وَلَا تُنْبِتُ كَلَأً، فَذَلِكَ مَثَلُ مَنْ فَقُهَ فِي دِينِ اللهِ وَنَفَعَهُ مَا بَعَثَنِي اللهُ بِهِ فَعَلِمَ وَعَلَّمَ وَمَثَلُ مَنْ لَمْ يَرْفَعْ بِذَلِكَ رَأْسًا وَلَمْ يَقْبَلْ هُدَى اللهِ الَّذِي أُرْسِلْتُ بِهِ»

(The parable of the guidance and knowledge with which Allah has sent me is that of an abundant rain falling on a land, some of which was fertile soil that absorbed rain water and brought forth vegetation and grass in abundance. And another portion of it was hard and held the rain water; and Allah benefited the people with it, they utilized it for drinking, making their animals drink from it, and for irrigation of the land for cultivation. And a portion of it was barren which could neither hold the water nor bring forth vegetation. The first is the example of the person who comprehends Allah's religion and gets benefit which Allah sent me with, by learnign and teaching others. The last example is that of a person who does not care for it and does not accept the guidance Allah sent me with.)

Surah: 7 Ayah: 59, Ayah: 60, Ayah: 61 & Ayah: 62

﴿ لَقَدْ أَرْسَلْنَا نُوحًا إِلَىٰ قَوْمِهِ فَقَالَ يَـٰقَوْمِ ٱعْبُدُواْ ٱللَّهَ مَا لَكُم مِّنْ إِلَـٰهٍ غَيْرُهُ إِنِّىٓ أَخَافُ عَلَيْكُمْ عَذَابَ يَوْمٍ عَظِيمٍ ﴿٥٩﴾

59. Indeed, We sent Nûh (Noah) to his people and he said: "O my people! Worship Allâh! You have no other Ilâh (God) but Him. (Lâ ilâha illallâh: none has the right to be worshipped but Allâh). Certainly, I fear for you the torment of a Great Day!"

﴿ قَالَ ٱلْمَلَأُ مِن قَوْمِهِ إِنَّا لَنَرَاكَ فِى ضَلَـٰلٍ مُّبِينٍ ﴿٦٠﴾

60. The leaders of his people said: "Verily, we see you in plain error."

﴿ قَالَ يَـٰقَوْمِ لَيْسَ بِى ضَلَـٰلَةٌ وَلَـٰكِنِّى رَسُولٌ مِّن رَّبِّ ٱلْعَـٰلَمِينَ ﴿٦١﴾

61. (Nûh (Noah)) said: "O my people! There is no error in me, but I am a Messenger from the Lord of the 'Alamîn (mankind, jinn and all that exists)!

﴿ أُبَلِّغُكُمْ رِسَـٰلَـٰتِ رَبِّى وَأَنصَحُ لَكُمْ وَأَعْلَمُ مِنَ ٱللَّهِ مَا لَا تَعْلَمُونَ ﴿٦٢﴾

62. "I convey unto you the Messages of my Lord and give sincere advice to you. And I know from Allâh what you know not.

Transliteration

59. Laqad arsalna noohan ila qawmihi faqala ya qawmi oAAbudoo Allaha ma lakum min ilahin ghayruhu innee akhafu AAalaykum AAathaba yawmin AAatheemin   60. Qala almalao min qawmihi inna lanaraka fee dalalin mubeenin   61. Qala ya qawmi laysa bee dalalatun walakinnee rasoolun min rabbi alAAalameena   62. Oballighukum risalati rabbee waansahu lakum waaAAlamu mina Allahi ma la taAAlamoona

Tafsir Ibn Kathir:

The Story of Nuh and His People

After Allah mentioned the story of Adam in the beginning of this Surah, He started mentioning the stories of the Prophets, the first then the latter of them. Allah mentioned the story of Nuh, because he was the first Messenger Allah sent to the people of the earth after Adam. His name was Nuh bin Lamak bin Matushalakh bin Khanukh. And Khanukh was, as they claim, the Prophet Idris. And Idris was the first person to write letters using pen, and he was the son of Barad bin Mahlil, bin Qanin bin Yanish bin Shith bin Adam, upon them all be peace. This lineage is mentioned by Muhammad bin Ishaq and other Imams who document lineage. `Abdullah bin `Abbas and several other scholars of Tafsir said that the first idol worship began when some righteous people died and their people built places of worship over their graves. They made images of them so that they could remember their righteousness and devotion, and thus, imitate them. When time passed, they made statues of them and later on worshipped these idols, naming them after the righteous people: Wadd, Suwa`, Yaghuth, Ya`uq and Nasr. After this practice became popular, Allah sent Nuh as a Messenger, all thanks are due to Him. Nuh commanded his people to worship Allah alone without partners, saying,

("O my people! Worship Allah! You have no other god but Him. Certainly, I fear for you the torment of a Great Day!") the torment of the Day of Resurrection, if you meet Allah while associating others with Him.

(The leaders of his people said) meaning, the general public, chiefs, commanders and great ones of his people said,

("Verily, we see you in plain error") because of your calling us to abandon the worship of these idols that we found our forefathers worshipping. This, indeed, is the attitude of evil people, for they consider the righteous people to be following misguidance. Allah said in other Ayat,

(And when they saw them, they said: "Verily, these have indeed gone astray!") (83:32) and,

(And those who disbelieve say of those who believe: "Had it been a good thing, they (the weak and poor) would not have preceded us thereto!" And when they have not let themselves be guided by it (this Qur'an), they say: "This is an ancient lie!") (46:11) There are several other Ayat on this subject.

((Nuh) said: "O my people! There is no error in me, but I am a Messenger from the Lord of all that exists!") meaning, there is nothing wrong with me, but I am a Messenger from the Lord of all that exists, Lord and King of all things,

("I convey unto you the Messages of my Lord and give sincere advice to you. And I know from Allah what you know not.") This is the attribute of a Messenger, that he conveys using plain, yet eloquent words, offers sincere advice and is knowledgeable about Allah; indeed, no other people can compete with the Prophets in this regard. In his Sahih, Muslim recorded that the Messenger of Allah said to his Companions on the Day of `Arafah, when their gathering was as large as it ever was,

«أَيُّهَا النَّاسُ إِنَّكُمْ مَسْؤُولُونَ عَنِّي فَمَا أَنْتُمْ قَائِلُونَ؟»

(O people! You will be asked about me, so what will you say) They said, "We testify that you have conveyed and delivered (the Message) and offered sincere advice." So he kept raising his finger to the sky and lowering it towards them, saying,

«اللَّهُمَّ اشْهَدْ اللَّهُمَّ اشْهَدْ»

(O Allah! Bear witness, O Allah! Bear witness.)

Surah: 7 Ayah: 63 & Ayah: 64

﴿ أَوَعَجِبْتُمْ أَن جَآءَكُمْ ذِكْرٌ مِّن رَّبِّكُمْ عَلَىٰ رَجُلٍ مِّنكُمْ لِيُنذِرَكُمْ وَلِتَتَّقُواْ وَلَعَلَّكُمْ تُرْحَمُونَ ۝ ﴾

63. "Do you wonder that there has come to you a Reminder from your Lord through a man from amongst you, that he may warn you, so that you may fear Allâh and that you may receive (His) Mercy?"

﴿ فَكَذَّبُوهُ فَأَنجَيْنَاهُ وَالَّذِينَ مَعَهُ فِى ٱلْفُلْكِ وَأَغْرَقْنَا ٱلَّذِينَ كَذَّبُواْ بِـَٔايَاتِنَا إِنَّهُمْ كَانُواْ قَوْمًا عَمِينَ ۝ ﴾

64. But they belied him, so We saved him and those along with him in the ship, and We drowned those who belied Our Ayât (proofs, evidences, verses, lessons, signs, revelations, etc.). They were indeed a blind people.

Transliteration

63. Awa AAajibtum an jaakum thikrun min rabbikum AAala rajulin minkum liyunthirakum walittaqoo walaAAallakum turhamoona   64. Fakaththaboohu faanjaynahu waallatheena maAAahu fee alfulki waaghraqna allatheena kaththaboo bi-ayatina innahum kanoo qawman AAameena

Tafsir Ibn Kathir:

Allah said that Nuh proclaimed to his people,

("Do you wonder..."), do not wonder because of this. Surely, it is not strange that Allah sends down revelation to a man among you as mercy, kindness and compassion for you, so that he warns you that you may avoid Allah's torment by associating none with Him,

Chapter 7: Al-Araf (The Heights), Verses 001-087

("and that you may receive (His) mercy.") Allah said,

(But they belied him) but they insisted on rejecting and opposing him, and only a few of them believed in him, as Allah stated in another Ayah. Allah said next,

(So We saved him and those along with him in the Fulk) the ark,

(And We drowned those who belied Our Ayat.) Allah said in another Ayah,

(Because of their sins they were drowned, then they were admitted into the Fire. And they found none to help them instead of Allah.) (71:25) Allah said,

(They were indeed a blind people.) meaning, blind from the Truth, unable to recognize it or find their way to it. Here, Allah said that He has taken revenge from His enemies and saved His Messenger and those who believed in him, while destroying their disbelieving enemies. Allah said in a another Ayah,

(Verily, We will indeed make victorious Our Messengers) (40:51). This is Allah's Sunnah (way) with His servants, in this life and the Hereafter, that the good end, victory and triumph is for those who fear Him. For example, Allah destroyed the people of Nuh, and saved Nuh and his believing followers. Ibn Wahb said that he was told that Ibn `Abbas said that eighty men were saved with Nuh in the ship, one of them was Jurhum, who spoke Arabic. Ibn Abi Hatim collected this statement, which was also narrated with a continuous chain of narration from Ibn `Abbas.

Surah: 7 Ayah: 65, Ayah: 66, Ayah: 67, Ayah: 68 & Ayah: 69

﴿ ۞ وَإِلَىٰ عَادٍ أَخَاهُمْ هُودًا ۗ قَالَ يَٰقَوْمِ ٱعْبُدُواْ ٱللَّهَ مَا لَكُم مِّنْ إِلَٰهٍ غَيْرُهُۥٓ ۚ أَفَلَا تَتَّقُونَ ﴿٦٥﴾ ﴾

65. And to 'Ad (people, We sent) their brother Hûd. He said: "O my people! Worship Allâh! You have no other Ilâh (God) but Him. (Lâ ilâha illallâh: none has the right to be worshipped but Allâh). Will you not fear (Allâh)?"

﴿ قَالَ ٱلْمَلَأُ ٱلَّذِينَ كَفَرُواْ مِن قَوْمِهِۦٓ إِنَّا لَنَرَىٰكَ فِى سَفَاهَةٍ وَإِنَّا لَنَظُنُّكَ مِنَ ٱلْكَٰذِبِينَ ﴿٦٦﴾ ﴾

66. The leaders of those who disbelieved among his people said: "Verily, we see you in foolishness, and verily, we think you are one of the liars."

﴿ قَالَ يَٰقَوْمِ لَيْسَ بِى سَفَاهَةٌ وَلَٰكِنِّى رَسُولٌ مِّن رَّبِّ ٱلْعَٰلَمِينَ ﴿٦٧﴾ ﴾

67. (Hûd) said: "O my people! There is no foolishness in me, but (I am) a Messenger from the Lord of the 'Alamîn (mankind, jinn and all that exists)!

﴿ أُبَلِّغُكُمْ رِسَٰلَٰتِ رَبِّى وَأَنَا۠ لَكُمْ نَاصِحٌ أَمِينٌ ﴿٦٨﴾ ﴾

68. "I convey unto you the Messages of my Lord, and I am a trustworthy adviser (or well-wisher) for you.

﴿ أَوَعَجِبْتُمْ أَن جَآءَكُمْ ذِكْرٌ مِّن رَّبِّكُمْ عَلَىٰ رَجُلٍ مِّنكُمْ لِيُنذِرَكُمْ وَٱذْكُرُوٓا۟ إِذْ جَعَلَكُمْ خُلَفَآءَ مِنۢ بَعْدِ قَوْمِ نُوحٍ وَزَادَكُمْ فِى ٱلْخَلْقِ بَصْۜطَةً فَٱذْكُرُوٓا۟ ءَالَآءَ ٱللَّهِ لَعَلَّكُمْ تُفْلِحُونَ ۝ ﴾

69. "Do you wonder that there has come to you a Reminder (and an advice) from your Lord through a man from amongst you to warn you? And remember that He made you successors after the people of Nûh (Noah), and increased you amply in stature. So remember the graces (bestowed upon you) from Allâh, so that you may be successful."

Transliteration

65. Wa-ila AAadin akhahum hoodan qala ya qawmi oAAbudoo Allaha ma lakum min ilahin ghayruhu afala tattaqoona 66. Qala almalao allatheena kafaroo min qawmihi inna lanaraka fee safahatin wa-inna lanathunnuka mina alkathibeena 67. Qala ya qawmi laysa bee safahatun walakinnee rasoolun min rabbi alAAalameena 68. Oballighukum risalati rabbee waana lakum nasihun ameenun 69. Awa AAajibtum an jaakum thikrun min rabbikum AAala rajulin minkum liyunthirakum waothkuroo ith jaAAalakum khulafaa min baAAdi qawmi noohin wazadakum fee alkhalqi bastatan faothkuroo alaa Allahi laAAallakum tuflihoona

Tafsir Ibn Kathir:

The Story of Hud, Peace be upon Him, and the Lineage of the People of `Ad

Allah says, just as We sent Nuh to his people, similarly, to the `Ad people, We sent Hud one of their own brethren. Muhammad bin Ishaq said that the tribe of `Ad were the descendants of `Ad, son of Iram, son of `Aws, son of Sam, son of Nuh. I say, these are indeed the ancient people of `Ad whom Allah mentioned, the children of `Ad, son of Iram who were living in the deserts with lofty pillars or statues. Allah said,

(Have you not seen how your Lord dealt with `Ad (people). Of Iram like (lofty) pillars. The like of which were not created in the land) (89:6-8) because of their might and strength. Allah said in another instance,

(As for `Ad, they were arrogant in the land without right, and they said: "Who is mightier than us in strength" See they not that Allah Who created them was mightier in strength than them. And they used to deny Our Ayat!) (41:15).

The Land of `Ad

The people of `Ad lived in Yemen, in the area of Ahqaf, which means sand mounds. Muhammad bin Ishaq narrated that Abu At-Tufayl `Amir bin Wathilah said that he heard `Ali (bin Abi Talib) saying to a man from Hadramawt (in Yemen), "Have you seen a red sand mound, where there are a lot of Arak and Lote trees in the area of so-and-so in Hadramawt Have you seen it" He said, "Yes, O Commander of the faithful! By Allah, you described it as if you have seen it before." `Ali said, `I have not seen it, but it was described to me." The man asked, "What about it, O Commander of the faithful" `Ali said, "There is the grave of Hud, peace be upon him, in its vicinity." Ibn Jarir recorded this statement, which gives the benefit of indicating that `Ad used to live in Yemen, since Prophet Hud was buried there. Prophet Hud was among the noble men and chiefs of `Ad, for Allah chose the Messengers from among the best, most honorable families and tribes. Hud's people were mighty and strong, but their hearts were mighty and hard, for they were among the most denying of Truth among the nations. Prophet Hud called `Ad to worship Allah alone without partners, and to obey and fear Him.

Debate between Hud and his People

(The leaders of those who disbelieved among his people said...) meaning, the general public, chiefs, masters and commanders of his people said,

("Verily, we see you in foolishness, and verily, we think you are one of the liars") meaning, you are misguided because you call us to abandon worshipping the idols in order to worship Allah Alone. Similarly, the chiefs of Quraysh wondered at the call to worship One God, saying,

("Has he (Muhammad) made the gods (all) into One God") (38:5).

((Hud) said: "O my people! There is no foolishness in me, but (I am) a Messenger from the Lord of all that exists!") Hud said, I am not as you claim. Rather, I brought you the Truth from Allah, Who created everything, and He is the Lord and King of all things,

("I convey unto you the Messages of my Lord, and I am a trustworthy adviser for you.") These, indeed, are the qualities of the Prophets: conveying, sincerity and honesty,

("Do you wonder that there has come to you a Reminder from your Lord through a man from among you to warn you") Prophet Hud said, do not wonder because Allah sent a Messenger to you from among yourselves to warn you about Allah's Days (His torment) and meeting with Him. Rather than wondering, you should thank Allah for this bounty.

("And remember that He made you successors (generations after generations) after the people of Nuh...") meaning, remember Allah's favor on you in that He made you among the offspring of Nuh, because of whose supplication Allah destroyed the people of the earth after they defied and opposed him.

("and increased you amply in stature.") making you taller than other people. Similarly, Allah said in the description of Talut (Saul),

(And has increased him abundantly in knowledge and stature.) (2:247) Hud continued,

("So remember the graces (bestowed upon you) from Allah.") in reference to Allah's favors and blessings

("so that you may be successful.")

Surah: 7 Ayah: 70, Ayah: 71 & Ayah: 72

﴿ قَالُوٓاْ أَجِئْتَنَا لِنَعْبُدَ ٱللَّهَ وَحْدَهُۥ وَنَذَرَ مَا كَانَ يَعْبُدُ ءَابَآؤُنَا فَأْتِنَا بِمَا تَعِدُنَآ إِن كُنتَ مِنَ ٱلصَّٰدِقِينَ ۝ ﴾

70. They said: "You have come to us that we should worship Allâh Alone and forsake that which our fathers used to worship. So bring us that wherewith you have threatened us if you are of the truthful."

﴿ قَالَ قَدْ وَقَعَ عَلَيْكُم مِّن رَّبِّكُمْ رِجْسٌ وَغَضَبٌ أَتُجَٰدِلُونَنِي فِىٓ أَسْمَآءٍ سَمَّيْتُمُوهَآ أَنتُمْ وَءَابَآؤُكُم مَّا نَزَّلَ ٱللَّهُ بِهَا مِن سُلْطَٰنٍ فَٱنتَظِرُوٓاْ إِنِّى مَعَكُم مِّنَ ٱلْمُنتَظِرِينَ ۝ ﴾

71. (Hûd) said: "Torment and wrath have already fallen on you from your Lord. Dispute you with me over names which you have named - you and your fathers - with no authority from Allâh? Then wait, I am with you among those who wait."

﴿ فَأَنجَيْنَٰهُ وَٱلَّذِينَ مَعَهُۥ بِرَحْمَةٍ مِّنَّا وَقَطَعْنَا دَابِرَ ٱلَّذِينَ كَذَّبُواْ بِـَٔايَٰتِنَا وَمَا كَانُواْ مُؤْمِنِينَ ۝ ﴾

72. So We saved him and those who were with him by a Mercy from Us, and We cut the roots of those who belied Our Ayât (proofs, evidences, verses, lessons, signs, revelations, etc.); and they were not believers.

Transliteration

70. Qaloo aji/tana linaAAbuda Allaha wahdahu wanathara ma kana yaAAbudu abaona fa/tina bima taAAiduna in kunta mina alssadiqeena   71. Qala qad waqaAAa AAalaykum min rabbikum rijsun waghadabun atujadiloonanee fee asma-in sammaytumooha antum waabaokum ma nazzala Allahu biha min sultanin faintathiroo innee maAAakum mina almuntathireena   72. Faanjaynahu waallatheena maAAahu birahmatin minna waqataAAna dabira allatheena kaththaboo bi-ayatina wama kanoo mu/mineena

Tafsir Ibn Kathir:

Allah mentions the rebellion, defiance and stubbornness of Hud's people, and their opposition to him, peace be upon him,

(They said: "You have come to us that we should worship Allah Alone") Later on, the disbelievers of Quraysh said,

(And (remember) when they said: "O Allah! If this (the Qur'an) is indeed the truth (revealed) from You, then rain down stones on us from the sky or bring on us a painful torment.") Muhammad bin Ishaq said that the people of Hud used to worship several idols, such as Suda', Samud and Al-Haba'. This is why Hud, peace be upon him, said to them,

("Rijs and wrath have already fallen on you from your Lord.") you deserve `Rijs' from your Lord because of what you said. Ibn `Abbas said that, `Rijs', means scorn and anger.

("Dispute you with me over names which you have named -- you and your fathers") (7:71). Hud said, do you dispute with me over these idols that you and your fathers made gods, even though they do not bring harm or benefit; did Allah give you authority or proof allowing you to worship them Hud further said,

("with no authority from Allah Then wait, I am with you among those who wait.") this is a threat and warning from the Messenger to his people.

The End of `Ad

So Allah said;

(So We saved him and those who were with him out of mercy from Us, and We severed the roots of those who belied Our Ayat; and they were not believers.) Allah mentioned several times in the Qur'an, the way the people of `Ad were destroyed stating that He sent a barren wind that destroyed everything it passed by. Allah said in another Ayah,

(And as for `Ad, they were destroyed by a furious violent wind! They were subjected to it for seven nights and eight days in succession, so that you could see men lying overthrown (destroyed), as if they were hollow trunks of date palms! Do you see any remnants of them) (69:6-8) When `Ad rebelled and transgressed, Allah destroyed them with a strong wind that carried them, one by one, up in the air and brought each one of them down on his head, thus smashing his head and severing it from its body. This is why Allah said,

(as if they were hollow trunks of date palms!) (69:7) Muhammad bin Ishaq said that `Ad used to live in Yemen between Oman and Hadramawt. They also spread throughout the land and defeated various peoples, because of the strength that Allah gave them. They used to worship idols instead of Allah, and Allah sent to them Prophet Hud, peace be upon him. He was from their most common lineage and was the best among them in status. Hud commanded them to worship Allah Alone and associate none with him. He also ordered them to stop committing injustice against the people. But they rejected him and ignored his call. They said, `Who is stronger than us' Some of them, however, followed Hud, although they were few and had to conceal their faith. When `Ad defied the command of Allah, rejected His Prophet, committed mischief in the earth, became arrogant and built high palaces on every high place -- without real benefit to them -- Hud spoke to them, saying,

("Do you build high palaces on every high place, while you do not live in them And do you get for yourselves palaces (fine buildings) as if you will live therein forever. And when you seize (somebody), seize you (him) as tyrants Have Taqwa of Allah, and obey me.") (26:128-131) However,

(They said: "O Hud! No evidence have you brought us, and we shall not leave our gods for your (mere) saying! And we are not believers in you. All that we say is that some of our gods have seized you with evil.") meaning, madness,

(He said: "I call Allah to witness, and bear you witness that I am free from that which you associate with Him. So plot against me, all of you, and give me no respite. I put my trust in Allah, my Lord and your Lord! There is not a moving creature but He has the grasp of its forelock. Verily, my Lord is on the straight path (the truth).") (11:53-56)."

Story of the Emissary of `Ad

Imam Ahmad recorded that Al-Harith Al-Bakri said: "I went to the Messenger of Allah to complain to him about Al-`Ala bin Al-Hadrami. When I passed by the area of Ar-Rabdhah, I found an old woman from Bani Tamim who was alone in that area. She said to me, "O servant of Allah! I need to reach the Messenger of Allah to ask him for some of my needs, will you take me to him" So I took her along with me to Al-Madinah and found the Masjid full of people. I also found a black flag raised high, while Bilal was holding a sword before the Messenger of Allah . I asked, "What is the matter with the people" They said, "The Prophet intends to send `Amr bin Al-`As (on a military expedition) somewhere." So I sat down. When the Prophet went to his house, I asked for permission to see him, and he gave me permission. I entered and greeted him. He said, "Was there a dispute between you and Bani Tamim" I said, "Yes. And we had been victorious over them. I passed by an old woman from Bani Tamim, who was alone, and she asked me to bring her to you, and she is at the door". So he allowed her in and I said, "O Allah's Messenger! What if you make a barrier between us and (the tribe of) Bani Tamim, such as Ad-Dahna' (Desert)" The old woman became angry and opposed me. So I said, "My example is the example of a sheep that carried its own destruction. I carried this woman and did not know that she was an opponent. I seek refuge with Allah and His Messenger that I become like the emissary of `Ad.' So the Prophet asked me about the emissary of `Ad, having better knowledge in it, but he liked to hear the story again. I said, "Once, `Ad suffered from a famine and they sent an emissary (to get relief), whose name was Qayl. Qayl passed by Mu`awiyah bin Bakr and stayed with him for a month. Mu`awiyah supplied him with alcoholic drinks, and two female singers were singing for him. When a month ended, Qayl went to the mountains of Muhrah and said, `O Allah! You know that I did not come here to cure an ill person or to ransom a prisoner. O Allah! Give `Ad water as You used to.' So black clouds came and he was called, `Choose which one of them you wish (to go to `Ad)!' So he pointed to one of the black clouds and he heard someone proclaiming from it, `Take it, as ashes that will leave none in `Ad.' And it has been conveyed to me that the wind sent to them was no more than what would pass through this ring of mine, but it destroyed them." Abu Wa'il said, "That is true. When a man or a woman would send an emissary, they would tell him, `Do not be like the emissary of `Ad (bringing disaster and utter destruction to them instead of relief).," Imam Ahmad collected this story in the Musnad. At-Tirmidhi recorded similar wording for it, as did An-Nasa'i and Ibn Majah.

Surah: 7 Ayah: 73, Ayah: 74, Ayah: 75, Ayah: 76, Ayah: 77 & Ayah: 78

﴿ وَإِلَىٰ ثَمُودَ أَخَاهُمْ صَٰلِحًا ۗ قَالَ يَٰقَوْمِ ٱعْبُدُوا۟ ٱللَّهَ مَا لَكُم مِّنْ إِلَٰهٍ غَيْرُهُۥ ۖ قَدْ جَآءَتْكُم بَيِّنَةٌ مِّن رَّبِّكُمْ ۖ هَٰذِهِۦ نَاقَةُ ٱللَّهِ لَكُمْ ءَايَةً ۖ فَذَرُوهَا تَأْكُلْ فِىٓ أَرْضِ ٱللَّهِ ۖ وَلَا تَمَسُّوهَا بِسُوٓءٍ فَيَأْخُذَكُمْ عَذَابٌ أَلِيمٌ ﴿٧٣﴾

73. And to Thamûd (people, We sent) their brother Sâlih. He said: "O my people! Worship Allâh! You have no other Ilâha (God) but Him. (Lâ ilâha illallâh: none has the right to be worshipped but Allâh). Indeed there has come to you a clear sign (the miracle of the coming out of a huge she-camel from the midst of a rock) from your Lord. This she-camel of Allâh is a sign unto you; so you leave her to graze in Allâh's earth, and touch her not with harm, lest a painful torment should seize you.

﴿ وَٱذْكُرُوٓا۟ إِذْ جَعَلَكُمْ خُلَفَآءَ مِنۢ بَعْدِ عَادٍ وَبَوَّأَكُمْ فِى ٱلْأَرْضِ تَتَّخِذُونَ مِن سُهُولِهَا قُصُورًا وَتَنْحِتُونَ ٱلْجِبَالَ بُيُوتًا ۖ فَٱذْكُرُوٓا۟ ءَالَآءَ ٱللَّهِ وَلَا تَعْثَوْا۟ فِى ٱلْأَرْضِ مُفْسِدِينَ ﴿٧٤﴾

74. "And remember when He made you successors after 'Ad (people) and gave you habitations in the land, you build for yourselves palaces in plains, and carve out homes in the mountains. So remember the graces (bestowed upon you) from Allâh, and do not go about making mischief on the earth."

﴿ قَالَ ٱلْمَلَأُ ٱلَّذِينَ ٱسْتَكْبَرُوا۟ مِن قَوْمِهِۦ لِلَّذِينَ ٱسْتُضْعِفُوا۟ لِمَنْ ءَامَنَ مِنْهُمْ أَتَعْلَمُونَ أَنَّ صَٰلِحًا مُّرْسَلٌ مِّن رَّبِّهِۦ ۚ قَالُوٓا۟ إِنَّا بِمَآ أُرْسِلَ بِهِۦ مُؤْمِنُونَ ﴿٧٥﴾

75. The leaders of those who were arrogant among his people said to those who were counted weak - to such of them as believed: "Know you that Sâlih is one

sent from his Lord." They said: "We indeed believe in that with which he has been sent."

﴿ قَالَ ٱلَّذِينَ ٱسْتَكْبَرُوٓاْ إِنَّا بِٱلَّذِىٓ ءَامَنتُم بِهِۦ كَٰفِرُونَ ﴿٧٦﴾ ﴾

76. Those who were arrogant said: "Verily, we disbelieve in that which you believe in."

﴿ فَعَقَرُواْ ٱلنَّاقَةَ وَعَتَوْاْ عَنْ أَمْرِ رَبِّهِمْ وَقَالُواْ يَٰصَٰلِحُ ٱئْتِنَا بِمَا تَعِدُنَآ إِن كُنتَ مِنَ ٱلْمُرْسَلِينَ ﴿٧٧﴾ ﴾

77. So they killed the she-camel and insolently defied the Commandment of their Lord, and said: "O Sâlih (Saleh)! Bring about your threats if you are indeed one of the Messengers (of Allâh)."

﴿ فَأَخَذَتْهُمُ ٱلرَّجْفَةُ فَأَصْبَحُواْ فِى دَارِهِمْ جَٰثِمِينَ ﴿٧٨﴾ ﴾

78. So the earthquake seized them, and they lay (dead), prostrate in their homes.

Transliteration

73. Wa-ila thamooda akhahum salihan qala ya qawmi oAAbudoo Allaha ma lakum min ilahin ghayruhu qad jaatkum bayyinatun min rabbikum hathihi naqatu Allahi lakum ayatan fatharooha ta/kulfee ardi Allahi wala tamassooha bisoo-in faya/khuthakum AAathabun aleemun 74. Waothkuroo ith jaAAalakum khulafaa min baAAdi AAadin wabawwaakum fee al-ardi tattakhithoona min suhooliha qusooran watanhitoona aljibala buyootan faothkuroo alaa Allahi wala taAAthaw fee al-ardi mufsideena 75. Qala almalao allatheena istakbaroo min qawmihi lillatheena istudAAifoo liman amana minhum ataAAlamoona anna salihan mursalun min rabbihi qaloo inna bima orsila bihi mu/minoona 76. Qala allatheena istakbaroo inna biallathee amantum bihi kafiroona 77. FaAAaqaroo alnnaqata waAAataw AAan amri rabbihim waqaloo ya salihu i/tina bima taAAiduna in kunta mina almursaleena 78. Faakhathat-humu alrrajfatu faasbahoo fee darihim jathimeena

Tafsir Ibn Kathir:

Thamud: Their Land and Their Lineage

Scholars of Tafsir and genealogy say that (the tribe of Thamud descended from) Thamud bin `Athir bin Iram bin Sam bin Nuh, and he is brother of Jadis son of `Athir, similarly the tribe of Tasm, and they were from the ancient Arabs, Al-`Aribah, before the time of Ibrahim, Thamud came after `Ad. They dwelled between the area of the Hijaz (Western Arabia) and Ash-Sham (Greater Syria). The Messenger of Allah passed by the area and ruins of Thamud when he went to Tabuk (in northern Arabia) during the ninth year of Hijrah. Imam Ahmad recorded that Ibn `Umar said, "When the Messenger of Allah went to the area of Al-Hijr in Tabuk with the people, he camped near the homes of Thamud, in Al-Hijr and the people brought water from the wells that Thamud used before. They used that water to make dough and placed the pots (on fire) for cooking. However, the Prophet commanded them to spill the contents of the pots and to give the dough to their camels. He then marched forth with them from that area to another area, near the well that the camel (as will follow) used to drink from. He forbade the Companions from entering the area where people were tormented, saying,

«إِنِّي أَخْشَى أَنْ يُصِيبَكُمْ مِثْلُ مَا أَصَابَهُمْ فَلَا تَدْخُلُوا عَلَيْهِم»

(I fear that what befell them might befall you as well. Therefore, do not enter on them.)" Ahmad narrated that `Abdullah bin `Umar said that the Messenger of Allah said while in the Hijr area,

«لَا تَدْخُلُوا عَلَى هَؤُلَاءِ الْمُعَذَّبِينَ إِلَّا أَنْ تَكُونُوا بَاكِينَ فَإِنْ لَمْ تَكُونُوا بَاكِينَ فَلَا تَدْخُلُوا عَلَيْهِمْ أَنْ يُصِيبَكُمْ مِثْلَ مَا أَصَابَهُم»

(Do not enter on these who were tormented, unless you do so while crying. If you are not crying, then do not enter on them, so that what befell them does not befall you, as well.) The basis of this Hadith is mentioned in Two Sahihs.

The Story of Prophet Salih and Thamud

Allah said,

(And to Thamud), meaning, to the tribe of Thamud, We sent their brother Salih,

(He said: "O my people! Worship Allah! You have no other god but Him.") All Allah's Messengers called to the worship of Allah alone without partners. Allah said in other Ayat,

(And We did not send any Messenger before you but We revealed to him (saying): "None has the right to be worshipped but I, so worship Me.") (21:25) and,

(And verily, We have sent among every Ummah a Messenger (proclaiming): "Worship Allah (Alone), and avoid Taghut (all false deities)") (16:36).

Thamud asked that a Camel appear from a Stone, and it did

Prophet Salih said,

("Indeed there has come to you a clear sign from your Lord. This she-camel of Allah is a sign unto you;") meaning, a miracle has come to you from Allah testifying to the truth of what I came to you with. Salih's people asked him to produce a miracle and suggested a certain solid rock that they chose, which stood lonely in the area of Hijr, and which was called Al-Katibah. They asked him to bring a pregnant camel out of that stone. Salih took their covenant and promises that if Allah answers their challenge, they would believe and follow him. When they gave him their oaths and promises to that, Salih started praying and invoked Allah (to produce that miracle). All of a sudden, the stone moved and broke apart, producing a she-camel with thick wool. It was pregnant and its fetus was visibly moving in its belly, exactly as Salih's people asked. This is when their chief, Jundu` bin `Amr, and several who followed him believed. The rest of the noblemen of Thamud wanted to believe as well, but Dhu'ab bin `Amr bin Labid, Al-Habbab, who tended their idols, and Rabbab bin Sum`ar bin Jilhis stopped them. One of the cousins of Jundu` bin `Amr, whose name was Shihab bin Khalifah bin Mikhlat bin Labid bin Jawwas, was one of the leaders of Thamud, and he also wanted to accept the message. However, the chiefs whom we mentioned prevented him, and he conceded to their promptings. The camel remained in Thamud, as well as, its offspring after she delivered it before them. The camel used to drink from its well on one day and leave the well for Thamud the next day. They also used to drink its milk, for on the days she drank water, they used to milk her and fill their containers from its milk. Allah said in other Ayat,

(And inform them that the water is to be shared between (her and) them, each one's right to drink being established (by turns)) (54:28) and,

(Here is a she-camel: it has a right to drink (water), and you have a right to drink (water) (each) on a day, known) (26:155) The camel used to graze in some of their valleys, going through a pass and coming out through another pass. She did that so as to be able to move easily, because she used to drink a lot of water. She was a tremendous animal that had a strikingly beautiful appearance. When she used to pass by their cattle, the cattle would be afraid of her. When this matter continued for a long time and Thamud's rejection of Salih became intense, they intended to kill her so that they could take the water for themselves every day. It was said that all of them (the disbelievers of Thamud) conspired to kill the camel. Qatadah said that he was told that, "The designated killer of the camel approached them all, including women in their rooms and children, and found out that all of them agreed to kill her." This fact is apparent from the wording of the Ayat,

(Then they denied him and they killed it. So their Lord destroyed them because of their sin, and made them equal in destruction!) (91:14), and,

(And We sent the she-camel to Thamud as a clear sign, but they did her wrong.) (17:59) Allah said here,

(So they killed the she-camel) Therefore, these Ayat stated that the entire tribe shared in agreeing to this crime, and Allah knows best.

Thamud kills the She-Camel

Imam Abu Ja`far Ibn Jarir and other scholars of Tafsir said that the reason behind killing the camel was that a disbelieving old woman among them named Umm Ghanm `Unayzah, the daughter of Ghanm bin Mijlaz, had the severest enmity among Thamud towards Salih, peace be upon him. She had beautiful daughters and she was wealthy, and Dhu'ab bin `Amr, one of the leaders of Thamud, was her husband. There was another noblewoman whose name was Saduf bint Al-Muhayya bin Dahr bin Al-Muhayya, who was of noble family, wealthy and beautiful. She was married to a

Muslim man from Thamud, but she left him. These two women offered a prize for those who swore to them that they would kill the camel. Once, Saduf summoned a man called Al-Habbab and offered herself to him if he would kill the camel, but he refused. So she called a cousin of hers whose name was Musaddi` bin Mihraj bin Al-Muhayya, and he agreed. As for `Unayzah bint Ghanm, she called Qudar bin Salif bin Jundu`, a short person with red-blue skin, a bastard, according to them. Qudar was not the son of his claimed father, Salif, but the son of another man called, Suhyad. However, he was born on Salif's bed (and thus named after him). `Unayzah said to Qudar, "I will give you any of my daughters you wish, if you kill the camel." Qudar bin Salif and Musaddi` bin Mihraj went along and recruited several mischievous persons from Thamud to kill the camel. Seven more from Thamud agreed, and the group became nine, as Allah described, when He said,

(And there were in the city nine men, who made mischief in the land, and would not reform.) These nine men were chiefs of their people, and they lured the entire tribe into agreeing to kill the camel. So they waited until the camel left the water well, where Qudar waited beside a rock on its path, while Musaddi` waited at another rock. When the camel passed by Musaddi` he shot an arrow at her and the arrow pierced her leg. At that time, `Unayzah came out and ordered her daughter, who was among the most beautiful women, to uncover her face for Qudar, encouraging Qudar to swing his sword, hitting the camel on her knee. So she fell to the ground and screamed once to warn her offspring. Qudar stabbed her in her neck and slaughtered her. Her offspring went up a high rock and screamed. `Abdur-Razzaq recorded from Ma`mar that someone reported from Al-Hasan Al-Basari that the offspring said, "O my Lord! Where is my mother" It was said that her offspring screamed thrice and entered a rock and vanished in it, or, they followed it and killed it together with its mother. Allah knows best. When they finished the camel off and the news reached Prophet Salih, he came to them while they were gathered. When he saw the camel, he cried and proclaimed,

("Enjoy yourselves in your homes for three days.") (11:65)

The Wicked Ones Plot to Kill Prophet Salih, But the Torment descended on Them

The nine wicked persons killed the camel on a Wednesday, and that night, they conspired to kill Salih. They said, "If he is truthful, we should finish him before we are finished. If he is a liar, we will make him follow his camel."

(They said: "Swear one to another by Allah that we shall make a secret night attack on him and his household, and thereafter we will surely say to his near relatives: `We witnessed not the destruction of his household, and verily, we are telling the truth.'" So they plotted a plot, and We planned a plan, while they perceived not.) (27:49-50) When they conspired to kill Salih and gathered at night to carry out their plot, Allah, to Whom belongs all might and Who protects His Messengers, rained down stones that smashed the heads of these nine people before the rest of the tribe. On Thursday, the first of the three days of respite, the people woke up and their faces were pale (yellow), just as Prophet Salih had promised them. On the second day of respite, Friday, they woke up and found their faces had turned red. On the third day of the respite, Saturday, they woke up with their faces black. On Sunday, they wore the fragrance of Hanut (the perfume for enshrouding the dead before burial) and awaited Allah's torment and revenge, we seek refuge with Allah from it. They did not know what will be done to them or how and from where the torment would come. When the sun rose, the Sayhah (loud cry) came from the sky and a severe tremor overtook them from below; the souls were captured and the bodies became lifeless, all in an hour.

(And they lay (dead), prostrate in their homes.) They became dead and lifeless and none among them, whether young, old, male or female, escaped the torment. The scholars of Tafsir said that none from the offspring of Thamud remained, except Prophet Salih and those who believed in him. A disbelieving man called Abu Righal was in the Sacred Area at the time and the torment that befell his people did not touch him. When he went out of the Sacred Area one day, a stone fell from the sky and killed him. `Abdur-Razzaq narrated that Ma`mar said that Isma`il bin Umayyah said that the Prophet passed by the gravesite of Abu Righal and asked the Companions if they knew whose grave it was. They said, "Allah and His Messenger know better." He said,

«هَذَا قَبْرُ أَبِي رِغَالٍ رَجُلٍ مِنْ ثَمُودَ كَانَ فِي حَرَمِ اللهِ فَمَنَعَهُ حَرَمُ اللهِ عَذَابَ اللهِ، فَلَمَّا خَرَجَ أَصَابَهُ مَا أَصَابَ قَومَهُ فَدُفِنَ هَاهُنَا وَدُفِنَ مَعَهُ غُصْنٌ مِنْ ذَهَبٍ، فَنَزَلَ الْقَوْمُ فَابْتَدَرُوهُ بِأَسْيَافِهِمْ فَبَحَثُوا عَنْهُ فَاسْتَخْرَجُوا الْغُصْنَ»

(This is the grave of Abu Righal, a man from Thamud. He was in the Sacred Area of Allah and this fact saved him from receiving Allah's torment. When he went out of the Sacred Area, what befell his people also befell him. He was buried here along with a branch made from gold.) So the people used their swords and looked for the golden branch and found it. `Abdur-Razzaq narrated that Ma`mar said that Az-Zuhri said that Abu Righal is the father of the tribe of Thaqif.

Surah: 7 Ayah: 79

﴿ فَتَوَلَّىٰ عَنْهُمْ وَقَالَ يَٰقَوْمِ لَقَدْ أَبْلَغْتُكُمْ رِسَالَةَ رَبِّي وَنَصَحْتُ لَكُمْ وَلَـٰكِن لَّا تُحِبُّونَ ٱلنَّـٰصِحِينَ ۝ ﴾

79. Then he (Sâlih) turned from them, and said: "O my people! I have indeed conveyed to you the Message of my Lord, and have given you good advice but you like not good advisers."

Transliteration

79. Fatawalla AAanhum waqala ya qawmi laqad ablaghtukum risalata rabbee wanasahtu lakum walakin la tuhibboona alnnasiheena

Chapter 7: Al-Araf (The Heights), Verses 001-087

Tafsir Ibn Kathir:

These are the words of admonishment that Salih conveyed to his people after Allah destroyed them for defying Him, rebelling against Him, refusing to accept the truth, avoiding guidance, and preferring misguidance instead. Salih said these words of admonishment and criticism to them after they perished, and they heard him (as a miracle for Prophet Salih from Allah). Similarly, it is recorded in the Two Sahihs that after the Messenger of Allah defeated the disbelievers in the battle of Badr, he remained in that area for three days, and then rode his camel, which was prepared for him during the latter part of the night. He went on until he stood by the well of Badr (where the corpses of the disbelievers were thrown) and said,

«يَا أَبَا جَهْلِ بْنَ هِشَامٍ يَا عُتْبَةَ بْنَ رَبِيعَةَ يَا شَيْبَةَ بْنَ رَبِيعَةَ وَيَا فُلَانَ بْنَ فُلَانٍ هَلْ وَجَدْتُمْ مَا وَعَدَ رَبُّكُمْ حَقًّا؟ فَإِنِّي وَجَدْتُ مَا وَعَدَنِي رَبِّي حَقًّا»

(O Abu Jahl bin Hisham! O `Utbah bin Rabi`ah! O Shaybah bin Rabi`ah! Did you find what your Lord has promised you (of torment) to be true, for I found what my Lord promised me (of victory) to be true.) `Umar said to him, "O Allah's Messenger! Why do you speak to a people who have rotted" He said,

«وَالَّذِي نَفْسِي بِيَدِهِ مَا أَنْتُمْ بِأَسْمَعَ لِمَا أَقُولُ مِنْهُمْ وَلَكِنْ لَا يُجِيبُونَ»

(By He in Whose Hand is my soul! You do not hear what I am saying better than they, but they cannot reply.) Similarly, Prophet Salih, peace be upon him, said to his people,

("I have indeed conveyed to you the Message of my Lord, and have given you good advice,") but you did not benefit from it because you do not like the Truth and do not follow those who give you sincere advice,

("but you like not good advisers.")

Surah: 7 Ayah: 80 & Ayah: 81

﴿ وَلُوطًا إِذْ قَالَ لِقَوْمِهِ أَتَأْتُونَ ٱلْفَٰحِشَةَ مَا سَبَقَكُم بِهَا مِنْ أَحَدٍ مِّنَ ٱلْعَٰلَمِينَ ۝ ﴾

80. And (remember) Lût (Lot), when he said to his people: "Do you commit the worst sin such as none preceding you has committed in the 'Alamîn (mankind and jinn)?

$$\text{﴿ إِنَّكُمْ لَتَأْتُونَ ٱلرِّجَالَ شَهْوَةً مِّن دُونِ ٱلنِّسَآءِ ۚ بَلْ أَنتُمْ قَوْمٌ مُّسْرِفُونَ ﴾}$$

81. "Verily, you practice your lusts on men instead of women. Nay, but you are a people transgressing beyond bounds (by committing great sins)."

Transliteration

80. Walootan ith qala liqawmihi ata/toona alfahishata ma sabaqakum biha min ahadin mina alAAalameena   81. Innakum lata/toona alrrijala shahwatan min dooni alnnisa-i bal antum qawmun musrifoona

Tafsir Ibn Kathir:

The Story of Prophet Lut, upon Him be Peace, and His People

Allah said,

(And (remember) Lout (Lot), when he said to his people:..) Lut (Lot) is the son of Haran the son of Azar (Terah), and he was the nephew of Ibrahim, peace be upon them both. Lut had believed in Ibrahim and migrated with him to the Sham area. Allah then sent Lut to the people of Sadum (Sodom) and the surrounding villages, to call them to Allah, enjoin righteousness and forbid them from their evil practices, their sin, and wickedness. It this area, they did things that none of the children of Adam or any other creatures ever did before them. They used to have sexual intercourse with males instead of females. This evil practice was not known among the Children of Adam before, nor did it even cross their minds, so they were unfamiliar with it before the people of Sodom invented it, may Allah's curse be on them. `Amr bin Dinar conmented on;

("...as none preceding you has committed in all of the nations.") "Never before the people of Lut did a male have sex with another male." This is why Lut said to them,

("Do you commit lewdness such as none preceding you has committed in all of the nations Verily, you practice your lusts on men instead of women.") meaning, you left women whom Allah created for you and instead had sex with men Indeed, this behavior is evil and ignorant because you have placed things in their improper places. Lut, peace be upon him, said to them:

("these (the girls of the nation) are my daughters (to marry lawfully), if you must act (so).") (15:71) So he reminded them of their women, and they replied that they do not desire women!,

(They said: "Surely, you know that we have neither any desire nor need of your daughters, and indeed you know well what we want!") (11:79) meaning, you know that we have no desire for women and you know what we desire with your guests.

Chapter 7: Al-Araf (The Heights), Verses 001-087

Surah: 7 Ayah: 82

﴿ وَمَا كَانَ جَوَابَ قَوْمِهِ إِلَّا أَن قَالُوٓا۟ أَخْرِجُوهُم مِّن قَرْيَتِكُمْ ۖ إِنَّهُمْ أُنَاسٌ يَتَطَهَّرُونَ ﴾

82. And the answer of his people was only that they said: "Drive them out of your town, these are indeed men who want to be pure (from sins)!"

Transliteration

82. Wama kana jawaba qawmihi illa an qaloo akhrijoohum min qaryatikum innahum onasun yatatahharoona

Tafsir Ibn Kathir:

So they answered Prophet Lut by trying to expel and banish him from their village, along with those who believed with him. Allah indeed removed Prophet Lut safely from among them, and He destroyed them in their land in disgrace and humiliation. They said (about Lut and the believers):

("These are indeed men who want to be pure (from sins)!") Qatadah commented, "They shamed them (Lut and the believers) with what is not a shame at all." Mujahid commented, "(Lut's people said about Lut and the believers,) They are a people who want to be pure from men's anuses and women's anuses!" Similar was narrated from Ibn `Abbas.

Surah: 7 Ayah: 83 & Ayah: 84

﴿ فَأَنجَيْنَاهُ وَأَهْلَهُ إِلَّا ٱمْرَأَتَهُ كَانَتْ مِنَ ٱلْغَابِرِينَ ﴾

83. Then We saved him and his family, except his wife; she was of those who remained behind (in the torment).

﴿ وَأَمْطَرْنَا عَلَيْهِم مَّطَرًا ۖ فَٱنظُرْ كَيْفَ كَانَ عَاقِبَةُ ٱلْمُجْرِمِينَ ﴾

84. And We rained down on them a rain (of stones). Then see what was the end of the Mujrimûn (criminals, polytheists and sinners).

Transliteration

83. Faanjaynahu waahlahu illa imraatahu kanat mina alghabireena 84. Waamtarna AAalayhim mataran faonthur kayfa kana AAaqibatu almujrimeena

Tafsir Ibn Kathir:

Allah says, We saved Lut and his family, for only his household believed in him.

Allah said in another Ayah,

(So We brought out from therein the believers. But We found not there any household of the Muslims except one (of Lut and his daughters)) (51: 35-36). Only his wife (from his family) did not believe, remaining on the religion of her people. She used to conspire with them against Lut and inform them of who came to visit him, using certain signals that they agreed on. This is why when Lut was commanded to leave by night with his family, he was ordered not to inform his wife or take her with him. Some said that she followed them, and when the torment struck her people, she looked back and suffered the same punishment as them. However, it appears that she did not leave the town and that Lut did not tell her that they would depart. So she remained with her people, as apparent from Allah's statement,

(except his wife; she was of the Ghabirin) meaning, of those who remained, or they say: of those who were destroyed, and this is the more obvious explanation. Allah's statement,

(And We rained down on them a rain) is explained by His other statement,

(And rained on them stones of baked clay, in a well-arranged manner one after another. Marked from your Lord; and they are not ever far from the wrongdoers.) (11:82-83). Allah said here,

(Then see what was the end of the criminals.) This Ayah means: `See, O Muhammad, the end of those who dared to disobey Allah and reject His Messengers.' Imam Ahmad, Abu Dawud, At-Tirmidhi, Ibn Majah, all recorded a Hadith (from) Ibn `Abbas who said that Allah's Messenger said;

«مَنْ وَجَدْتُمُوهُ يَعْمَلُ عَمَلَ قَوْمِ لُوطٍ فَاقْتُلُوا الْفَاعِلَ وَالْمَفْعُولَ بِهِ»

(Whoever is found doing the act of the people of Lut, then kill them; the doer and the one it is done to.)

Surah: 7 Ayah: 85

﴿ وَإِلَىٰ مَدْيَنَ أَخَاهُمْ شُعَيْبًا ۗ قَالَ يَـٰقَوْمِ ٱعْبُدُوا۟ ٱللَّهَ مَا لَكُم مِّنْ إِلَـٰهٍ غَيْرُهُۥ ۖ قَدْ جَآءَتْكُم بَيِّنَةٌ مِّن رَّبِّكُمْ ۖ فَأَوْفُوا۟ ٱلْكَيْلَ وَٱلْمِيزَانَ وَلَا تَبْخَسُوا۟ ٱلنَّاسَ أَشْيَآءَهُمْ وَلَا تُفْسِدُوا۟ فِى ٱلْأَرْضِ بَعْدَ إِصْلَـٰحِهَا ۚ ذَٰلِكُمْ خَيْرٌ لَّكُمْ إِن كُنتُم مُّؤْمِنِينَ ﴾

85. And to (the people of) Madyan (Midian), (We sent) their brother Shu'aib. He said: "O my people! Worship Allâh! You have no other Ilâh (God) but Him. (Lâ ilâha illallâh (none has the right to be worshipped but Allâh))" Verily, a clear proof (sign) from your Lord has come unto you; so give full measure and full weight and wrong not men in their things, and do not mischief on the earth after it has been set in order, that will be better for you, if you are believers.

Transliteration

85. Wa-ila madyana akhahum shuAAayban qala ya qawmi oAAbudoo Allaha ma lakum min ilahin ghayruhu qad jaatkum bayyinatun min rabbikum faawfoo alkayla waalmeezana wala tabkhasoo alnnasa ashyaahum wala tufsidoo fee al-ardi baAAda islahiha thalikum khayrun lakum in kuntum mu/mineena

Tafsir Ibn Kathir:

Story of Shu`ayb, upon him be Peace, and the Land of Madyan

Muhammad bin Ishaq said, "They (the people of Madyan) are the descendents of Madyan, son of Midyan, son of Ibrahim. Shu`ayb was the son of Mikil bin Yashjur. And in the Syrian language, his name was Yathrun (Jethro)". I (Ibn Kathir) say, Madyan was the name of the tribe and also a city that is close to Ma`an on route to the Hijaz (from Ash-Sham). Allah said in another Ayah,

(And when he arrived at the water (a well) of Madyan he found there a group of men watering (their flocks).) (28:23) They are also the people of Al-Aykah (the Woods), as we will mention later on, Allah willing, and our trust is in Him.

(He said: "O my people! Worship Allah! You have no other God but Him") and this is the call of all Messengers,

("Verily, a clear proof (sign) from your Lord has come unto you;") meaning, `Allah has presented the proof and evidences of the truth of what I brought you.' He then advised them and commanded them to give full measure and full weight and not to wrong men in their dealings, meaning, to refrain from cheating people in buying and selling. They used to treacherously avoid giving full weight and measure. Allah said in other Ayat,

(Woe to Al-Mutaffifin (those who give less in measure and weight)...) (83:1) until He said,

(before the Lord of all that exists) (83:6). These Ayat contain a stern warning and sure promise that we ask Allah to save us from. Shu`ayb was called `Speaker of the Prophets', because of his eloquent words and eloquent advice, and Allah stated that Shu`ayb said:

Surah: 7 Ayah: 86 & Ayah: 87

﴿ وَلَا تَقْعُدُواْ بِكُلِّ صِرَاطٍ تُوعِدُونَ وَتَصُدُّونَ عَن سَبِيلِ ٱللَّهِ مَنْ ءَامَنَ بِهِۦ وَتَبْغُونَهَا عِوَجًا ۚ وَٱذْكُرُوٓاْ إِذْ كُنتُمْ قَلِيلًا فَكَثَّرَكُمْ ۖ وَٱنظُرُواْ كَيْفَ كَانَ عَٰقِبَةُ ٱلْمُفْسِدِينَ ﴾ ۸٦

86. "And sit not on every road, threatening, and hindering from the Path of Allâh those who believe in Him, and seeking to make it crooked. And remember when

you were but few, and He multiplied you. And see what was the end of the Mufsidûn (mischief-makers, corrupts, liars).

﴿ وَإِن كَانَ طَآئِفَةٌ مِّنكُمْ ءَامَنُواْ بِٱلَّذِىٓ أُرْسِلْتُ بِهِۦ وَطَآئِفَةٌ لَّمْ يُؤْمِنُواْ فَٱصْبِرُواْ حَتَّىٰ يَحْكُمَ ٱللَّهُ بَيْنَنَا وَهُوَ خَيْرُ ٱلْحَـٰكِمِينَ ۝ ﴾

87. "And if there is a party of you who believes in that with which I have been sent and a party who do not believe, so be patient until Allâh judges between us, and He is the Best of judges."

Transliteration

86. Wala taqAAudoo bikulli siratin tooAAidoona watasuddoona AAan sabeeli Allahi man amana bihi watabghoonaha AAiwajan waothkuroo ith kuntum qaleelan fakaththarakum waonthuroo kayfa kana AAaqibatu almufsideena   87. Wa-in kana ta-ifatun minkum amanoo biallathee orsiltu bihi wata-ifatun lam yu/minoo faisbiroo hatta yahkuma Allahu baynana wahuwa khayru alhakimeena

Tafsir Ibn Kathir:

Prophet Shu`ayb forbade his people from setting up blockades on the roads, saying,

("And sit not on every road, threatening,") threatening people with death if they do not give up their money, as they were bandits, according to As-Suddi. Ibn `Abbas, Mujahid and several others commented:

("And sit not on every road, threatening.") the believers who come to Shu`ayb to follow him." The first meaning is better, because Prophet Shu`ayb first said to them,

("on every road...") He then mentioned the second meaning,

("and hindering from the path of Allah those who believe in Him, and seeking to make it crooked.") meaning, you seek to make the path of Allah crooked and deviated,

("And remember when you were but few, and He multiplied you.") meaning, you were weak because you were few. But you later on became mighty because of your large numbers. Therefore, remember Allah's favor.

("And see what was the end of the mischief-makers. ") from the previous nations and earlier generations. See the torment and punishment they suffered, because they disobeyed Allah and rejected His Messengers. Shu`ayb continued;

("And if there is a party of you who believes in that with which I have been sent and a party who does not believe,") that is, if you divided concerning me,

("so be patient") that is, then wait and see,

("until Allah judges between us,"), and you,

("and He is the best of judges.") Surely, Allah will award the best end to those who fear and obey Him and He will destroy the disbelievers.

www.ingramcontent.com/pod-product-compliance
Lightning Source LLC
Chambersburg PA
CBHW081111080526
44587CB00021B/3543